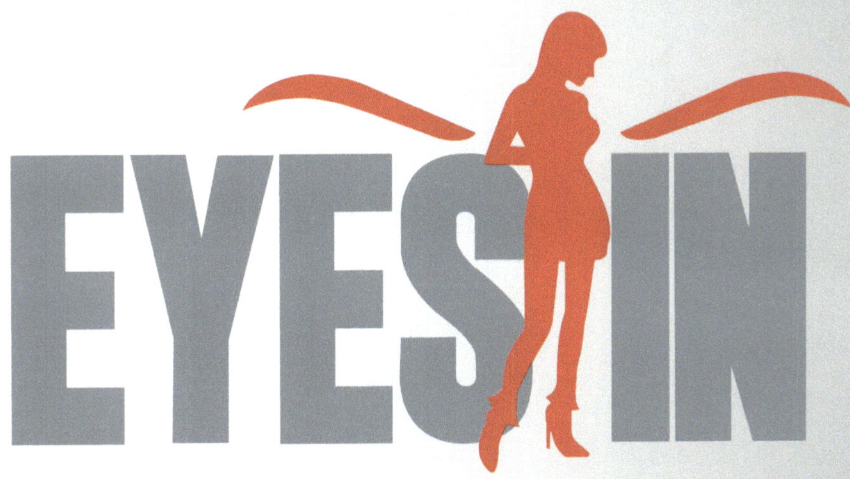

art | architecture | beauty | books | culinary arts | culture | design | fashion | film
health | music | photography | real estate | travel

World's Innovative Creators & Their Masterpieces

In this edition:

Photographer Jonathan Alpeyrie
Images of War

Bestselling Author David Baldacci

Innovative Cancer Detection by Dr. Rainer Ehmann & Dr. Thorston Walles

Eyes in

ITALY, ENGLAND, NEW YORK, L.A., VENEZUELA, SOUTH-KOREA, NEW JERSEY, BARCELONA, AUSTRIA, PITTSBURGH, PARIS, BOSTON, VIRGINIA, LONDON

Innovative Artist Manfred Kielnhofer from Austria

Fashion Designer Toni Francesc

The Hairrestoration Specialists in New York - Dr. Gary Hitzig & Dr. Amiya Prasad

Photo by Manfred Kielnhofer

COLLECTOR'S ITEM Nr. 9

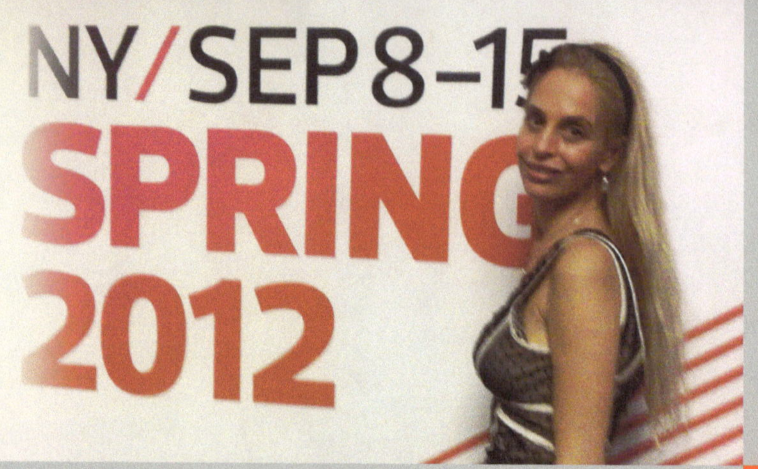

EYES IN

Dear Reader,

According to author David Baldacci, reading John Irving's "The World According to Garp" convinced him that he wanted to be a novelist. Absolute power — in which a thief finds himself accidentally connected to a murder involving the president and the ensuing cover up — was hardly Irvingesque, but it did begin Baldacci's friendly relationship with the best seller lists, which has continued over his writing career.

Brilliant minds inspire and produce new innovative creators as author John Irving did for author David Baldacci. With EYES IN™ we hope to be an endless form of aspiration and inspiration for existing, current and future creators so that innovation will continue to be an endless road towards improvement, sustainability, safety, beauty and happiness.

On this long track we hope that this EYES IN™ issue 9 will add enjoyment during this travel. Including author David Baldacci, various contributing creators will express their thoughts and masterpieces within the issue. From innovation in architecture to health - no boundaries stop us - EYES IN™ brings you everywhere - showing connections to different disciplines that make meaning to a future for all of us.

Enjoy reading. Best wishes!

Vivian Van Dijk, Author, Art Director
and Editor-in-Chief

EYES IN™ Team

Contact: press@eyesin.com
Vivian_Van_Dijk@eyesin.com

Vivian Van Dijk - Author, Art Director and Editor-in-Chief
Christian Zagarskas - Red Fish Creative - Web Developer & Marketing Strategist
Andy Boehm - Web Developer
Neal Henry - Designer
Michelle Wandres - Designer
Amanda Rinker - Editor
Cari Cooney - Editor
Tracy Hayes Odena - Editor
Cheryl Knight - Editor
Dayle Fraschilla - Editor
Kessel Nelson - Editor
Tonia Roemer - Editor
Jay Hogben - Video Editor
Phil Kin - Editor & Photographer
Neha Dey - Web Editor

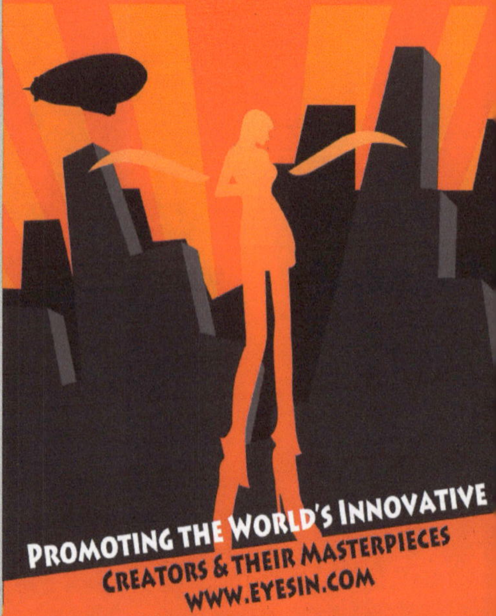

Contents

Visit us at www.eyesin.com

ISBN 978-0-9859043-0-2

Published by EYES IN Corp.
Vivian Van Dijk
339 East 85th Street 1C
New York, New York 10028

EYES IN™ is a Publication from EYES IN™ Corp.

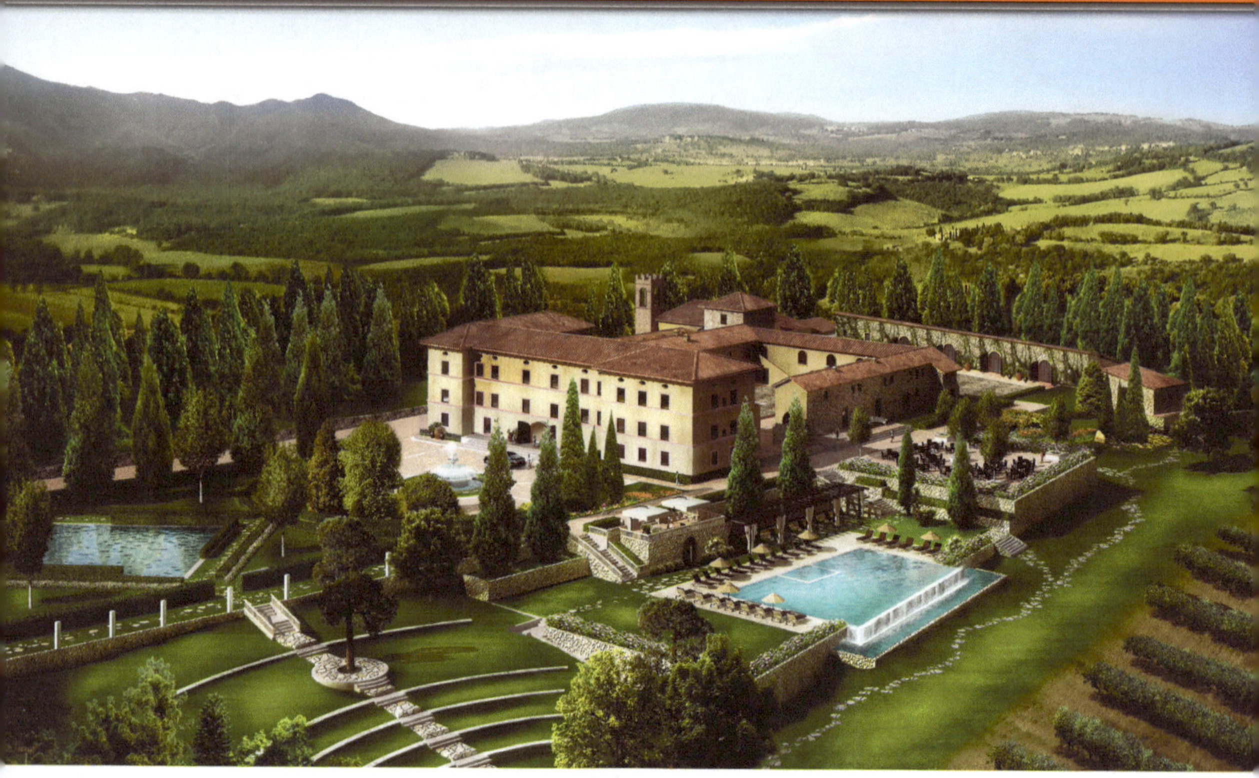

Castello Di Casole Villas and Hotel

An innovative real estate investment that makes the dream of home ownership in Tuscany, Italy a reality.

Imagine yourself basking in the sun-drenched landscape of rolling hills and endless vineyards. Imagine living in Tuscany, Italy – possibly the greatest repository of art in the world with its extraordinary paintings, sculptures, frescoes and architectural masterpieces. And, to leave behind the bothersome details of reservations and maintenance; to enjoy the breathtaking surroundings of Tuscany, Italy – now known as home.

You don't have to imagine it any longer. Castello Di Casole makes the dream of ownership in Tuscany a reality.

This 4,200 square foot Tuscan property and estate will be transformed into villas and a hotel offering the remarkable choice of whole ownership or residential interests through the Private Residence Club Program.

Castello Di Casole is in the rolling hills of central Tuscany. It's landscape is dotted with vineyards and olive tree orchards. This quaint estate is located near the mythic cities of Florence, Siena and San Gimignano and is considered one of the largest private landholdings in all of Italy. The Italian coast is just a scenic one hour drive to the west.

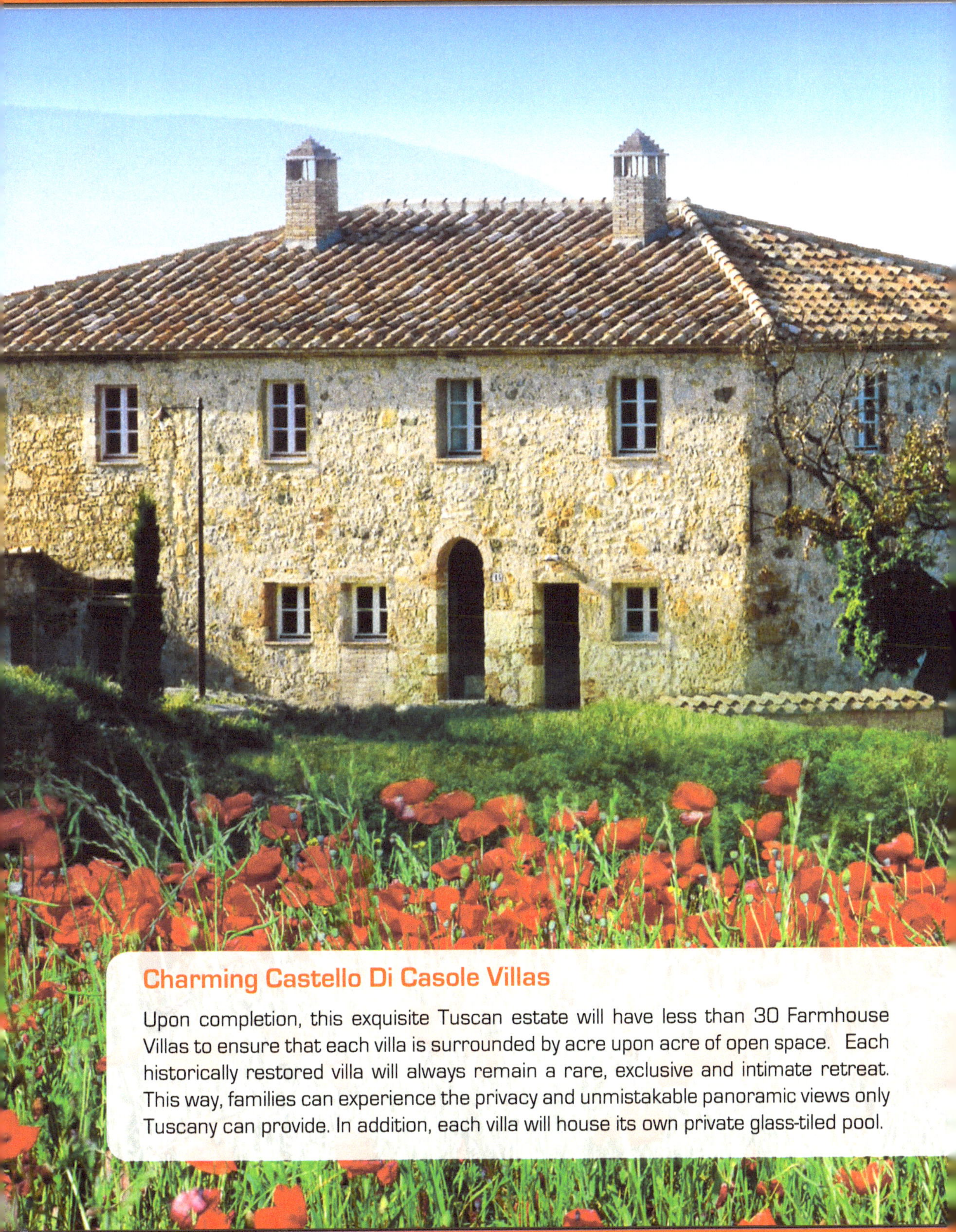

Charming Castello Di Casole Villas

Upon completion, this exquisite Tuscan estate will have less than 30 Farmhouse Villas to ensure that each villa is surrounded by acre upon acre of open space. Each historically restored villa will always remain a rare, exclusive and intimate retreat. This way, families can experience the privacy and unmistakable panoramic views only Tuscany can provide. In addition, each villa will house its own private glass-tiled pool.

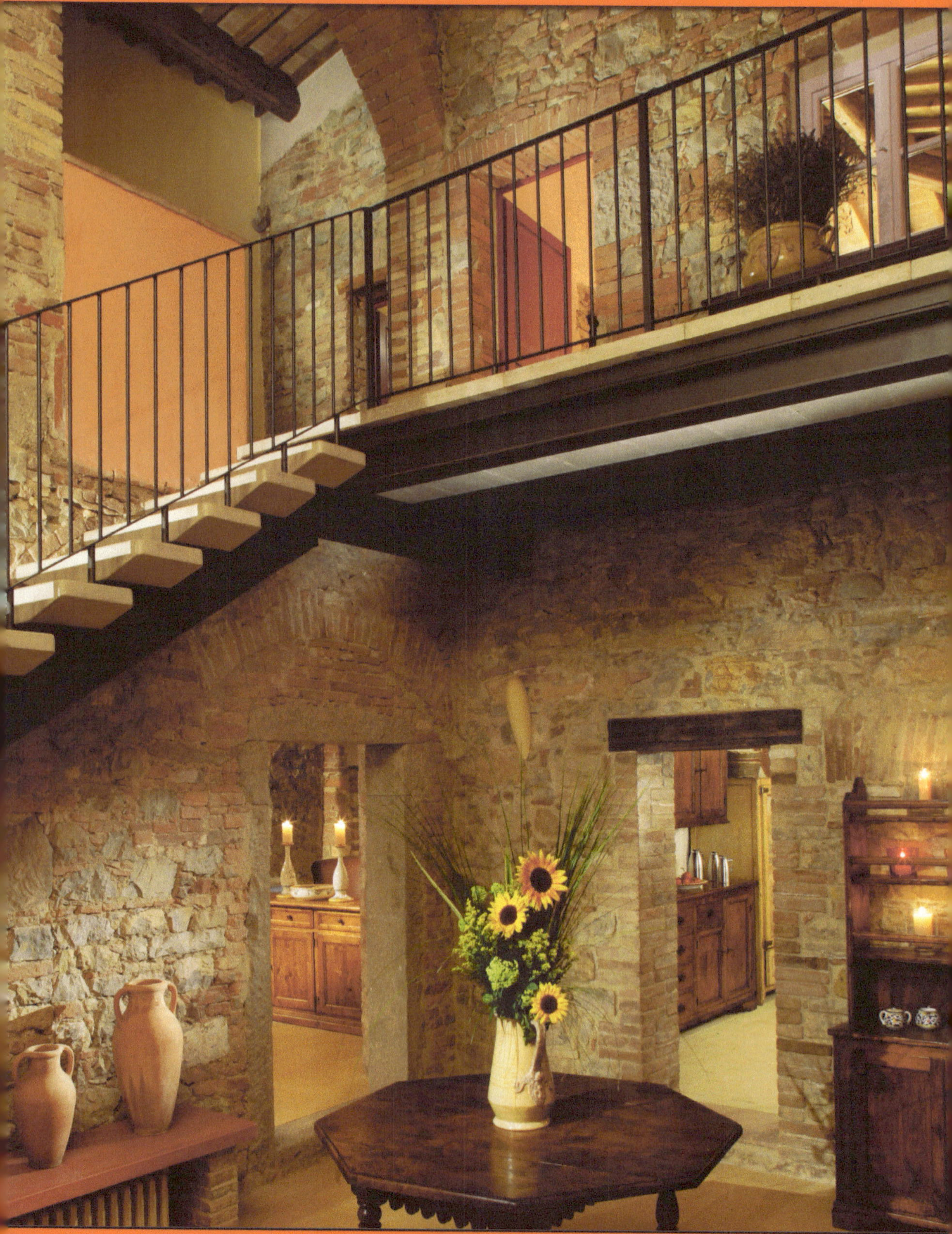

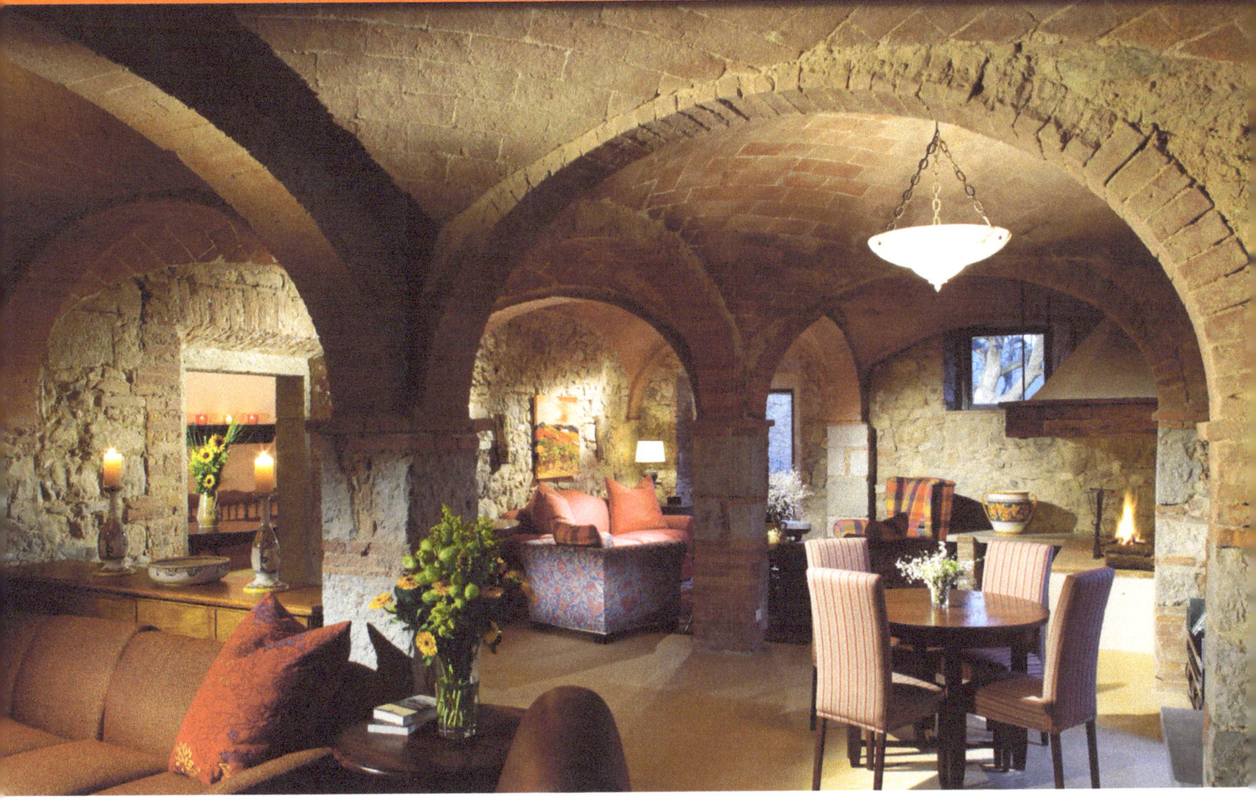

Five-Star Boutique Castello Di Casole Hotel

The unique Castello property is currently under restoration to create the enchanting, five-Star hotel with 41 private suites. The Castello will offer a true Tuscan lifestyle with fine and casual dining rooms open to terraces and a pool. A world-class spa and fitness center inspire the region's natural approach to diet and exercise. The hotel will also offer boutiques with unique souvenirs and fine Italian products. Hotel Castello Di Casole is slated open in the spring of 2012.

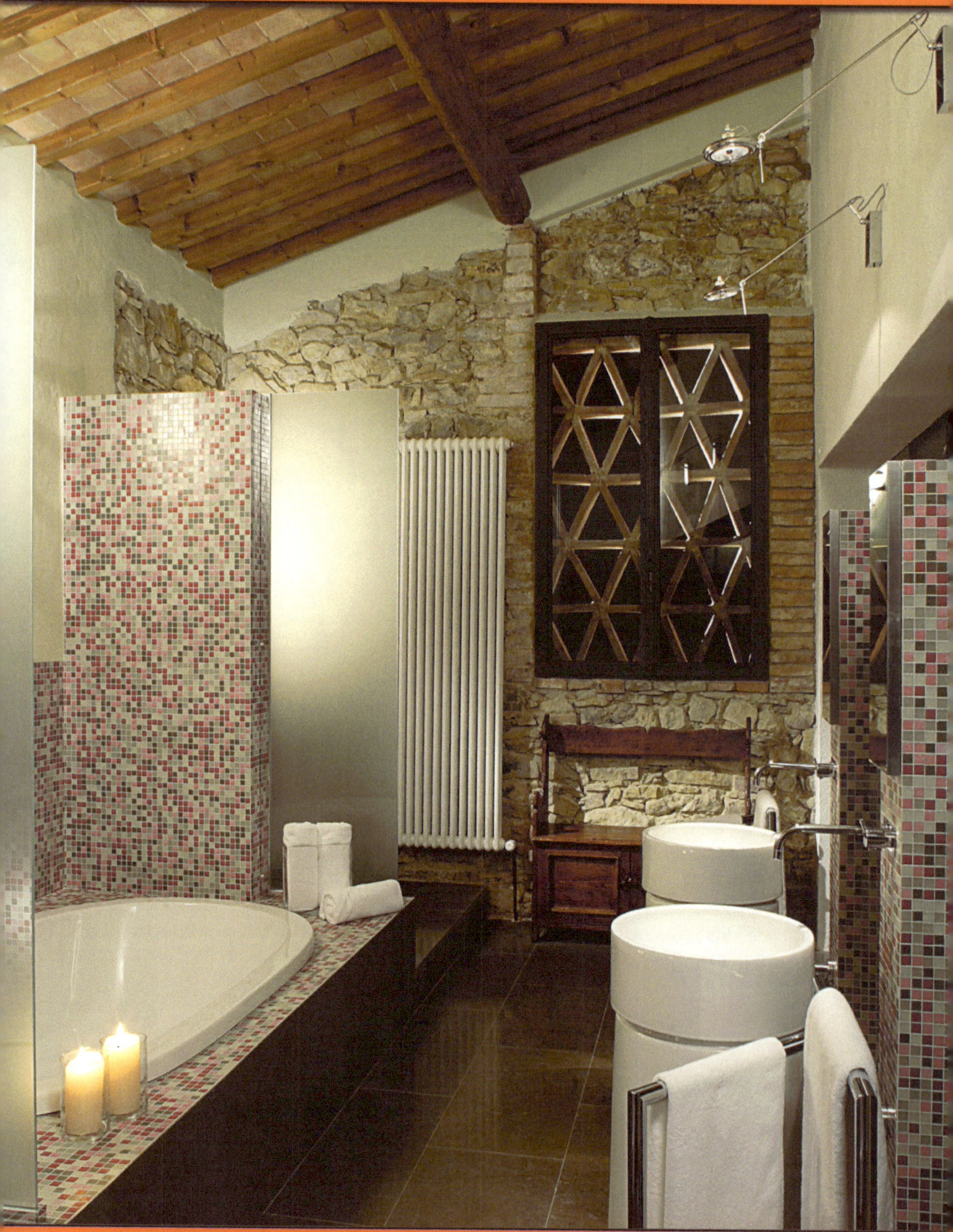

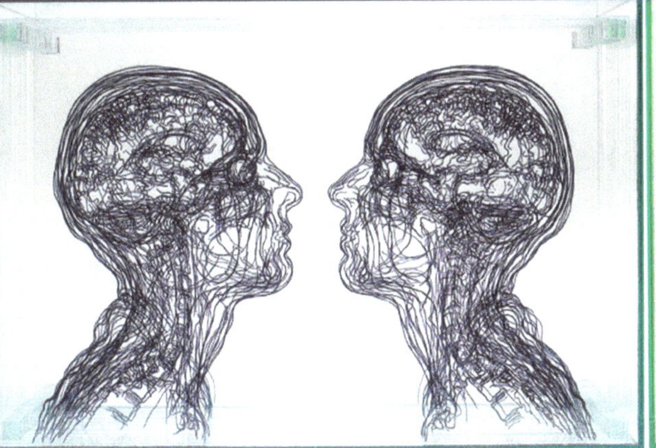

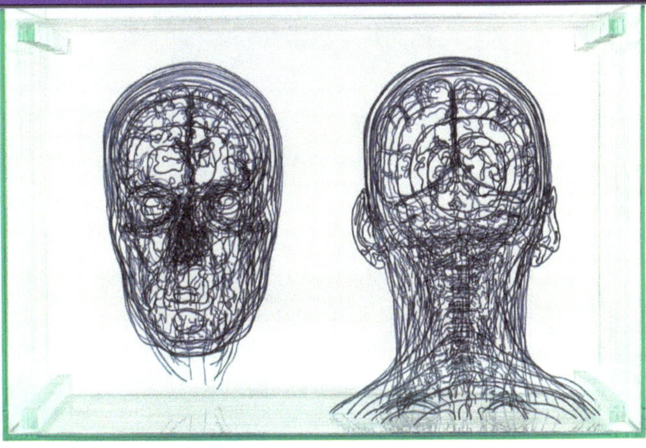

Artist Angela Palmer

Angela Palmer studied at the Royal College of Art, London, and The Ruskin School, University of Oxford, receiving both a scholarship and the Fitzgerald Prize. In 2009 she literally brought London to a standstill with the installation of her 'Ghost Forest' in Trafalgar Square. This group of ten enormous tree stumps from the rainforests of Ghana, spotlit and grouped on plinths, then travelled to Copenhagen to coincide with the UN Climate Change Conference. Palmer's main body of work is on a more manageable scale. The works illustrated here are derived from MRI and CT scans of bodies, both human and animal. The artist interprets these scans in delicate drawings or engravings on glass, which hint at the fragility of life as the forms disappear and then reform as you walk around each piece. The main work illustrated above is based upon a 2,000 year old child mummy in the collection of the Ashmolean Museum in Oxford, and a version of this piece is installed in the museum. Further examples of her work are in many important collections in the UK, the USA and the UAE.

About the Waterhouse & Dodd Gallery

Waterhouse & Dodd, formed in 1987, is a well known international dealership specializing in Impressionist, modern and contemporary fine art, with two galleries in the heart of London's art dealing district (Cork Street, serving as a base for international contemporary art and Savile Row, our centre of operations for secondary market dealing) and a further gallery in Greene Street, New York that specializes in contemporary art. They represent a wide range of European, American and Middle Eastern artists, from young emerging talents to well-established names. They exhibit a variety of media. The gallery has an active program of exhibitions in Cork Street and Greene Street NY, and also participate in a number of prestigious art fairs; these include TEFAF in Maastricht, the International Fine Art Fair in New York, Art Dubai, Abu Dhabi Art, The American Fine Art Fair in Palm Beach, The London Art Fair, SCOPE Miami and Basel, Art Miami, and Art Hamptons.

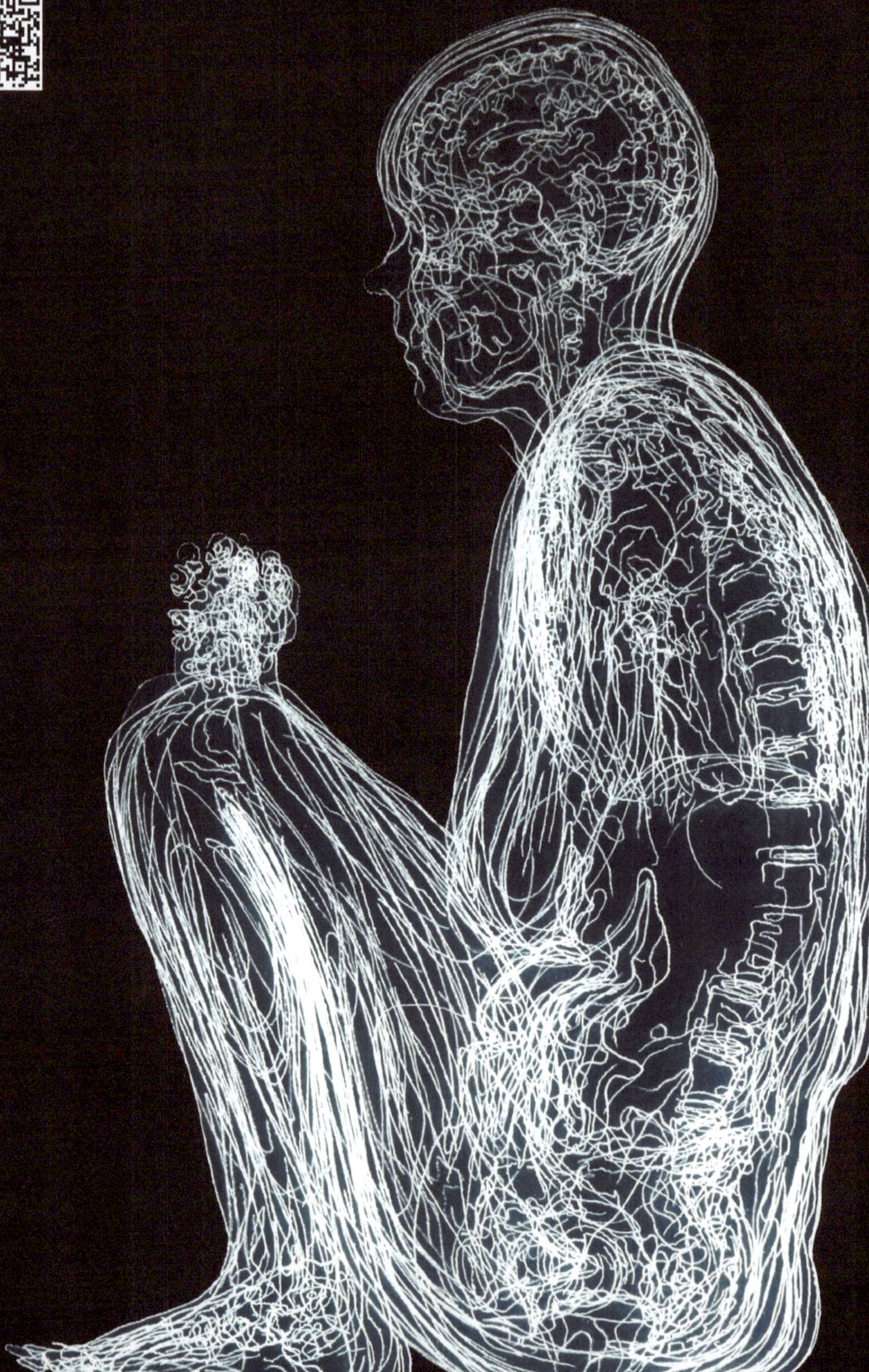

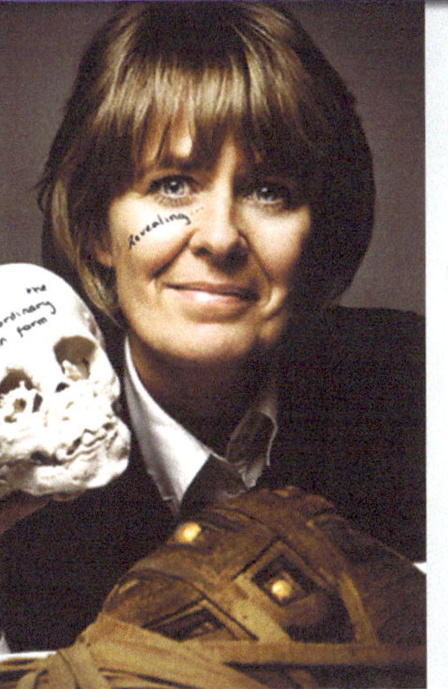

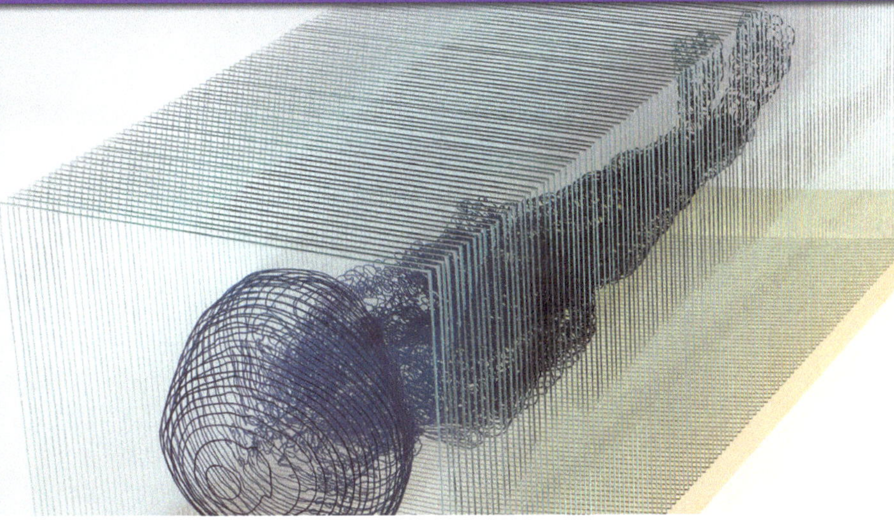

A Conversation with Angela Palmer

As a child, what did you want to become (profession-wise)?

I wanted to be a journalist and an artist.

In which town did you grow up?

Edinburgh.

Do you think your background has influenced your current art style? If so, what specific element in your background is most pervasive in influencing your current art style?

Many people have commented that at the core of my work is a desire to 'map'; the work is almost always accompanied with a narrative, often the result of months of research involving many specialists. In a way it is old fashioned story-telling, perhaps largely informed by my background in journalism. A common theme running through all my projects is the collision between art and science, and almost without exception the work is the result of collaborations with scientists in every conceivable discipline, from engineers specializing in bio-fluidics, to dust-mite and spider experts, radiologists, veterinary scientists, pediatric dentists and specialists in ancient Egyptian dyes.

What inspires you in the job of being an artist?

An endless curiosity about the natural world.

In which way do you consider yourself an innovative creator?

With all my work I strive to disrupt the senses and I use all manner of experimentation to achieve this. It can involve anything from adapting cutting edge technology to creating a work which is a simple juxtaposition of objects. But my work is almost always achieved in collaboration with specialists, mostly scientists who have been extraordinarily generous with their time and expertise.

Do you have any other creative ambitions or dreams to which you aspire?

Dreams and ambitions abound - it's time I need. I probably have four or five projects bubbling away at any one time.

Which basic elements of creativity did your family teach you?

A sense of curiosity.

How did you get the idea for creating your art work?

My environmental work was inspired by a very vivid dream. In the dream, I went to the most polluted and then cleanest place in the world wearing an identical white outfit. The outfit was like a blank canvas on which I captured the atmospheric extremes of these wildly different places, and in my dream the outfits were exhibited in a completely white gallery. When I awoke I resolved to re-enact the dream, which took me off to Linfen in Shanxi Province in China and to Cape Grim in the north west tip of Tasmania. The results were shown at the Welcome Trust gallery in London. Inspired by this work, I became determined to illustrate environmental issues through visual means, and my research led me to rainforest destruction. I went on to create the Ghost Forest, a major installation in which I brought 10 rainforest trees from a commercially logged primary forest to Europe from Africa. The trees were first shown in Trafalgar Square, then in Copenhagen outside the Danish Parliament and they are now on the lawn of the Pitt Rivers and Museum of Natural History in Oxford. The absence of the trees' trunks is intended as a metaphor for the absence of the planet's 'lungs' through continued deforestation.

I have also been making work based on details derived from MRI and CAT scans which I engrave or draw onto multiple sheets of glass, layer upon layer. This technique allows me to use the scientific anatomy of the human body stripped of its recognizable features. Most of my work is based on MRI scans of myself – rebuilding the body, slice by slice, to create a self-portrait. While the works may not be instantly recognizable as a portrait, they are objective representations – removing the familiar to expose the extraordinary architecture of the internal human form. The inspiration for this work came from an exhibit in Oxford's History of Science Museum, constructed by the Nobel Laureate Dorothy Hodgkin in the mid 1940s. She drew the electron density contour images of the penicillin molecule on horizontal sheets of Perspex. I adapted this method by drawing details of the scanned human form on multiple sheets of glass, presented in three dimensions on a vertical plane.

Do you have a favorite artist yourself?

There are so many!

Are you ever afraid you will run out of inspiration and creativity in your job?

Never.

What is the most difficult thing in your job?

Time - I always feel guilty that I don't give enough time to my family!

What is the most fun part of your job?

Collaboration - the scientists I work with never cease to inspire me with some new insight or innovation.

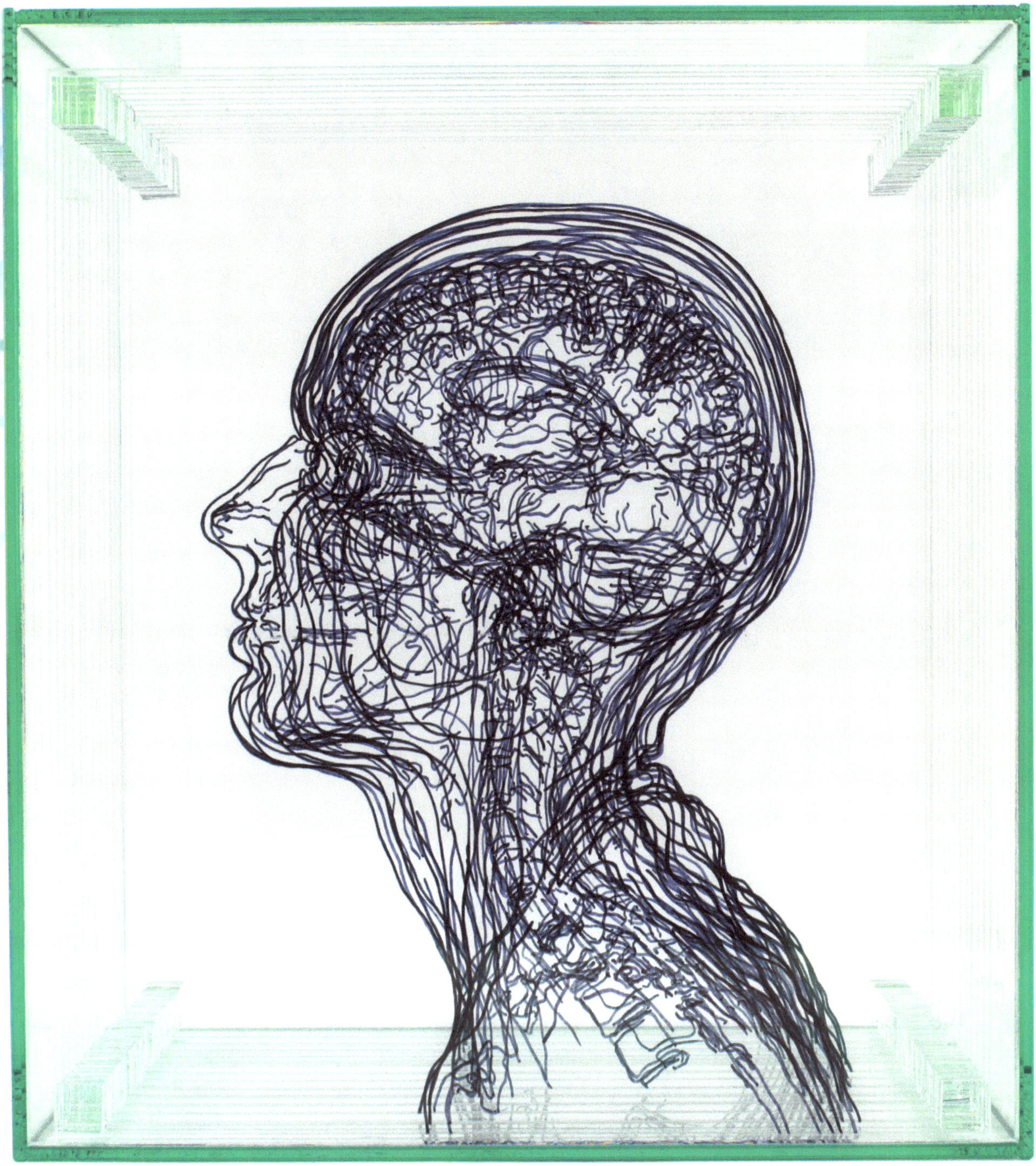

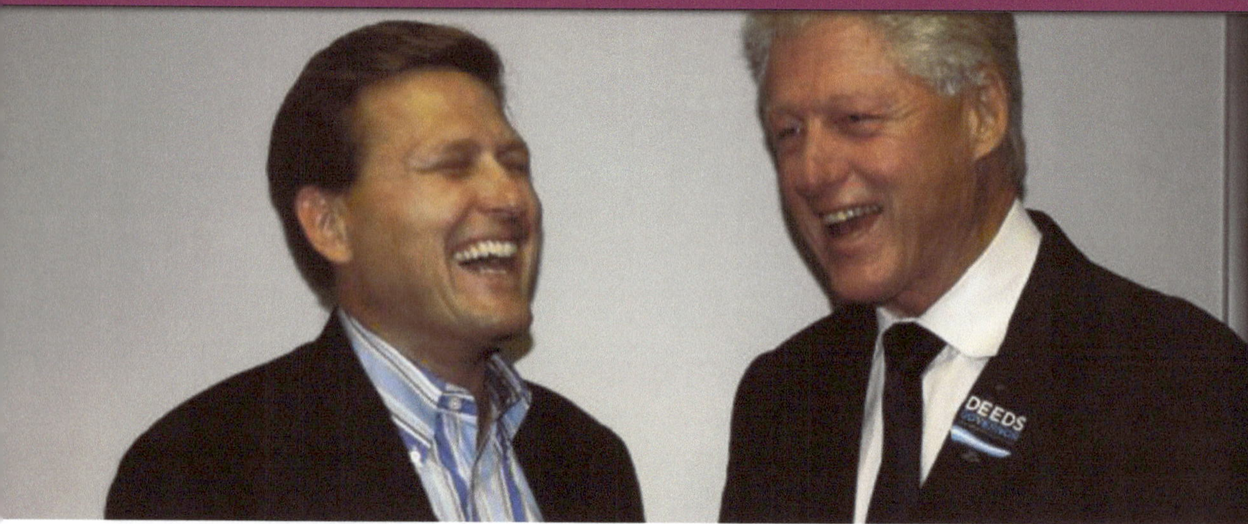

Author David Baldacci

Internationally acclaimed bestselling author David Baldacci shocked the publishing world when he burst onto the literary scene with his incredible first novel, "Absolute Power." Since then he has written 22 additional bestselling works, including "Wish You Well," "Last Man Standing," "The Christmas Train," "Split Second," "The Camel Club," "The Collectors," "Stone Cold," "The Sixth Man" and "One Summer." He has also published two young adult novels: "Freddy and the French Fries: Fries Alive!" and "Freddy and the French Fries: The Adventures of Silas Finklebean." He published a novella for the Dutch entitled "Office Hours," which was written for Holland's Year 2000 "Month of the Thriller," and authored a short story, "The Mighty Johns," as part of a mystery anthology published in 2002.

Baldacci was born in 1960 in Virginia, where he currently resides. He received a bachelor's degree in political science from Virginia Commonwealth University and a law degree from the University of Virginia. He practiced law for nine years in Washington, D.C., as both a trial and corporate attorney.

Baldacci's works have appeared in numerous magazines, newspapers, journals and other publications worldwide. He has authored seven original screenplays. His books — all of which have been national and international best sellers — have been translated into more than 45 languages and sold in more than 80 countries; over 110 million copies are in print worldwide.

Baldacci is also a contributing editor for Parade magazine, which has a circulation of over 75 million readers. Castle Rock entertainment made "Absolute Power" (Warner Books/Grand Central Publishing, 1996) into a major motion picture starring Clint Eastwood and Gene Hackman. The novel, "Absolute Power," won Britain's W. H. Smith's Thumping Good Read award for fiction in 1997 and was nominated for a literary award in Italy.

"Absolute Power" was selected for People Magazine's "Page Turner of the Week" and won the 1996 Gold Medal Award for Best Mystery/Thriller from the Southern Writers Guild.

Baldacci's authoritative legal thrillers operate on the irresistible notion that a sinister undercurrent threads through the country's most powerful institutions. While his stories hinge on the complex machinations behind the presidency, the FBI, the Supreme Court, and other spheres of influence, Baldacci finds his way into a mystery through the eyes of the innocents. Semi-innocents, at least: small players who often don't realize they're players at all end up hunting down answers, and their hunt becomes the reader's.

According to Baldacci, reading John Irving's "The World According to Garp" convinced him that he wanted to be a novelist. "Absolute Power" — in which a thief finds himself accidentally connected to a murder involving the president and the ensuing cover up — was hardly Irvingesque, but it did begin Baldacci's friendly relationship with the best seller lists, which has continued over his writing career.

Baldacci's style is brief and plot-driven, but he's not afraid to linger on macabre and vivid details, such as a rosary clenched in a plane crash victim's hand or hard-learned lessons from a sniper's life... pack your food so you can find it at night, by touch. These small but memorable — indeed, almost cinematic — details give his books another layer that distinguishes them from the average potboiler.

Although the author has occasionally departed from his usual fare (examples include the tenderhearted coming-of-age tale "Wish You Well" and the holiday-themed adventure "The Christmas Train," it is high-octane thrillers that are his true stock in trade. Whether it's a taut standalone or a new installment in his "Camel Club" series, readers know when they crack the spine of a new Baldacci book that they're in for an action-packed page-turner.

David contributes to, and is involved in, several philanthropic efforts. He is currently an ambassador for the National Multiple Sclerosis Society. His greatest efforts are dedicated to his family's own Wish You Well Foundation. Established by Michelle and David Baldacci, the foundation supports family literacy in the United States by fostering and promoting the development and expansion of new and existing literacy and educational programs. For more information, call 703-476-6032.

About David Baldacci

Baldacci was a trial lawyer and a corporate lawyer for nine years in Washington, D.C. He worked his way through college as a Pinkerton security guard and by washing and detailing 18-wheel trucks.

Baldacci writes under his own name except when published in Italy, where he uses a pseudonym because it is the homeland of his ancestors.

Bill Clinton selected "The Simple Truth" as his favorite novel of 1998, according to Baldacci's Website.

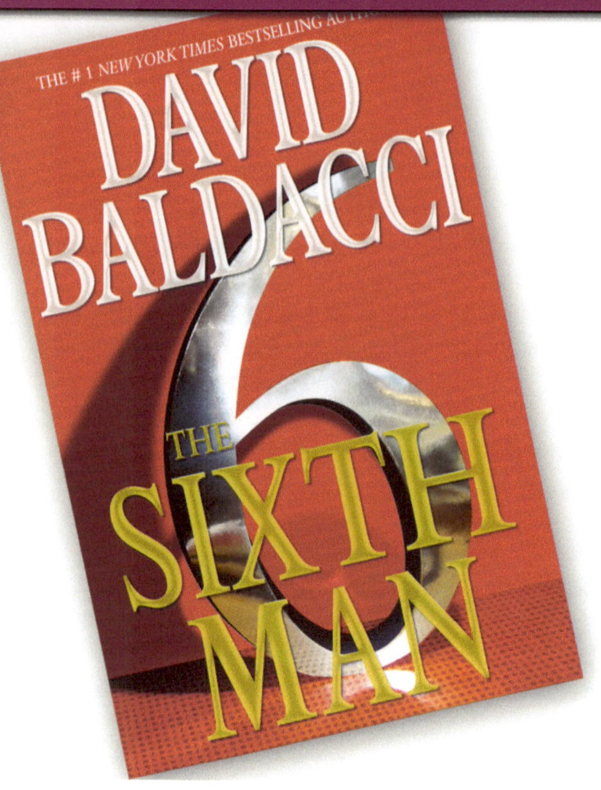

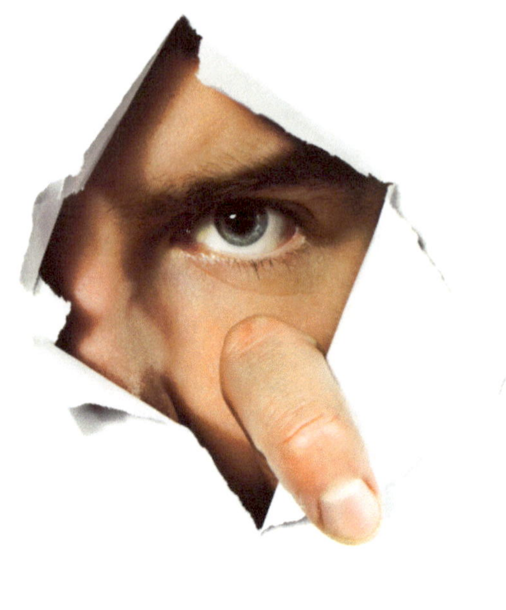

The Sixth Man (Sean King and Michelle Maxwell Series #5)

After the #1 New York Times best sellers "Split Second," "Hour Game," "Simple Genius" and "First Family," Sean King and Michelle Maxwell return in their most shocking case: a high-stakes struggle where the relentless needs of national security run up against the absolute limits of the human mind.

Edgar Roy — an alleged serial killer held in a secure, fortress-like Federal Supermax facility — is awaiting trial. He faces almost certain conviction. Sean King and Michelle Maxwell are called in by Roy's attorney, Sean's old friend and mentor Ted Bergin, to help work the case. But their investigation is derailed before it begins — en route to their first meeting with Bergin, Sean and Michelle find him murdered. It is now up to Sean and Michelle to ask the questions no one seems to want answered: Is Roy a killer? Who murdered Bergin?

With help from some surprising allies, they continue to pursue the case. But the more they dig into Roy's past, the more they encounter obstacles, half-truths, dead-ends, false friends, and escalating threats from every direction. Their persistence puts them on a collision course with the highest levels of the government and the darkest corners of power. In a terrifying confrontation that will push Sean and Michelle to their limits, the duo may be permanently parted.

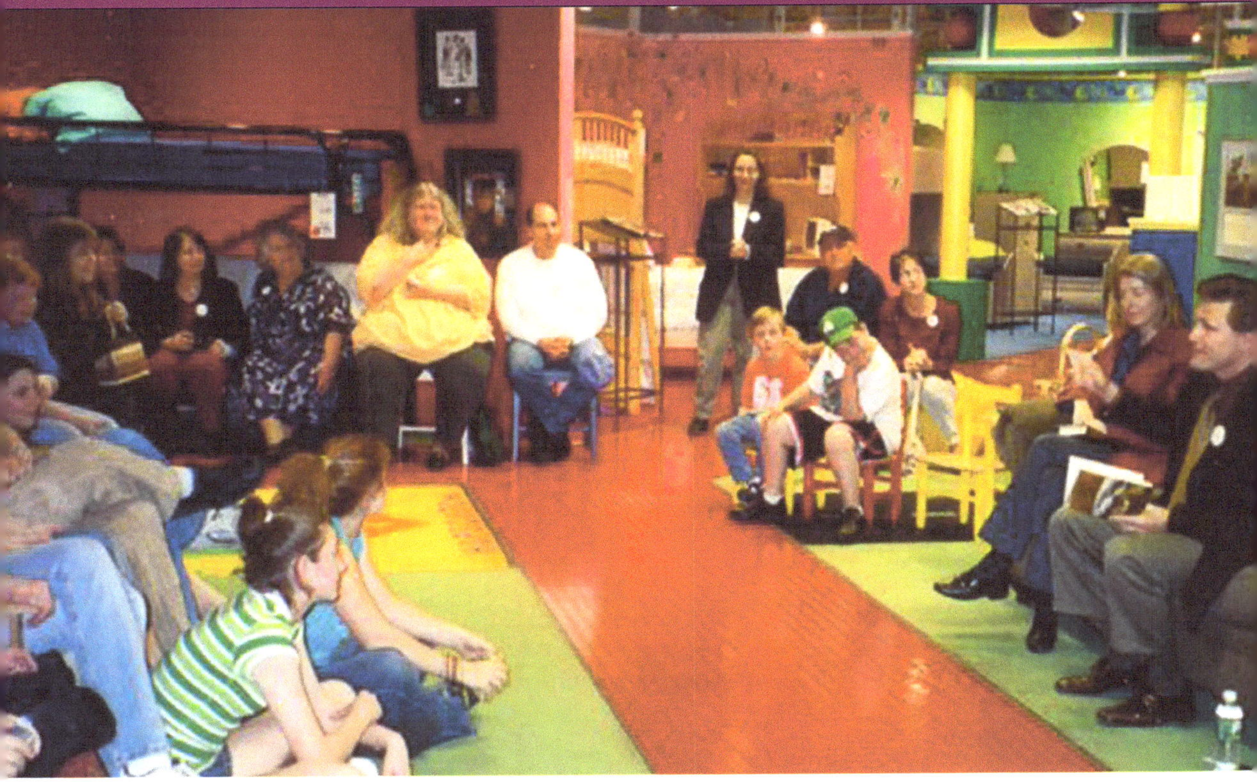

A Conversation with David Baldacci

How did you become a writer?

I started writing very early while in high school. I continued through college and while I pursued a law degree at the University of Virginia. During my years as an active attorney, I wrote in the late-evening and anytime I had a spare moment. It was my private passion.

Do you conduct your own research?

For me, doing my own research is essential to the writing process. Until I am in the midst of a chapter, paragraph, or even dialogue between characters, I never know what my research can bring to the story. Bottom line — if I cut corners on being less than thorough with the research, the story will suffer.

Do you accept story ideas from others?

I have so many stories I want to tell and explore that I am not able to accept story ideas from others. With my current and projected work schedule, honestly, I would not be able to give outside ideas the thought and writing time that they would need.

Where will you be signing books in the coming months?

I enjoy getting out from behind the writer's solitary desk and talking with readers and fellow authors. My Website will list the cities where I will be signing.

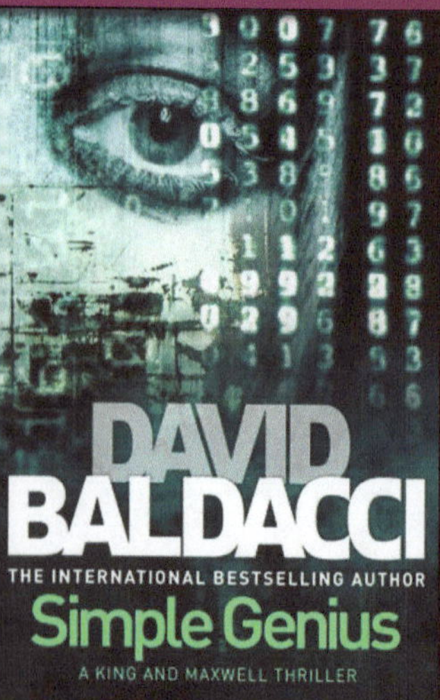

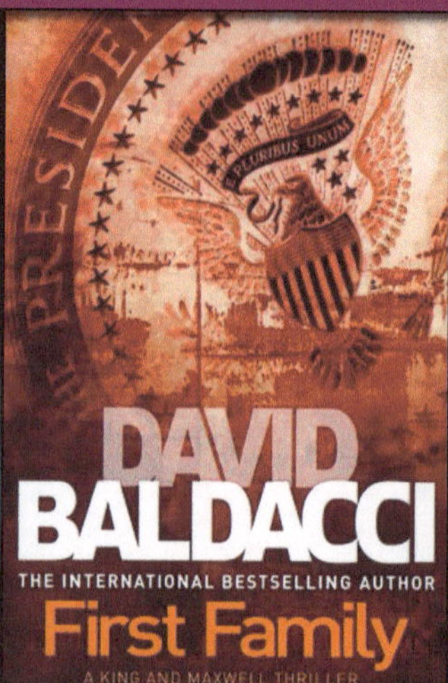

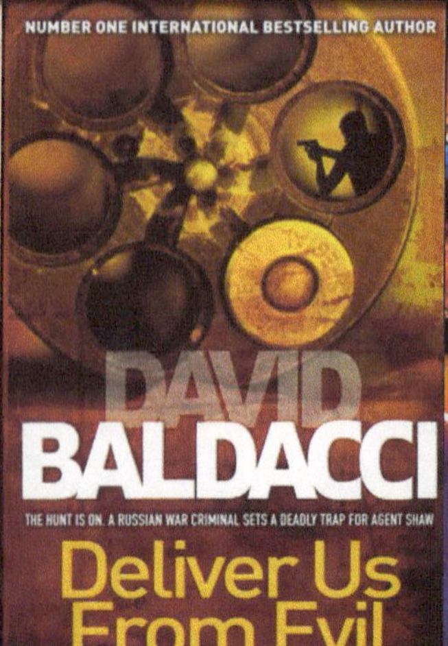

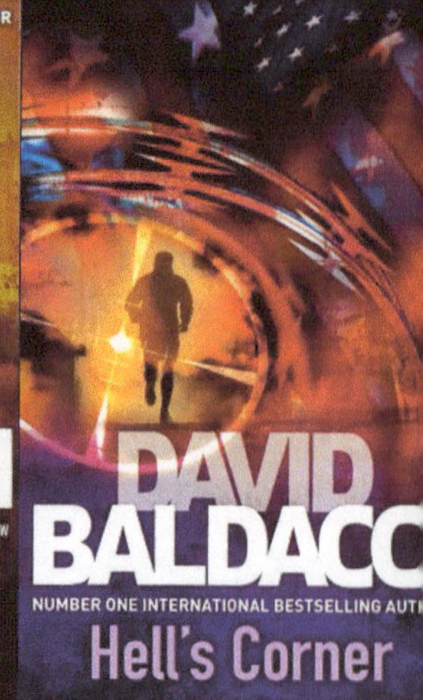

What's next?

I'm finishing up the fall 2011 book and thinking about the spring 2012 book. I receive thousands of e-mails through the website about another "Camel Club adventure." I don't think I'm finished with John Carr and the gang, so I'm thinking about bringing them back soon. In the meantime, try my latest release "One Summer" (U.S. release: June 14, 2011) and look for my newest thriller, Zero Day, on November 1, 2011!

Where do you get your book ideas and themes?

I am always thinking about and seeking story ideas. As a writer, you can never "turn off" your passion for the written word and love of a great story. So I watch life, listen intently, and basically drive everyone around me a bit crazy as I absorb every environment in which I find myself. And believe me, being naturally curious uncovers many possible story lines. Writers have to see the world exactly as it is, and then go a step further and realize the potential of what could be there.

How many books do you have in print?

I have over 110 million copies of my books in print worldwide, translated into more than 45 languages and sold in more than 80 countries.

What authors or books do you enjoy and admire?

I admire many of the traditional southern scribes: Flannery O'Connor, Lee Smith, Eudora Welty, Harper Lee, Walker Percy and Truman Capote. Since college, I have been reading and re-reading works by Anne Tyler and John Irving. I've also been reading Graham Greene and Patricia Highsmith, and am a big fan of David McCullough. And I am never far from a well-read copy of Mark Twain.

What television and/or movie projects are you working on currently?

I have several film projects being considered, and I continue to work with producers in Los Angeles on getting my books to the "big screen." Keep checking the website (http://davidbaldacci.com/) for updates.

How do you pronounce your last name?

This question comes up frequently. It should be pronounced ball-DA-chee.

How do I get a book signed?

I host an online book signing that coincides with the U.S. release date of each novel. I sign and send out up to four bookplates for your books free of charge, in the U.S. and overseas.

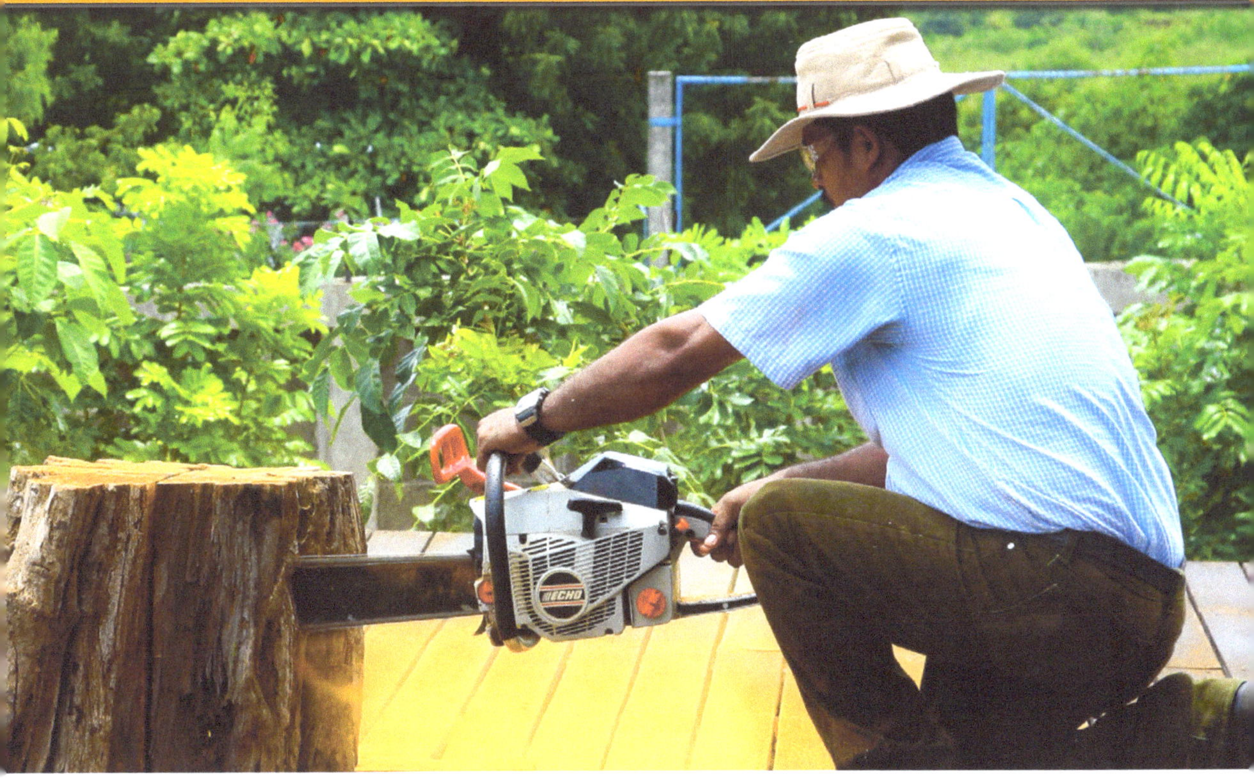

Designer John Houshmand

"Trees are the guardians of everything sacrosanct. They hold secrets of the past and relinquish everything necessary to sustain the future."

Born in 1954, John Houshmand was raised by a Dutch-American mother and an Iranian father. Houshmand has always danced between Eastern philosophy and Western principles. He spent his youth abroad in the Philippines, Great Britain, Iran and Israel.

Educated at Yale University, Houshmand received a bachelor's degree in art history in 1978. During his education, he explored the worlds of professional photography and ceramic arts. Because working with his hands proved a natural extension of his inner vision, John immersed himself in an assortment of artistic realms. He studied under the direction of Professor Emeritus of Sculpture Erwin Hauer.

Houshmand produced and recorded eclectic world jazz albums playing guitar, bass and percussion. Ultimately, it was his love for nature that led him to begin crafting homes, log chalets and bridges in the Northwest. Having relocated to New York in 1980, Houshmand launched a career by co-partnering Clark Construction, a preeminent NYC-based contracting firm.

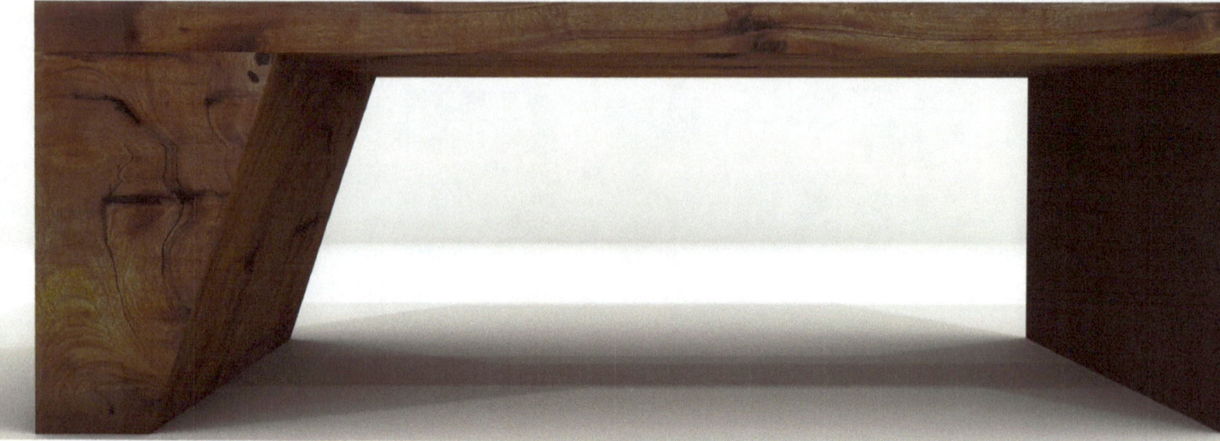

His inventive essence and exceptional life experiences have harmonized to produce his latest masterful creation. His current endeavor involves designing and crafting an exclusive line of functional art, ironically disguised as furniture. John's work embodies the simplicity of Eastern aesthetics, a vibrant celebration of nature, and a deep reverence for all things esoteric. His unique relationship with the natural world has manifested into a 900-acre farm in upstate New York, which is where he creates his furniture today.

Houshmand's collection of urban organic furniture is a celebration of the natural and vital, fusing together the basic elements of nature with timeless materials and esoteric design sensibility.

"In our world, mankind strips all life from its underlying individuality in exchange for the uniform of mass production," Houshmand said. "Trees are truly becoming a lost species."

The success of this collection revolves around the balance of precise and high-risk intervention with the art of minimal intrusion. Engaging the basic elements of wood, glass and steel, each piece is individually handcrafted to heighten and reveal their underlying splendors.

Challenging the division between fine and functional arts, Houshmand strives to provide an elevated view of nature's vibrant intensity through the ironic earthly beauty of each unique piece.

"Trees are the guardians of everything sacrosanct. They hold secrets of the past and relinquish everything necessary to sustain the future," Houshmand explained. "They bare their souls providing us with the air we breathe, the shelter in which we live, and the food that nourishes our very beings. We allow trees to do the talking. We simply listen."

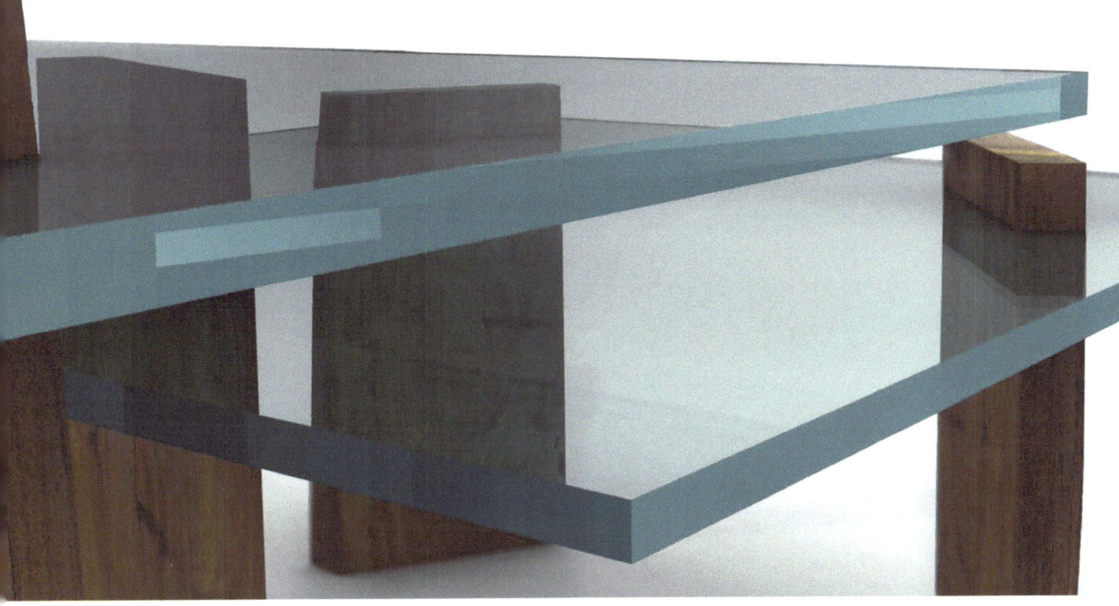

A Conversation with John Houshmand

As a child, what did you want to become (profession-wise)?

As a child, I went through the evolution of heroes ... astronaut, president and so on. In college, I wanted a panchromatic education with no career target. Later, I wanted to know all that is knowable. Now I just want to make things that bring the future into the present, and make it a better, wiser, more beautiful one.

In which town did you grow up?

I spent five years in Los Angeles and then 11 in Manila, Philippines. My father is Iranian and my mom is Dutch/American. I am an immigrant to planet Earth.

Do you think your background has influenced your current design style? If so, what specific element in your background is most pervasive in influencing your current design style?

My background has so many pieces that it is more of a mosaic, with tiles that range from a suburban American childhood, a tropical youth, an international geography, elemental experiences, and so many other story parts.

What inspires you in the job of being a designer?

Capturing an essential potential outside of time/space and making it real. And, of course, testing it against a calculus of beauty, meaning and inspiration... the vertical axis.

In which way do you consider yourself an innovative creator?

I feel my vector is to take the most exquisite aspects of organic and inorganic life on this planet and then marry these to a truly elemental design sense that borders on the platonic.

Do you have any other creative ambitions or dreams to which you aspire?

I want to learn to play the cello, the saxophone and learn theoretical physics. And, I'd like to become a great father and a successful farmer.

Which basic elements of creativity did your family teach you?

My family taught me to be global, honest, aspire to the best, and to appreciate the world around me.

How did you get the idea for this design style?

In dreams.

Do you have a favorite designer yourself?

Zumthor, Holl, and many musical composers whom I fancy to be excellent designers in the ephemeral world that might teach a few solid designers a thing or two.

Are you ever afraid you will run out of inspiration and creativity in your job?

No.

What is the most difficult thing in your job?

Doing the business side of it all.

What is the most fun part of your job?

Inspiration, love of uses, and seeing something new dancing between one's own existence and the world around. The world is made new, larger, and more vibrant each time. There is nothing like the passage of a real idea into your brain to get you high.

Do you expect your way of designing to change in the future?

I hope so. It starts now.

Do you embrace the changes in the design industry regarding social media and technology influences?

Only those that have a value component. Technology ultimately becomes transparent and is not a thing in and of itself. All is constant and value — and silence and beauty. GIGO.

Do you aspire to collaborate in your creations with an artist from another artistic discipline?

I always love collaborating with any person in any discipline. Stretches in all the right places.

Do you like art? Do you have any preferences for an artist? And/or for creators of artistic work?

I love art. Art and music are the quantum portals into our 3D existence. They give us the vibrations that evolve our existence when of appropriate quality. Do not forget, ALL impressions are food, and all food has qualities and attributes. Eat well daily and eat better each day than the one before. Your mission here on Earth is to bring up the vibratory level of the planet and humanity, and it starts with yourself.

Preferences are many: Keith Jarrett, Pat Metheny, the architects mentioned above, John Luther Adams, Rothko, Bach, and on and on...

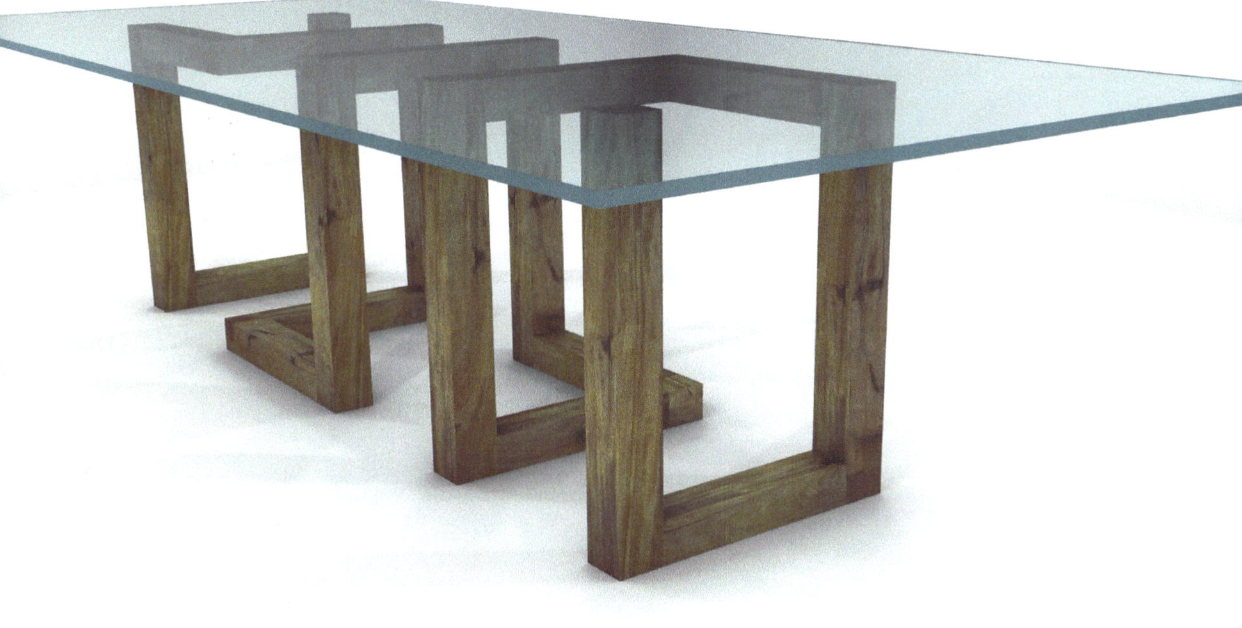

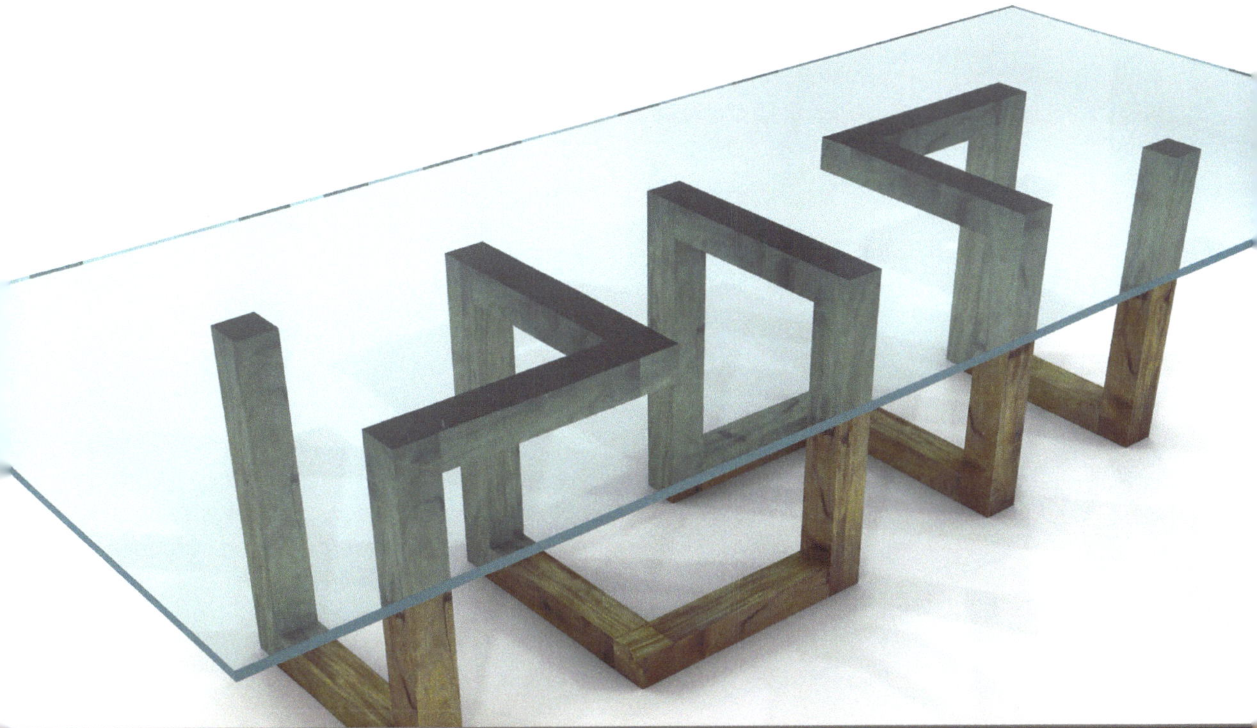

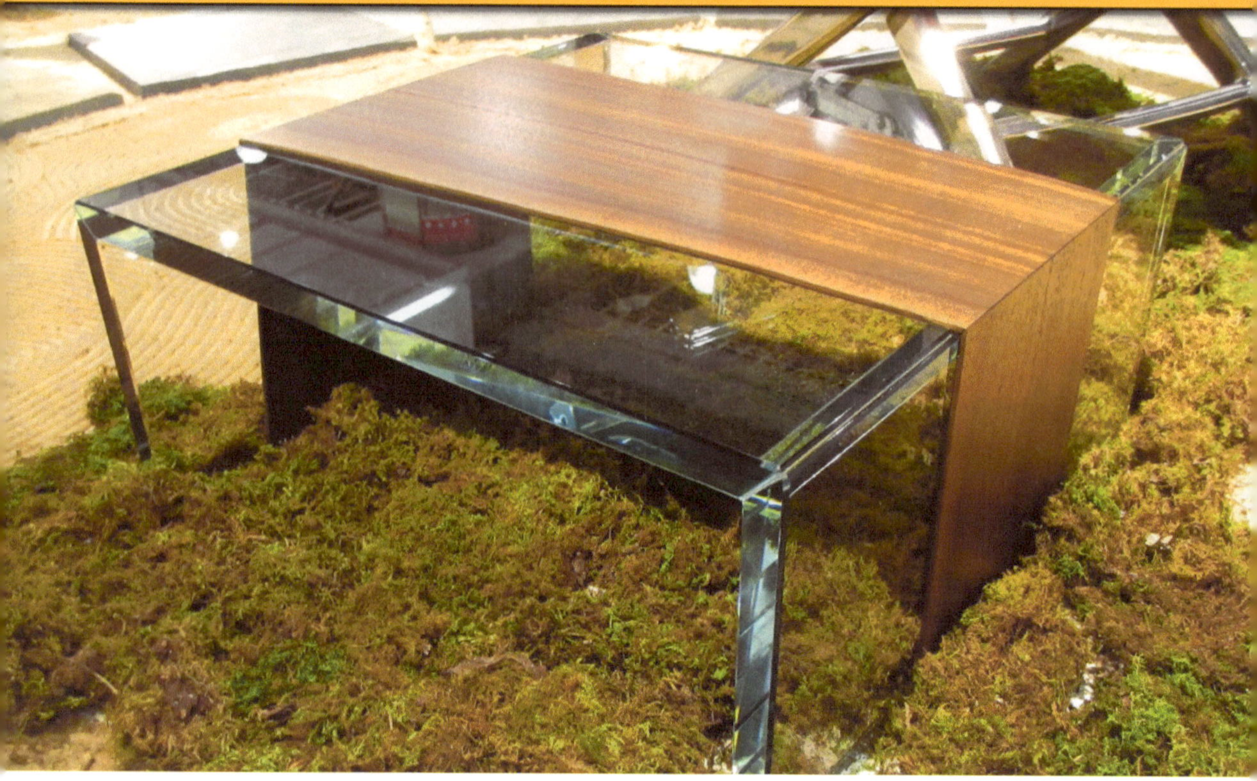

If so, why is that? What special quality do you like in their work or personalities?

A great artist/composer/creator has the power to bring YOU and your existence into a new reality, open you up to new dimensions, and raise your consciousness. Once each experience has taken root that becomes your new psychic platform. And you seek out the next rung on the ladder. Of course, it can be beautiful, exciting and inspirational, but sometimes it can be disturbing and challenging.

In which way do you think design and art are different and/or similar?

Design and art are an odd marriage. Design can be simply the well-ordered placement of things — the presentation of aesthetics in 3D. But to enter the world of art, there must be a component of meaning, and that is either subjective or objective depending on whom you ask. I believe it must be measured against a calculus that is objective. But therein we get into metaphysics.

Do you follow any philosophical or psychological approach in making your designs?

Bring up the vibration level...

What is your favorite building in the world?

I really like my house in Mexico (www.retreatmexico.com). And the one in my head I want to build next.

What is your favorite hotel?

No favorite hotels. The experience of a hotel has so much to do with the locale it is in, and a hole in the wall in Heaven can have as much power as a palace in a ghetto.

What would be your ideal home?

Again, it is in my head.

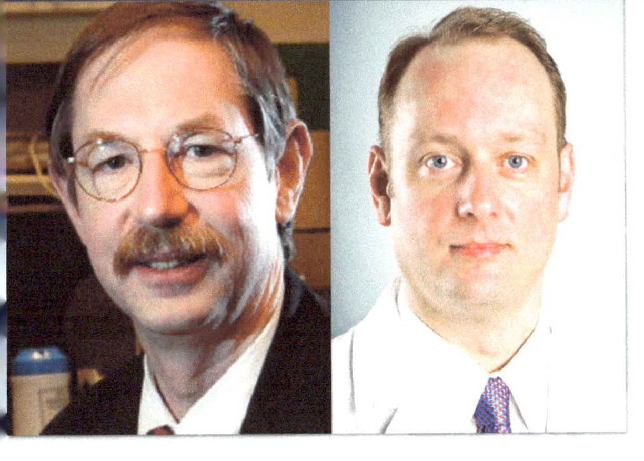

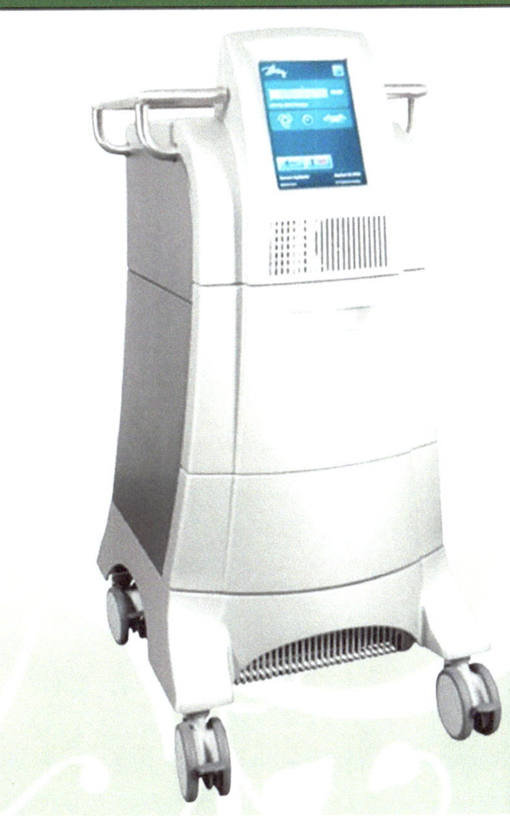

CoolSculpting by ZELTIQ

Offers Cutting-Edge Procedure to Fight Fat

What is CoolSculpting®?

CoolSculpting® is a revolutionary method of targeting specific fatty areas of the body and reducing those fat cells in a non-invasive manner. The process uses cooling technology to gradually break down the fat without damaging the surrounding tissue.

The Innovative Creators

Harvard scientists R. Rox Anderson, MD and Dieter Manstein, Md, Phd of The Wellman Center of Photomedicine at Massachusetts General Hospital in Boston invented the concept called Cryolipolysis, which is the basis of the CoolSculpting® procedure.

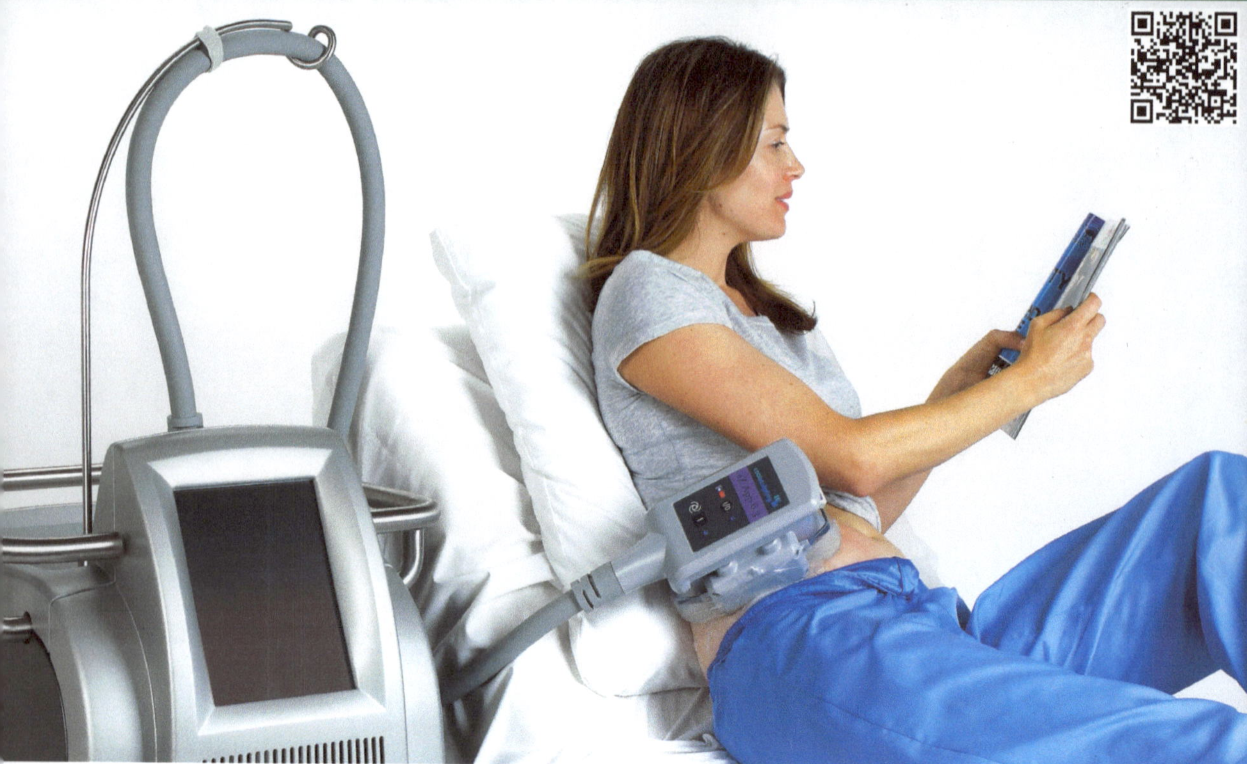

The Science Behind CoolSculpting®

Cryolipolysis is a non-invasive method of cooling fat tissue to break down the fat cells. The chilled cells undergo a cellular death and are eliminated over time. This process is most effective in "spot reduction" of fat—not large areas of fatty tissue.

The CoolSculpting® Procedure

Using a cooling applicator made by ZELTIQ™, a San Francisco Bay medical device company, doctors can target specific areas of fat. The applicator cup creates pressure from a vacuum which draws the fat tissue between the cooling applicator's panels. The procedure can take from one to three hours.

Patients resume their daily activities immediately as the body begins ridding itself of these fat cells through its natural metabolic process. Patients usually see a twenty percent reduction of fat in the targeted areas within two to four months.

What makes CoolSculpting® Different?

This FDA-cleared, patented, and non-invasive technology makes scars, needles, lasers, anesthesia, and long recoveries a thing of the past. Patients can read or check their email while undergoing the procedure, and they experience no "down-time" afterward. CoolSculpting® is ideal for anyone who wants to remove specific areas of fat in an easy and gentle manner.

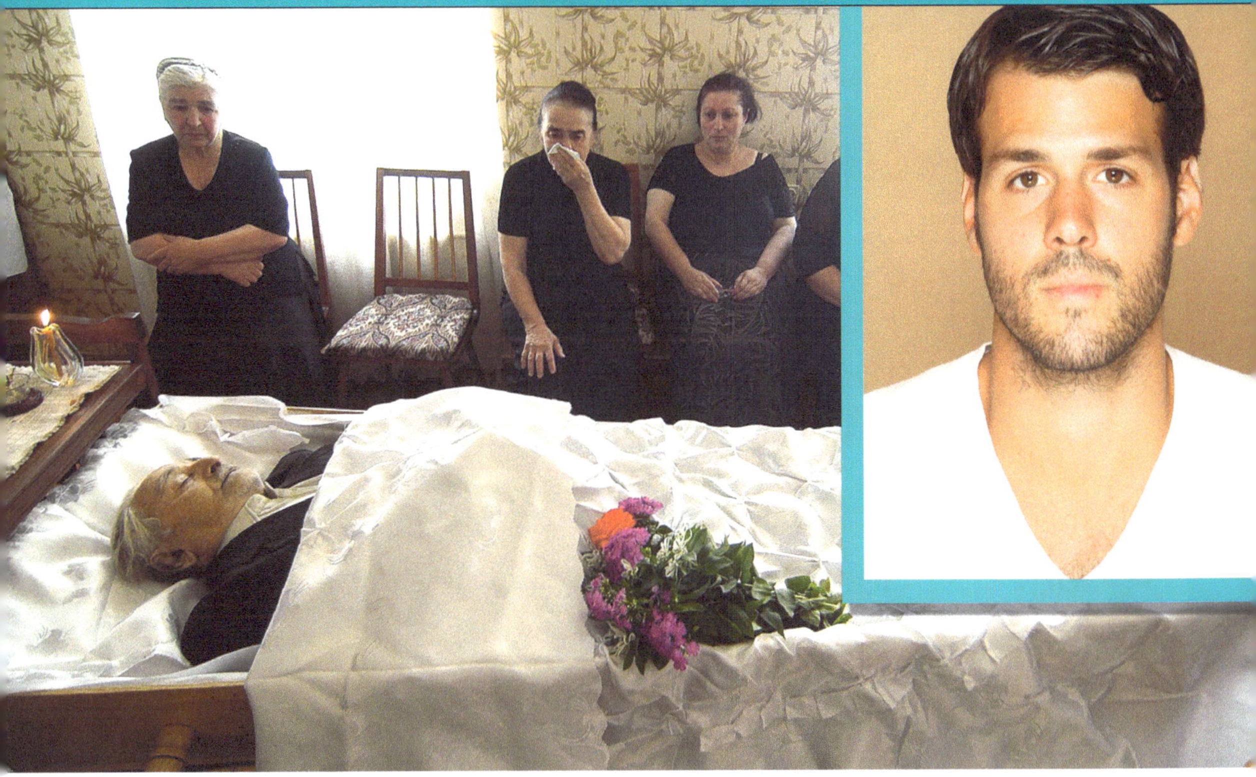

Photographer Jonathan Alpeyrie Images of War

Jonathan Alpeyrie was born in Paris in 1979 and moved to the United States in 1993. He graduated from The Lycée Français de New York (The French High School of New York City) in 1998, before going to the University of Chicago to earn his BA in medieval history. Jonathan started his career shooting photographs for local Chicago newspapers during his undergraduate years. He did his first photo essay in 2001 while traveling the South Caucasus. After graduating in 2003, he went to the Congo to work on various essays. Getty Images took notice of these photos and Jonathan signed a contributor contract with them in early 2004.

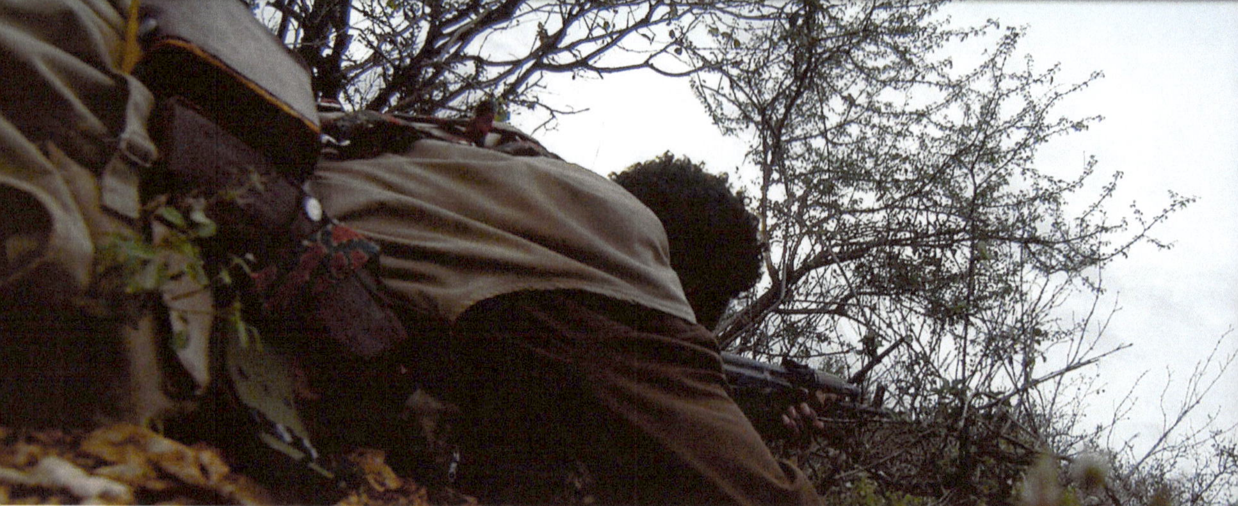

A Conversation with Jonathan Alpeyrie

As a child, what did you want to become (profession-wise)?

At first I wanted to be a fighter pilot, then later an army officer.

In which town did you grow up?

I grew up in Paris, then NYC.

Do you think your background has influenced your current photography style? If so, what specific element in your background is most pervasive in influencing your current photography style?

Yes. Many members of my family fought in major conflicts, like WWI, WWII, the Spanish Civil War, the War of Indochina. A lot of classic war photos came out of that– with Robert Capa and Henrie Huet's work.

What inspires you in the job of being a photographer?

My strong connection with history inspires me, as I am a history major from the University of Chicago. What better way to live these historical events then to photograph them?

In which way do you consider yourself an innovative creator?

I do not consider myself a creator. I consider myself a historical collector.

Do you have any other creative ambitions or dreams to which you aspire?

Time will tell.

Which basic elements of creativity did your family teach you?

My mother is an artist/painter. Composition in photography is crucial. It is the same in painting.

How did you get the idea for creating your photography?

Through my own experience and the way conflict photography was shot.

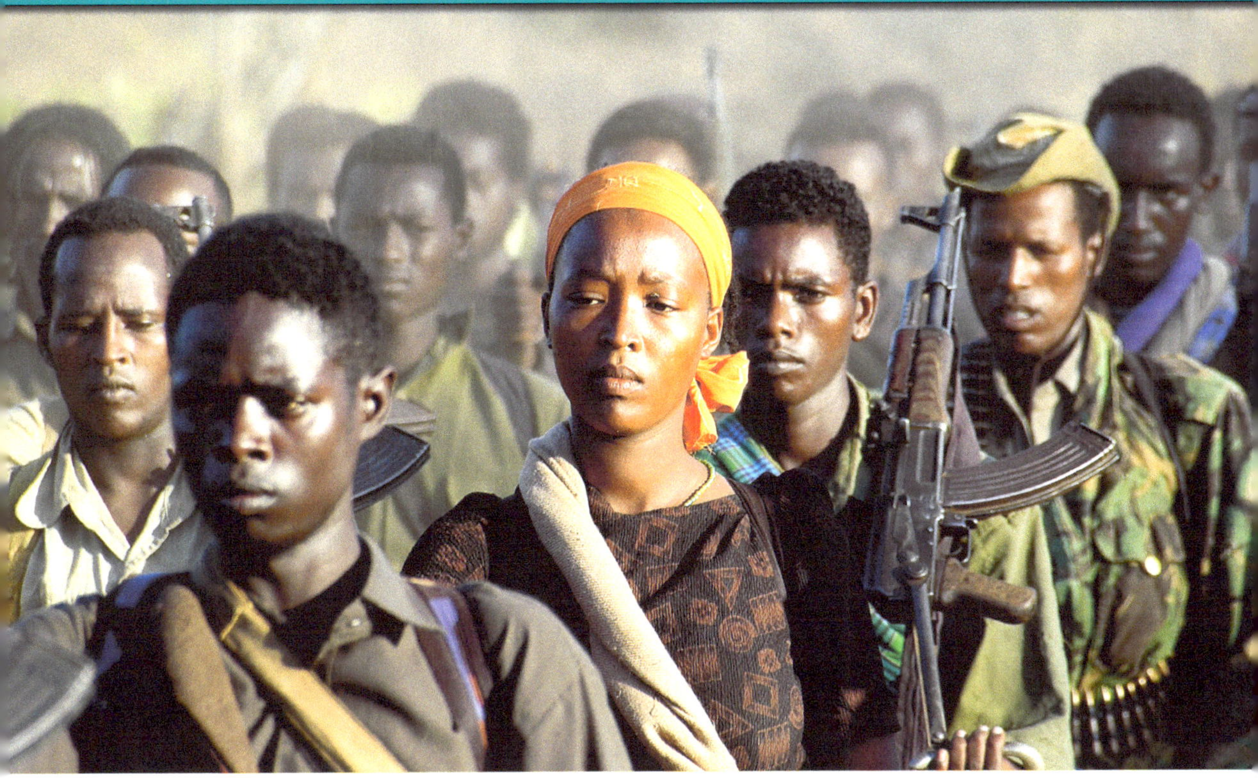

Do you have a favorite photographer yourself?

No.

Are you ever afraid you will run out of inspiration and creativity in your job?

No. There is an unlimited pool of ideas and events.

What is the most difficult thing in your job?

War.

What is the most fun part of your job?

War.

Do you expect your way of creating photography to change in the future?

It's impossible to tell.

Do you embrace the changes in the photography industry regarding social media and technology influences?

Not at all. I understand how technology is helping us, but it is not making us better photographers. Also, I truly dislike the way world media has transformed itself into a people-frenzy oriented machine— which feeds information to people— because it is what sells.

Do you like art? Do you have any preferences for an artist? And/or for creators of artistic work? (Creators can also be chefs, designers, fashion designers or inventors.)

I mostly appreciate very old and traditional art, from antiquity to medieval art.

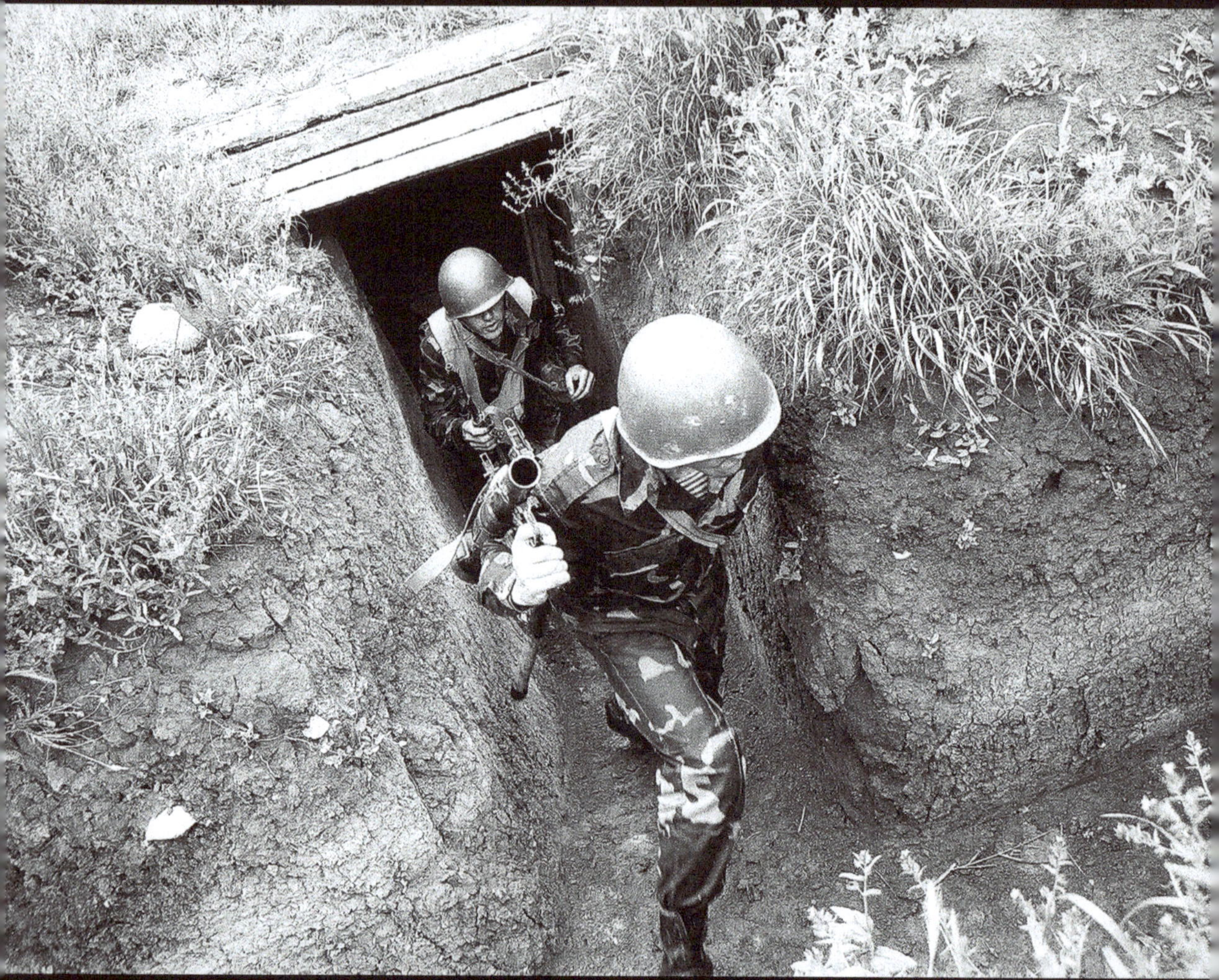

If so, why is that? What special quality do you like in their work or personalities?

I have a very strong connection with old Western traditions seen in Antic art, but also in medieval Christian art as well.

Could we feature your favorite photographer, author, artist, designer, architect, filmmaker, etc. in our publication and/or online?

Photographer: Henrie Huet
Author: Gustave Flaubert
Artist: Amedeo Modigliani
Architect: Phidias (Greek Sculptor)
Filmaker: Mel Gibson

In which way do you think photography, art and design are different and/or similar?

War photography differs mostly because of the experience one lives and goes through to take these photos. A photojournalist has to live his own experience in order to get the shot he needs. A pure artist or designer has a different relationship with the world, perhaps a more virtual one.

Do you aspire to collaborate in your creations with an artist from another artistic discipline?

Modigliani (Amedeo Modigliani, an Italian artist who worked mainly in France. Best known for painting and sculptures with mask-like faces and elongated forms).

Do you have a favorite company or exciting other creator with whom you would like to work?

No.

Do you follow any philosophical or psychological approach in your photography?

I have a very Western approach to my work and the way I chose my assignments on the field. Western influences are strong in my work, showing its influence in the world, and how globalization (a Western push), is changing human behavior and decision making.

What is your favorite building in the world? (If more than one, please list more, and if you like, please add motivation to your favorite(s).)

The Parthenon.

What is your favorite hotel? (If more than one, please list more, and if you like, please add motivation to your favorite(s).)

The Manaslu Hotel in Kathmandu, Nepal.

What would be your ideal home? (If more than one, please list more, and if you like, please add motivation to your dream home(s).)

I'd buy an island off Greece.

Do you have any dreams for the future?

I don't organize my life in terms of dreams, but more with goals and objectives. A successful career is a major goal for me.

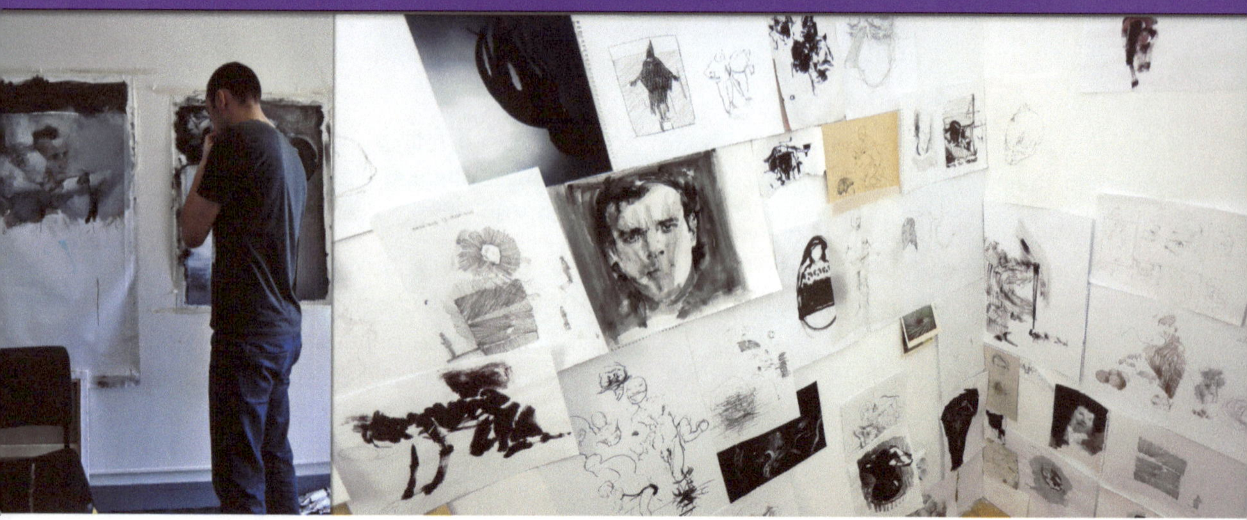

Innovative Artist - Razvan Boar

Ana Cristea Gallery in New York recently presented (May 19 - June 25, 2011) the first solo show in the U.S. of Romanian artist Razvan Boar (b. 1982). Boar is one of the most promising and original talents emerging from a new generation of painters in Romania, a country that has recently produced an important movement in contemporary painting.

At first sight, Boar's characters might appear deliciously seductive. However, once a viewer's gaze lingers on a particular painting, they are drawn into the scenario the artist imagines for them. Initially, these scenarios might appear quite straight forward, even familiar, but the work's familiarity is not merely rooted in commonplace contemporary imagery; it springs from Boar's attentiveness to art's great past masters.

The one constant of Boar's work is that no matter what the dress, social status or position of his sitters, their humanity burns out from the work; it is confrontational and unavoidable.

Razvan Boar's works, meticulously rendered paintings and drawings, withhold themselves. They are oblique in their exploration of social or political change in the lives of their protagonists. Things are happening, but somewhere in the middle distance. His subjects are indifferent to our gaze, fully absorbed in their own worlds, as we, through looking, become absorbed in ours.

It is perhaps this area, where the image breaks down into its effects, that the artist is exploring altogether. The recipient of the Constantin Brâncusi fellowship granted by the Romanian Cultural Institute, Razvan Boar is currently working in Paris at Cité Internationale des Arts. Recent shows include "Portraits of Ambiguity" at Ana Cristea Gallery and "Portraits and Self portraits" curated by Liliana Popescu at Knoll Galerie as part of the project "EAST by SOUTH WEST, curated by_vienna 2011." The Ana Cristea Gallery exhibition was made possible with the support of the Romanian Cultural Institute in New York.

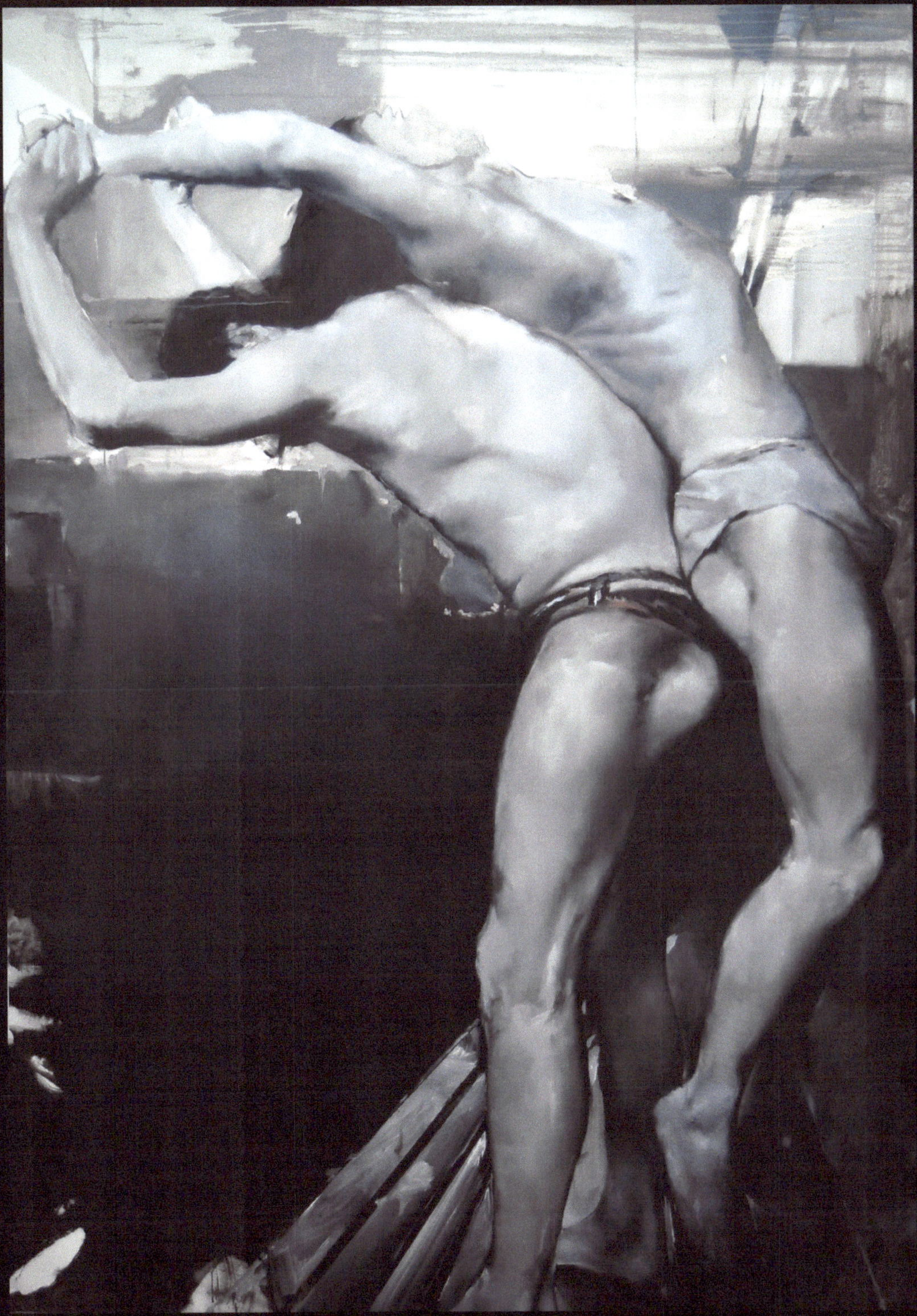

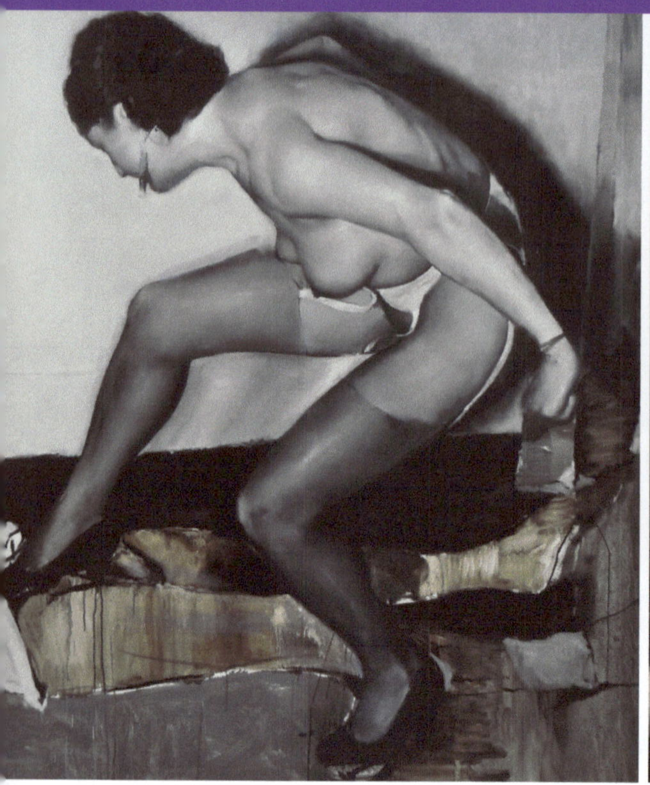

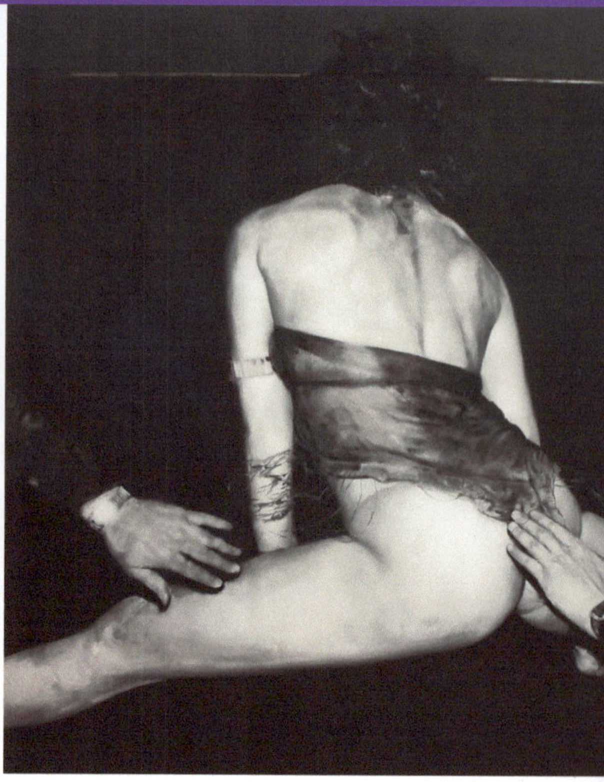

The Ana Cristea Gallery

Since its inception in October 2009, Ana Cristea Gallery has established a strong international program, showcasing some of the most interesting artists to emerge in recent years from Central and Eastern Europe. These artists include Razvan Boar (Romania), Zsolt Bodoni (Hungary), Alexander Tinei (Republic of Moldova) and Daniel Pitin (Czech Republic), all of whom were first introduced to a New York audience by the gallery.

Ana Cristea has also featured young, local artists like Michael Brown, Andrew Sendor and Joe Diebes. The gallery will continue to develop its program by focusing primarily on international and local new talent in painting, sculpture, video and photography.

Romanian Cultural Institute

The Romanian Cultural Institute in New York (RCINY) aims to promote Romanian culture throughout the U.S. and internationally, as well as to build sustainable, creative partnerships among American and Romanian cultural organizations. RCINY acts as a catalyst and proponent of initiatives across artistic fields, striving to foster understanding, cultural diplomacy, and scholarly discourse by enriching public perspectives of contemporary Romanian culture. RCINY is currently the president of the European Union National Institutes for Culture (EUNIC) network in New York City. For the past five years, RCINY has been an active enabler and supporter of the presence and promotion of contemporary Romanian visual artists in the U.S.

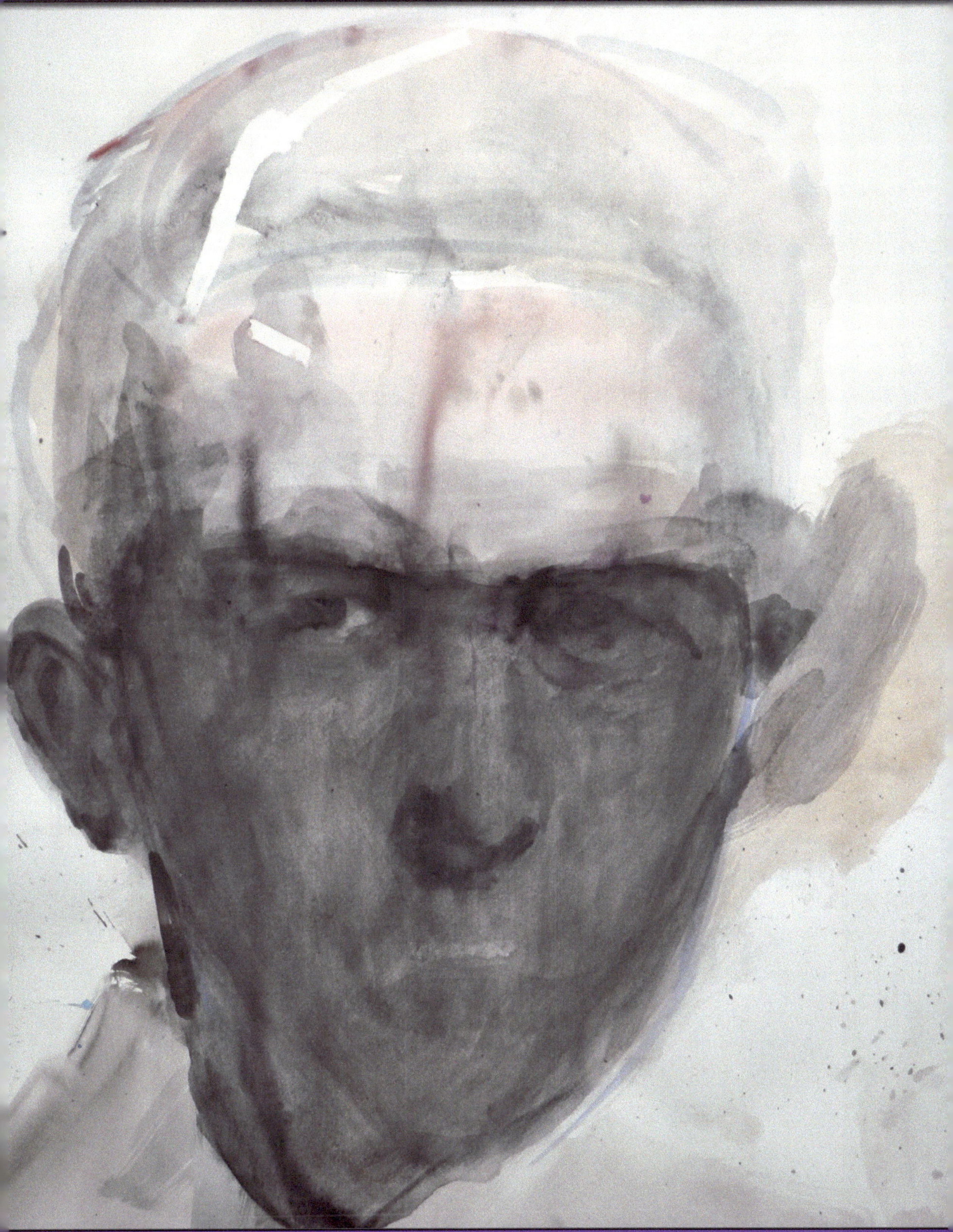

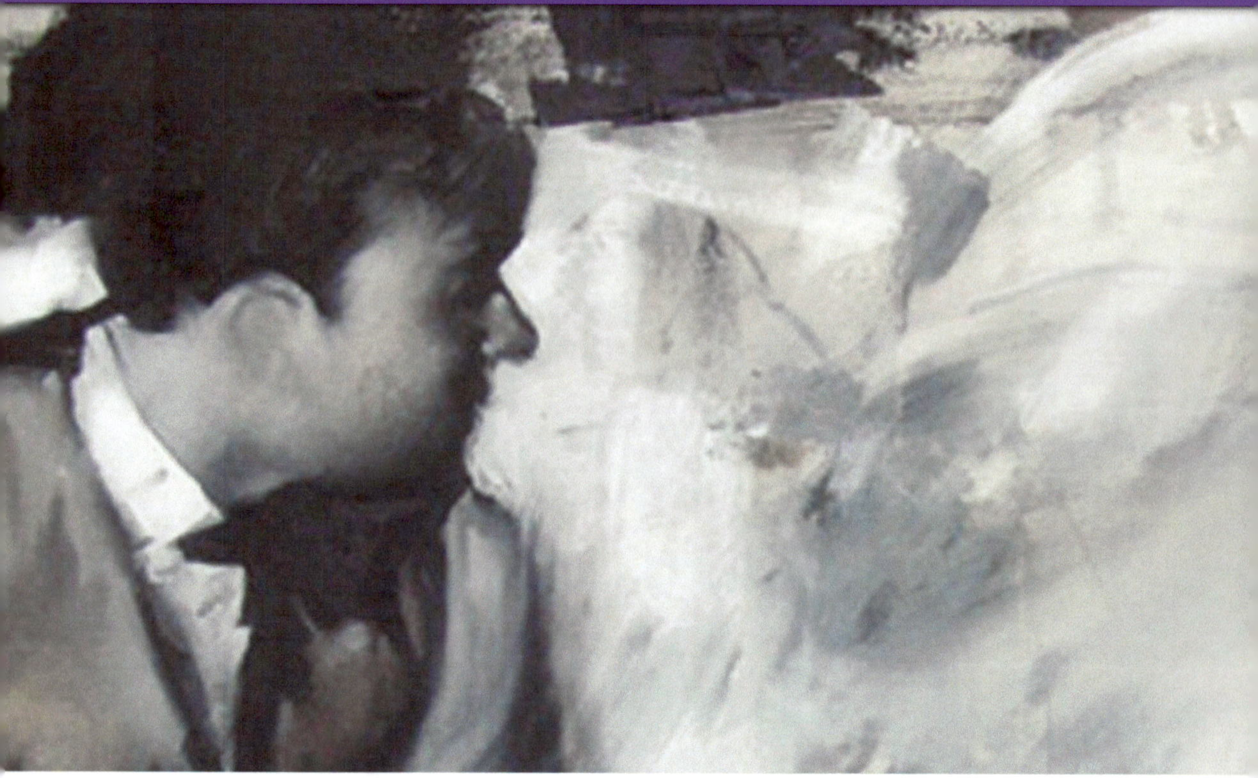

A Conversation with Razvan Boar

As a child, what did you want to become profession-wise?

I had always been fascinated with animals, and when I was really small, I wanted to become a shepherd. Afterwards, I thought my next job had to be an astronaut. I had a strong passion for drawing since I can remember, but I never considered that this would have been the work of an artist.

Where did you grow up?

I grew up in Lugoj, a nice small town in Western Romania that has large Hungarian and German minorities.

Do you think your background influenced your current art style? If so, what specific element in your background is most pervasive in influencing your current art style?

Certainly your background influences you, but it's difficult to identify a specific element that can be held responsible for the way I am or for the way I see things. Art wasn't my first choice in high school; I studied biology and chemistry.

I think this "dabbling" before turning to art enriched me in some ways. I know now that my family contributed a great deal to building my character. It was something that we had in the family; perhaps it was a way of making things unique and original.

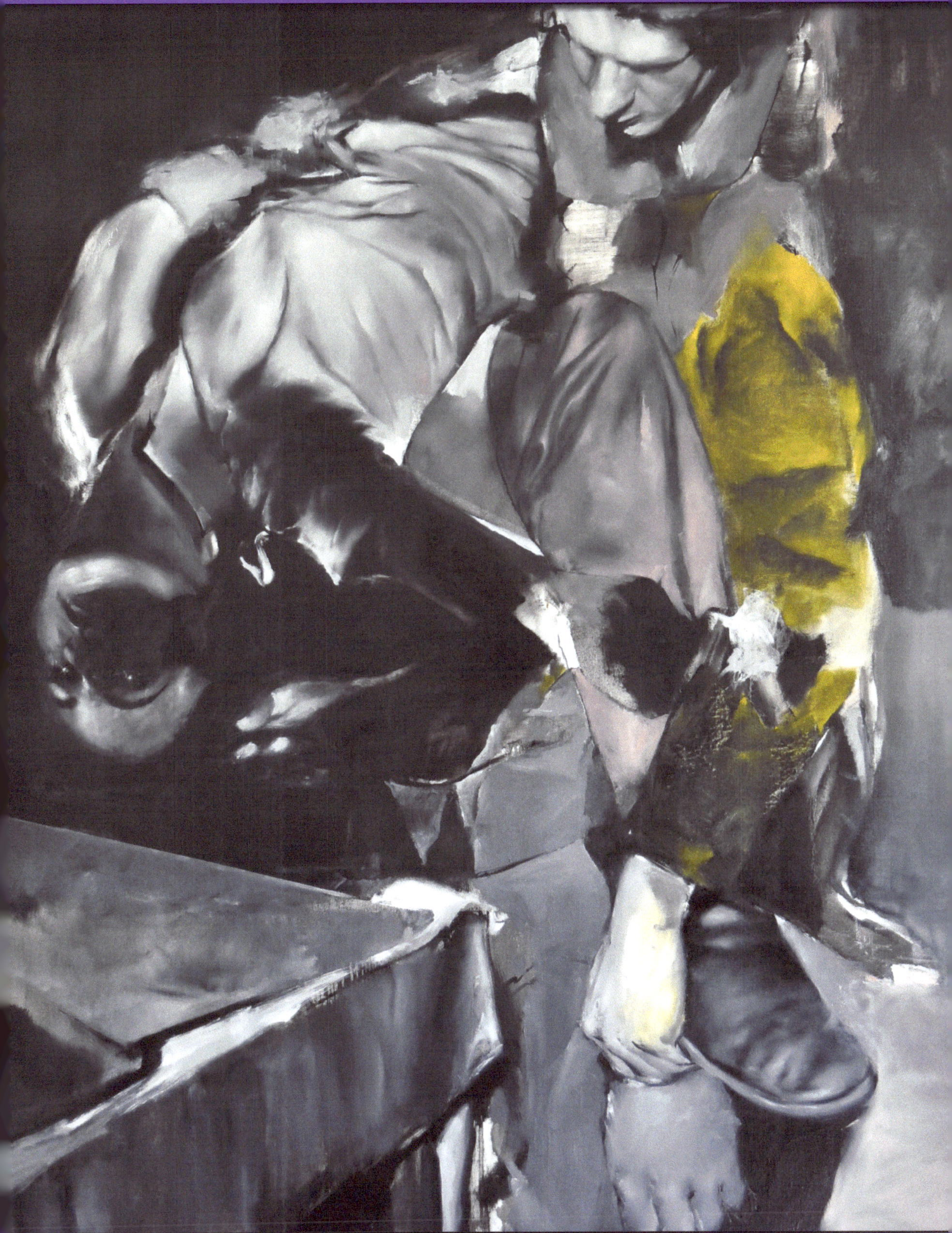

Could you describe the masterpieces you have created?

I'd rather look at it as my work — I wouldn't call it "masterpieces." Some works became more important than others, but I try to approach every piece with the same consideration. If I were to describe the work that I consider to be the most important, I would mention my portraits first. Then, I would continue to explain my work by specifying my interventions and interpretations upon the human body. That's the general idea. My work is really a praise of mankind.

Which basic elements of creativity did your family teach you?

I mentioned earlier that my family was special in some ways. My parents produced things (without being artists) that were considered by others to be unique and beautiful, and I guess I learned just by being there and watching.

How did you get the idea for creating your artwork?

Work comes from work really.

What is the most difficult thing in your job?

Keeping up with deadlines. Also, being able to work every day — to have the same rhythm.

What is the most fun part of your job?

I would rather call it the rewarding part. That's when I'm happy with the outcome of my work and when others enjoy it too.

Do you expect your way of creating artwork to change in the future?

My work is different now than it was a year ago, so a few changes could happen in the future. A big part of my work consists of experimenting, trying different solutions to problems I'm facing, and criticizing my own thoughts, ideas and matter. I'm constantly rearranging my stuff, planning works and generating ideas.

Do you embrace the changes in the art industry regarding social media and technology influences?

Yes.

Do you aspire to collaborate in your creations with an artist from another artistic discipline?

I would like to do that.

Do you have a favorite company or exciting other creator with whom you would like to work?

I could name a few of them, but for now, I'm not planning to collaborate with other artists for specific projects.

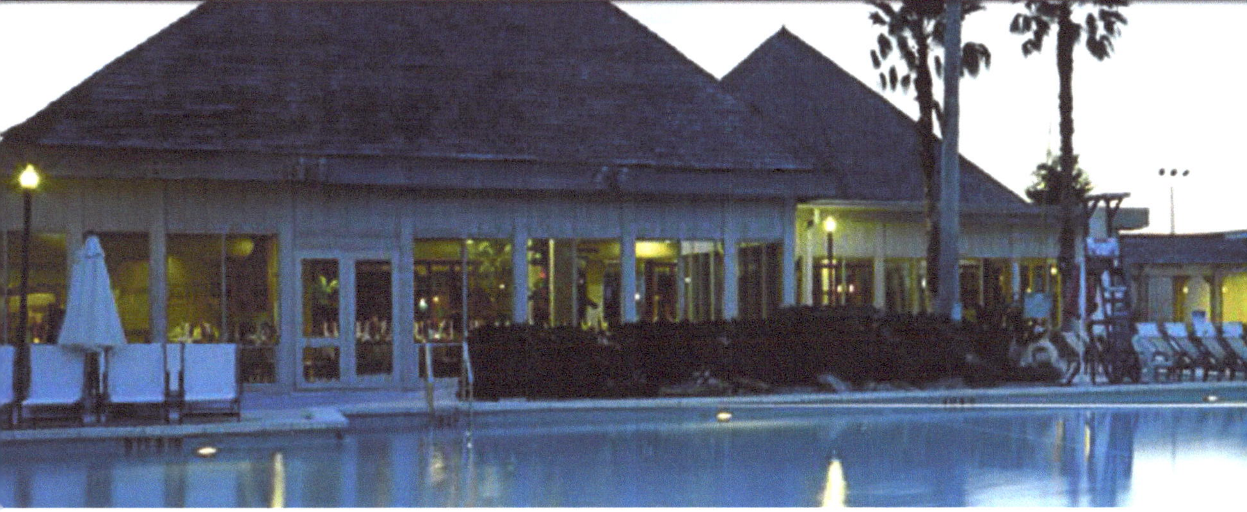

The Sandpiper Club Med Miami

A Flagship of Club Med Resorts

You are invited to experience Sandpiper Bay as you've never experienced it before. This newly renovated hotel is the innovative creation of Francois Champsaur – a world renowned French Interior Designer.

The Sandpiper is located in Sandpiper Bay, Florida and considered the only all-inclusive family resort in the United States. This 216-acre resort is secluded in the beautiful landscape of Port St. Lucie and surrounded by natural swamps and lush tropics. Club Med Sandpiper Bay offers visitors everything from a premium, full-service fitness spa to golf and tennis academies. If you are looking for a quiet haven to escape everyday life, Club Med Sandpiper Bay also offers secluded oasis spots of rest and relaxation. This is truly a resort to meet everyone's needs.

Meet Francois Champsaur

Francois Champsaur was born in Marseilles (south of France) and attributes his upbringing and art studies in Marseilles as two great influences on his work. Francois also gives credit to his mother, a ceramist, for giving him, "a great sense of color and harmony." Among other things, Francois specializes in developing interior and structural design together. This specialty is seen in The Sandpiper Project that presented its own design demands. "The Sandpiper project was unique because the challenge was to reinstate the importance of the site and natural heritage into the hotel and gardens area. The main idea was to open the rooms and common areas (pools, restaurants and alleys) on the St. Lucie River and Sandpiper Bay," said Francois. One example of this goal achieved is the new River Pool that provides breathtaking views of the river and its elaborate vegetation.

Francois is currently working on a variety of projects including a hotel in the 8th District of Paris and Yearlings Auction Hall in Deauville that is due to open in mid-August with rare Yearlings sales.

Luxury at its Best

The Sandpiper Club Med Miami offers luxurious accommodations, tennis, golf and fitness academies, yoga and spa wellness options, gourmet dining and excursions. This premier resort is also touted as a top family resort.

An Assortment of Room Options

At the Sandpiper, you have your pick of lavish room accommodations. You have five options to choose from: The Club Room, Club Family Room, Deluxe Room, Deluxe Family Room and the Club Room Pre-renovated. Each room offers a spacious bedroom with a private terrace and a large bathroom. The Deluxe and Deluxe Family Rooms offer added services that include bathrobe and slippers, mini bar stocked with soft drinks (refilled daily), turndown service, priority housekeeping, branded toiletries, welcome gift and pick up/drop off luggage service in front of room. In addition, the Deluxe Family Room has a private room for parents and a separate bedroom for children along with a large living space.

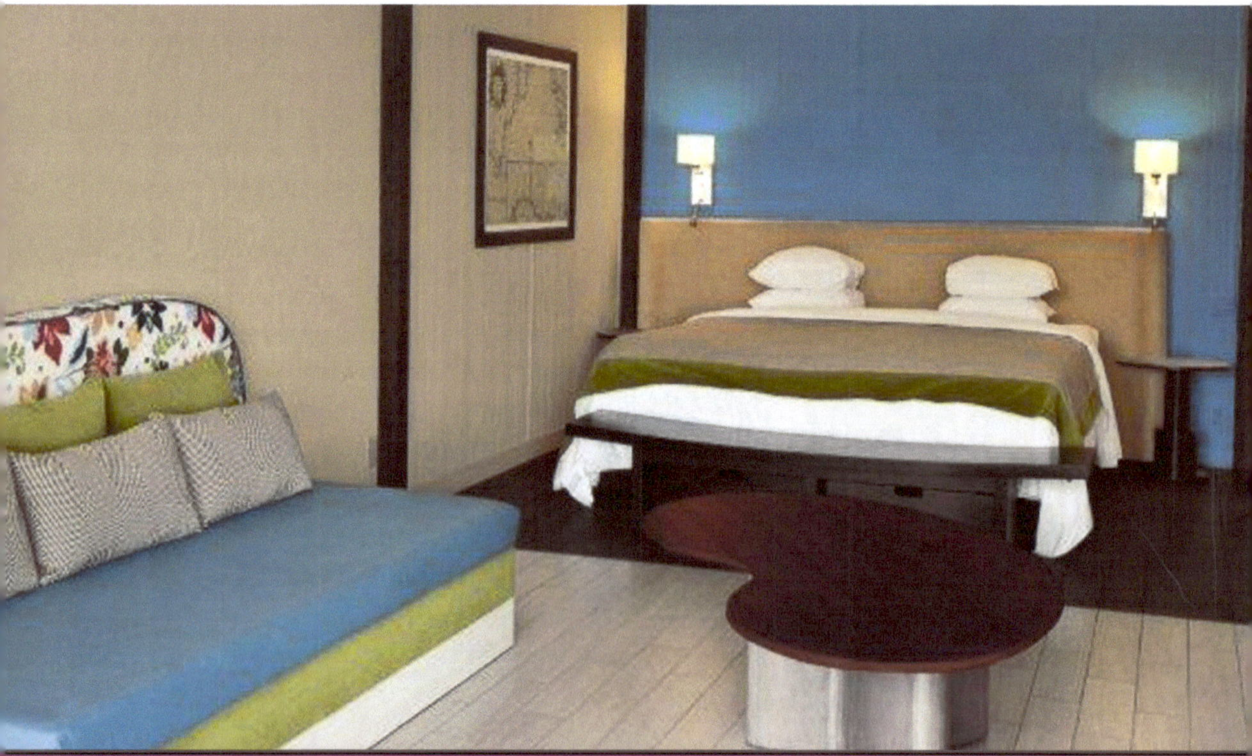

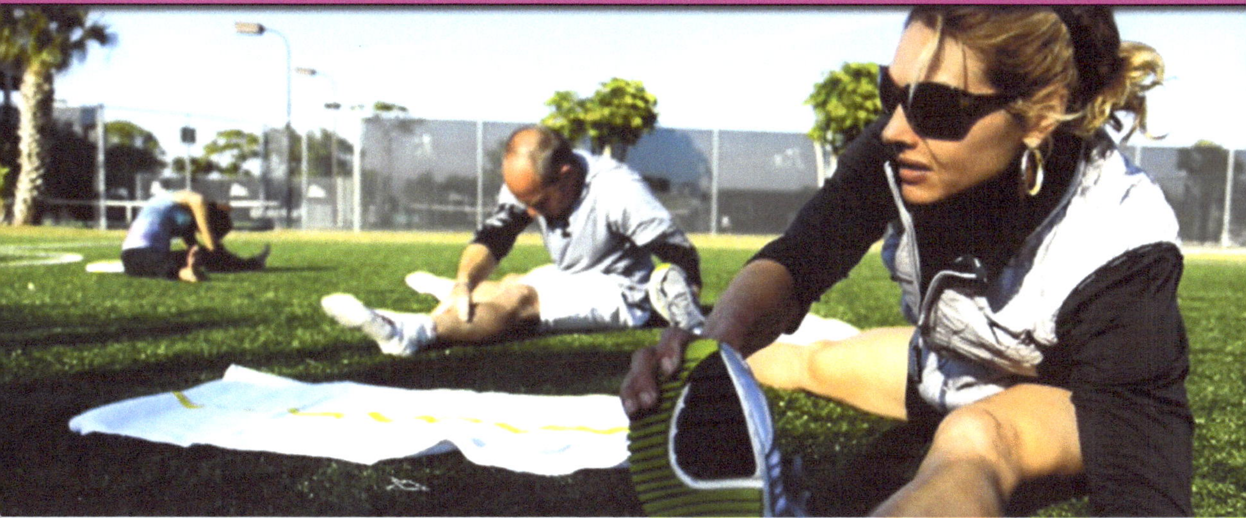

Top-Ranked Academies

The Club Med Golf Academy offers an on-site 18-hole golf course with 15 world-renowned courses within 25 minutes with a service to arrange tee times at any of the courses. Golf instructor and professional coaches Brad Brewer (serves as Golf Channel's lead online instructor), Don Law (award-winning junior golf instructor) and LPGA Master Professional Marie-Claire De Bortoli have created a top-ranked training program for any golf enthusiast.

If tennis is your sport, the Club Med Tennis Academy is sure to help you reach your goals. Gabe Jaramillo, helped develop eight number one and 26 top ten players in the world, will be one of your instructors. Also, you will learn from Scott Del Mastro, known to help hone in on individual technique and with training that is personalized.

Wellness Redefined

The new Club Med Fitness Academy is run by Heather Gollnick who is a professional triathlete and five time Ironman Champion. Along with her husband, Todd, they lead the Club Med racing series that implements everything from 5K and 10K running races to fitness and sports specialty camps. Club Med also offers high quality yoga programs. The programs range from beginner to experienced levels. Yoga is practiced in serene outdoor spots that overlook the St. Lucie River.

World-Class Dining

The Sandpiper will meet your every craving with two world-class restaurants. The Market Place offers diversified cuisines that include: Asian, Italian, Mexican, Regional American and International rotisseries. For your a la carte healthy dining options, Soleil has a fresh juice menu, salads, wraps, a light grill and full bar service. Each night, the executive chef creates specialty dishes native to Southern Florida.

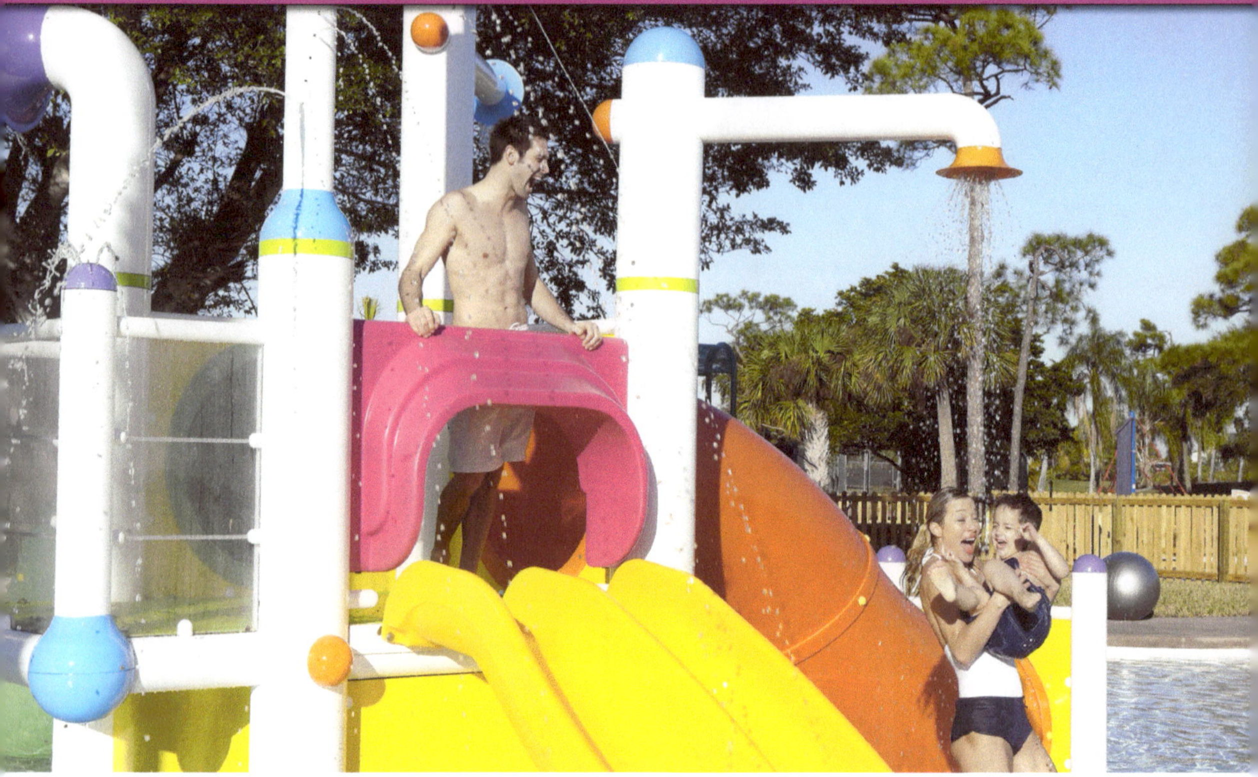

Adventure-Filled Excursions

If you are looking for some adventure on the water, Club Med Sandpiper Bay offers on-site, off-site Orlando and off-site South Florida excursions. Special excursions are available for individuals, couples and families. This is a great way to enjoy the St. Lucie River, a sunset cruise or a tour of nearby attractions.

Activities for Kids

Club Med is also known for its outstanding children's programs that include: The Kidz Village – an age-specific sports club, Britto Art Center, special kids programs in music, arts studio, dance and circus, a mini club childcare center and much more. When its time to vacation, come escape the grind of everyday life and experience the relaxation and freedom that comes from a vacation that meets your every need.

For more information on The Sandpiper Club Med Miami, please call (800) Club Med or visit: www.clubmed.us/sandpiperbay.

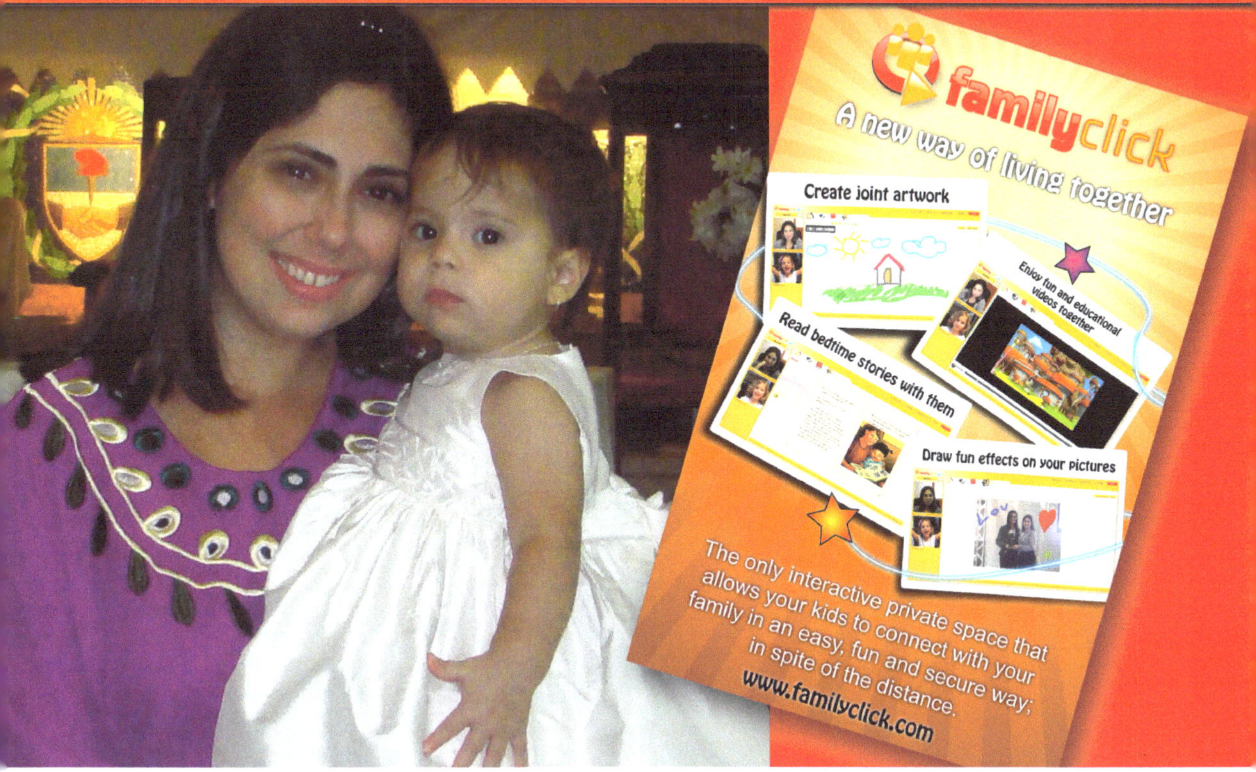

Entrepreneur Marie Molinet

Innovative Creator of Family Click

In the world of telecommuting, competing with Internet video chatting moguls like Skype and ooVoo can seem like a daunting task, but innovative entrepreneur Marie Molinet is willing to accept the challenge. Launched in 2010, Marie cofounded, along with her children and in-laws, FamilyClick; a way to give families the opportunity to create their own cocoon where they can interact in real-time while they video chat. Families using the program can get together across thousands of miles to read books, watch children's programs and draw together. Anything that you would do in your own family room can now be done on your own virtual, private place.

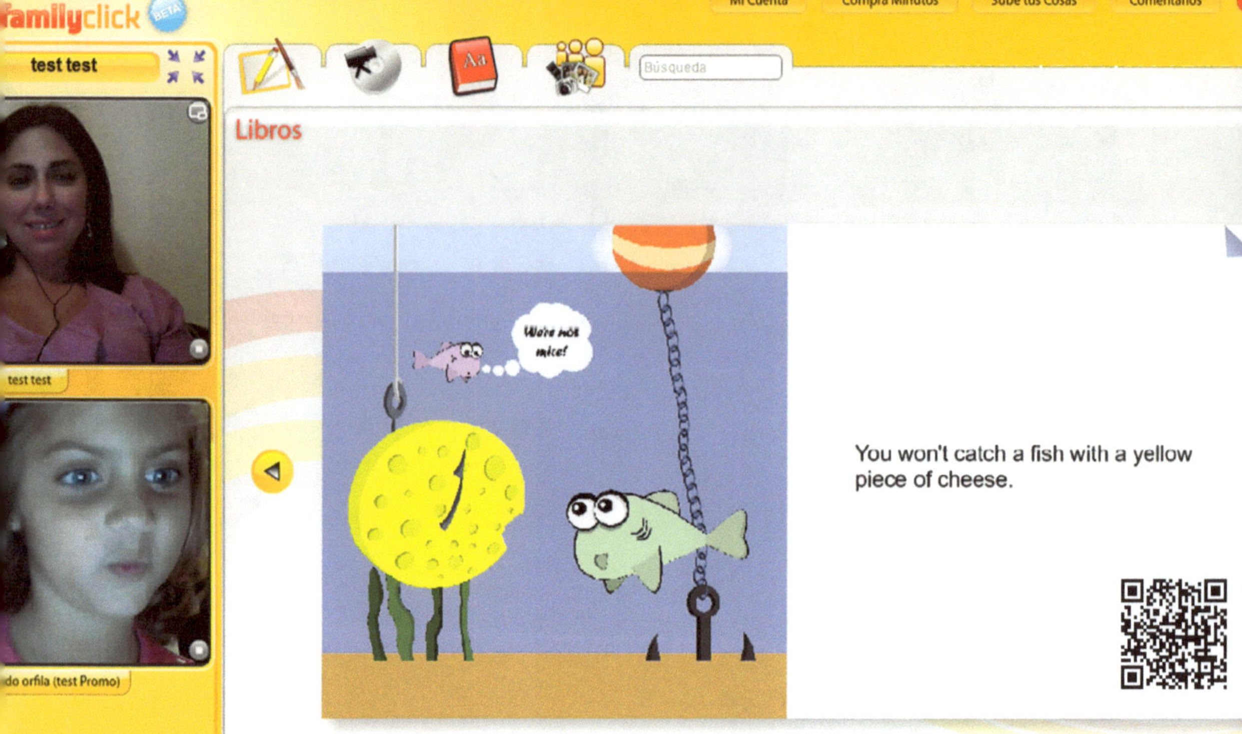

"Children's security is our core philosophy," says Marie. FamilyClick groups are strictly private. Only the owner of the group can invite people to join, and has to do so via email. There is no search feature on FamilyClick, so no one can find a specific user or their group. Also, the website is designed to have no intrusive advertising, and blocks predators from sending unwanted "friend requests." Focusing on family connections, privacy and security are major factors in distinguishing FamilyClick from their corporate competition.

FamilyClick was the third prize winner of the renowned Enterprise 2010 competition and continues to become a household success. Marie hopes to have FamilyClick become the all-in-one family room, playroom and activity room for relatives and schools, and all those that believe communicating with kids is more than just looking at them through a webcam.

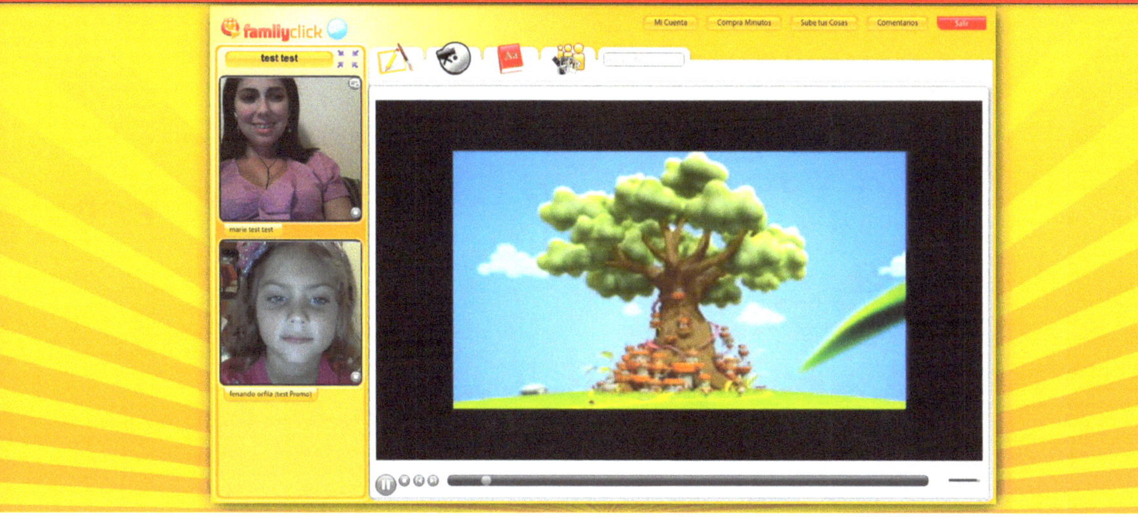

A Conversation with Innovator Marie Molinet

As a child, what did you want to become (profession-wise)?

I always loved science, particularly research. I find the research and discovery process very thrilling. Perhaps someday I will just pick up and go back to school. I think it's never too late to learn and reinvent oneself.

In which town did you grow up?

I grew up in San Juan, Puerto Rico, but spent a lot of time, especially the summers, in the United States where my father lives.

Do you think your background has influenced your entrepreneurial style? If so, what specific element in your background is most pervasive in influencing your current entrepreneurial style?

My background has definitely been defining. I come from a multicultural background. My parents are Cuban, I was born and raised in Puerto Rico, my step mom is American and my husband is Argentine. I've also lived in four different countries and have traveled to many more. This has inspired me to make sure that www.familyclick.com is as multicultural and multilingual as possible. This will also be the case for any future business I develop.

Having also suffered great personal loss in my childhood has impacted me. My parents divorced when I was five and my mother passed away when I was sixteen. Holding on to family even when apart has become essential for me. My entrepreneurial style has also been shaped by that. My style is making sure that family is first, no matter what I do; and in spite of spending many, many hours working on the start-up, I always make sure that my daughters are not neglected.

What inspires you in the job of being an entrepreneur?

The growth and learning process [inspires me]. I find it exhilarating to see something, an idea a possible business, be born, grow, mature and so forth. It is just like the life cycle. To me, even failure is perfectly natural. Again, it's the equivalent of death in the natural life cycle.

In which way do you consider yourself an innovative creator?

Dreaming opens possibilities to new ideas. I think that I am a good dreamer. For instance I've dreamt about the possibility of my daughters reading a book together with my father, even if he is in Atlanta and we are in Puerto Rico. And FamilyClick was born. I see myself as an innovative creator in the area of family advocacy.

Do you have any other creative ambitions or dreams to which you aspire?

Well, at this time I'm completely focused on FamilyClick. I don't have anything specific in mind right now but I would like to work and create an organization to help Latino children in the United States.

How did you get the idea for your business?

It just happened after a very frustrating video-chat between my daughter, who at the time was two years old, and my mother-in-law. My daughter was not interested in video chatting and my mother-in-law was doing everything possible to keep her entertained. She raised books up to the webcam, she played children's music on her end, but nothing worked to keep my daughter's attention. My husband and I were stuck in the middle trying to keep our daughter focused and just frustrated with the process. That's when, after that call, my husband and I started talking and saying that there had to be a better way to keep our daughter interested in a video-chat with her grandmother.

Do you have a favorite entrepreneur yourself?

I'm a huge fan of Reed Hastings, founder of Netflix. I think the Netflix story is one I and any media entrepreneur can learn a lot from. He changed the movie rental business, made it his own and simply because he was tired of getting charged late fees. He really was a game changer, and most importantly listened to what his customers were saying. Non-tech related, I'm also an admirer of Lynn Hughes, founder of the Comfort Zone Camp, a non-profit bereavement camp for children who have lost a parent or sibling. I wish there had been a camp like that around when my mother passed away.

Do you expect your entrepreneurship to change in the future?

Not really. Entrepreneurship gives me a good mix between personal development and family time.

Do you embrace the changes in the entrepreneurship industry regarding social media and technology influences?

I think we all have to embrace these changes, but only to the level they are a real advantage or a real benefit to any venture. It's not something that should be done just because everyone else is doing it. If it doesn't fit into your model, then why force it?

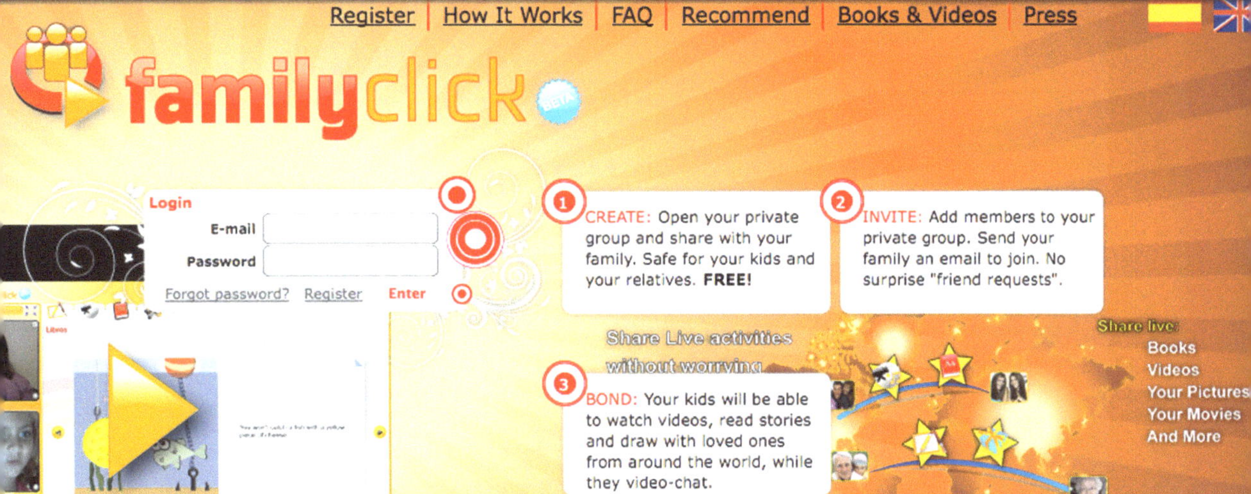

In which way do you think entrepreneurialism, art and design are different and/or similar?

All of them follow the same life cycle I mentioned before. In art and design you also have an initial idea and then you work hard to see it come to life.

Do you aspire to collaborate in your creations with an artist from another artistic discipline?

I already work with a number of designers, as well children authors and illustrators due to the nature of the venture. It's a great experience! You learn a lot from the exchange.

Did you follow any philosophical or psychological approach in creating your business?

Even if this is my first venture, I tried all the time to do two things. First, to keep the children that are using this website safe and secure. Children's security is our core philosophy. Second, respect for all the content suppliers and their intellectual property. No matter if they are big or small; all are helping us develop FamilyClick further.

Do you have any dreams for the future?

My dream is to have FamilyClick become the all-in-one family room, playroom and activity room for families, schools, and all entities that believe communicating with kids is more than just looking at them through a webcam.

Is there anything else you would like to add to this interview?

I want to thank the publication for giving me the honor of including me with such an amazing group of artists, innovators, and creators... especially in such an early stage of the venture.

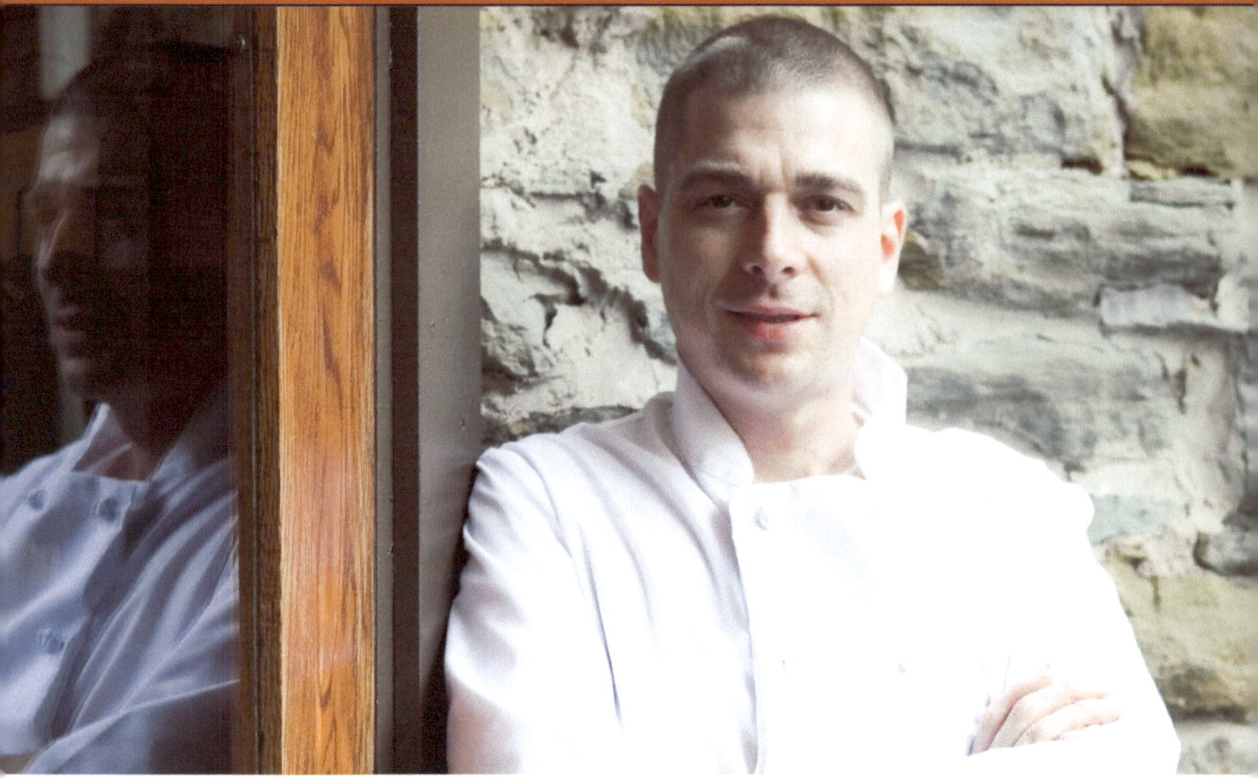

Innovative Chef Christopher J. Corimski

Chris Corimski, a Pittsburgh native chef, has emerged from the rolling hills of Pennsylvania to join the high standard of culinary art professionals. Chris is the cooking mastermind currently working at Girasole (Italian for "sunflower") creating nightly meat, fish and chicken specials, as well as preparing seasonal menu items. At the 2011, 8th Annual Flavors of Pittsburgh, Chris was among the few premier chefs chosen to arrange meals at the fundraiser for the fight against liver cancer. Chef Chris Corimski's Veal Osso Bucco recipe was featured at the event.

A Conversation with Chef Chris Corimski

As a child, what did you want to become (profession-wise)?

I really wanted to be an archaeologist. When I watched Indiana Jones and the Raiders of the Lost Ark, it inspired me. It was either that or race car driver. I like to drive fast.

Do you think your background has influenced your current culinary style? If so, what specific element in your background is most pervasive in influencing your current culinary style?

With hard working parents, I cooked a lot for myself. Also, the Culinary Arts program from Beattie Tech (A.W. Beattie Career Center) helped me decide on my career. Not only did it get me out of high school, but it honestly pointed me in the direction of where I wanted to go in life. Beattie Tech offered a program in which high school juniors prepped food, while the seniors cooked for a buffet open to the public. We would also cook morning breakfast for students, which included egg sandwiches and more.

Also, when I was a kid, I grew up in the rural Sarver, PA, picking berries on the side of the road with mom and dad. This inspired me to cook with fresh ingredients. I like to cook seasonally, just like the seasonal menu at Girasole.

What inspires you in the job of being a chef?

I've worked with Bill Fuller from the big Burrito Restaurant Group. Andre Lemaire from Le Perroquet Bistro Francais also inspires me. Both of these men have high work ethic and great attention to detail. I strive to be like that every day.

In which way do you consider yourself an innovative creator?

I shoot for strong attention to detail and consistency in what I make. I'm always a perfectionist with my food, though it is a constant quest for perfection. Girasole's has the seasonal menu and I enjoy using these ingredients even in my personal recipes. Travel and experiencing new things also helps broaden my culinary expertise. I've traveled to Europe and South America several times with my wife Paulina, experiencing new tastes to become more cultured in the art of food.

Do you expect your way of creating culinary art works to change in the future?

Yes, of course! Again with the way I travel and branch out, the more things I try the better. I want to experiment in the future with more of the different ingredients, flavors, and spices I find in my travels.

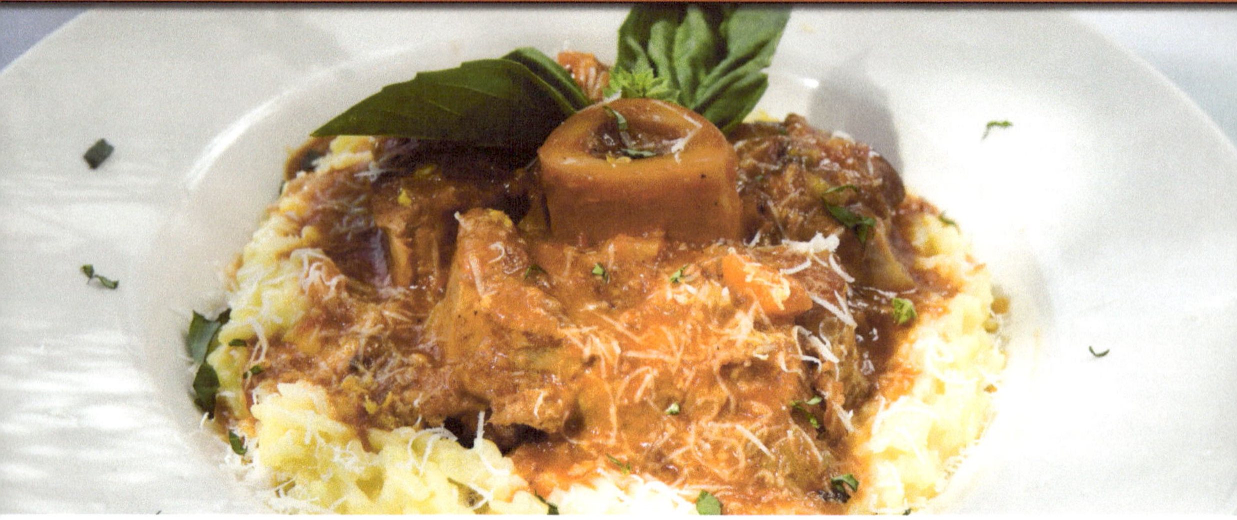

Veal Osso Bucco

INGREDIENTS

6, 8 oz. veal shanks, cross-cut
Olive oil

FOR THE MIREPOIX

2 carrots, diced small
1/2 celery stalk, diced small
5 cloves garlic, minced
2 cups white wine
1/2 lemon juice
1/2 orange juice
1, 16 oz. can of San Marzano tomatoes
1 bay leaf
10 sprigs fresh thyme
Chicken stock as needed

FOR THE GREMOLATA

1 lemon zest
1/4 cup basil, chopped
1/4 cup Parmesan Reggiano

DIRECTIONS

1. Seal veal shanks on both sides in olive oil.

2. Prepare the mirepoix by mixing together the onion, carrots, celery and garlic.

3. In a medium roasting pan, sauté the mirepoix on low heat until translucent. Add the wine, lemon juice and orange juice and cook until reduced by 1/3.

4. Add the San Marzano tomatoes, bay leaf, fresh thyme, and enough chicken stock to cover the veal. Bring to a boil on the stove top. Remove from heat and cool for 5 minutes. Cover pan tightly with foil and bake in a 400 degree oven for 2 1/2 to 3 hours.

5. Prepare the gremolata by mixing the lemon zest, basil and Parmesan Reggiano.

6. Braising is complete when the veal begins to fall away from the bone. Cool slightly and garnish with the gremolata mixture.

Serves 4-6.

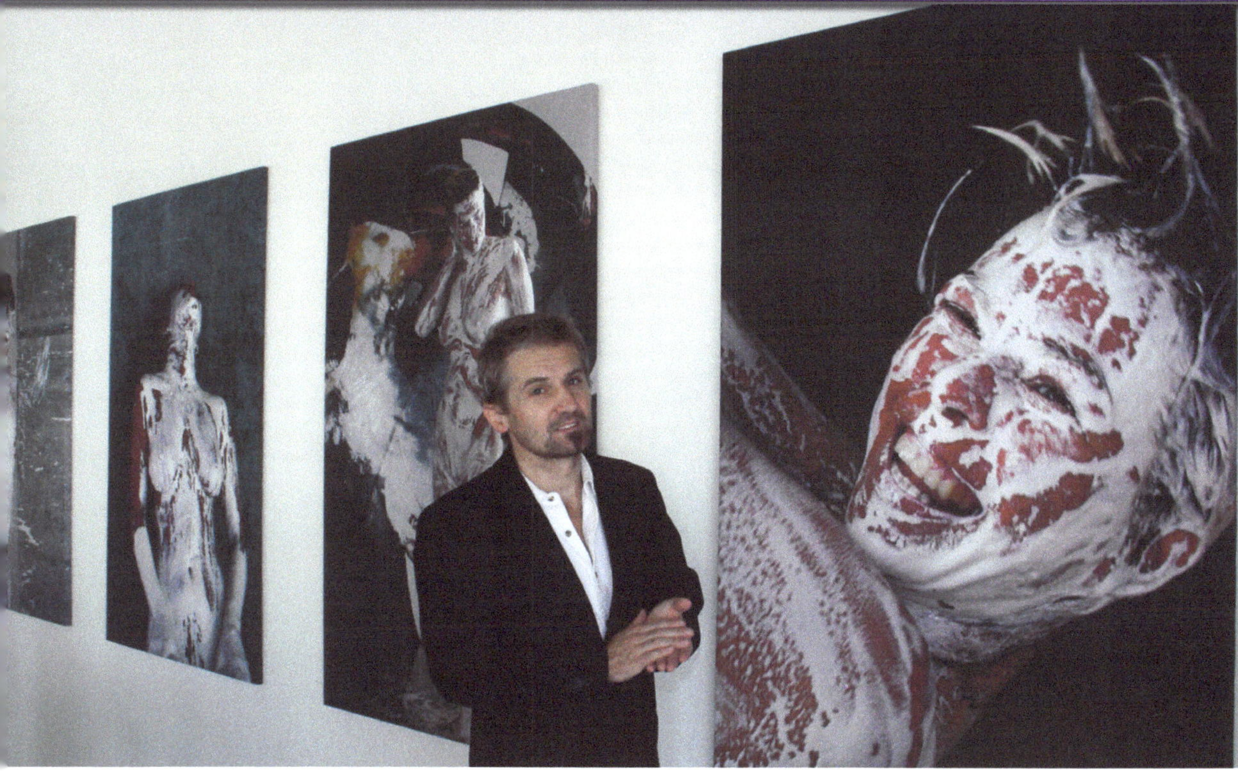

Artist and Designer Manfred Kielnhofer

Manfred Kielnhofer was born in Haslach an der Mühl, Austria. He currently lives and works in Linz, Austria, where he opened the gallery Art Park in 2005. Kielnhofer's work spans the mediums of painting, film, photography, installation, performance and sculpture.

A self-taught abstract painter, Kielnhofer recently used a naked female body as a "canvas" for one of his best works. His artistry is predominantly concerned with the human figure and its various forms and movements. The "figure" is an integral part of his work, and he often uses the human form as a tool, either in place of a canvas or in a collaboration to produce large-scale installations or performances. Kielnhofer has exhibited widely throughout Austria, and his work has recently been featured in exhibitions in New York and Miami.

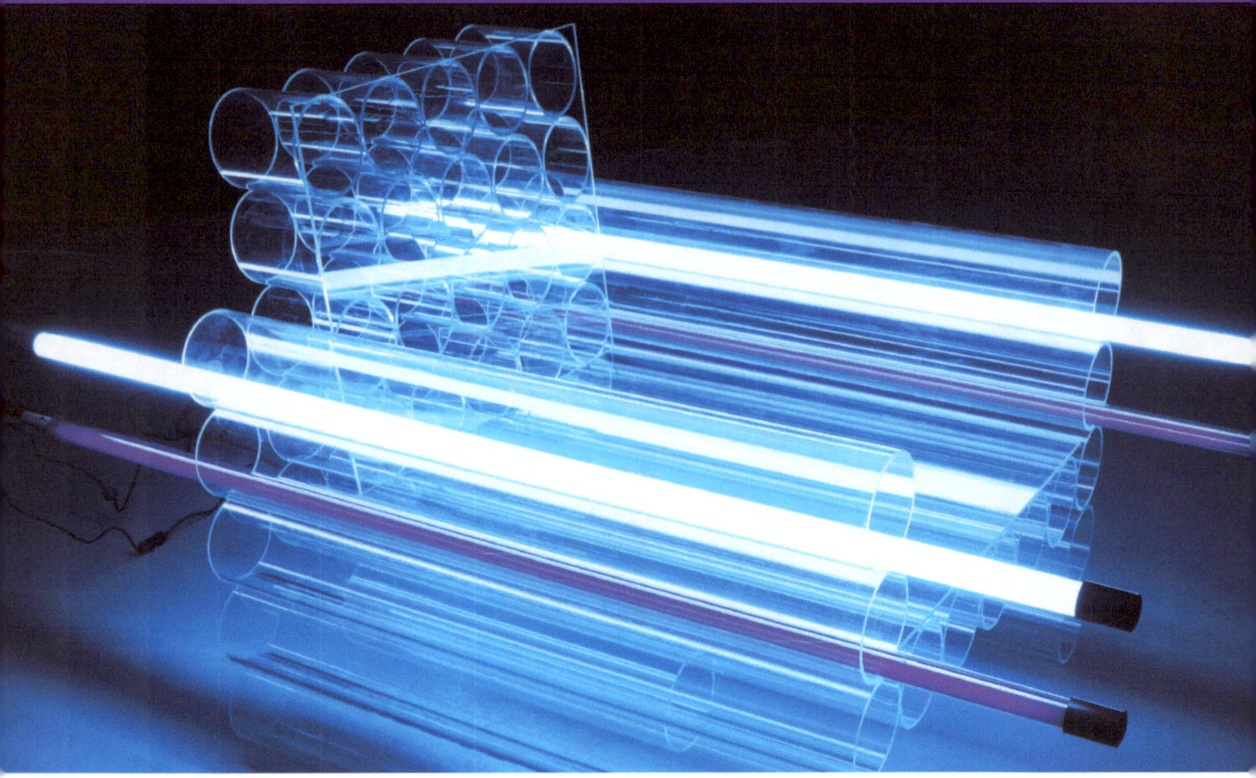

"The focus of my art is the peculiarities of the human nature," Kielnhofer said. "As an artist, the natural form and movement of the human body poses me a great deal of challenge. The different perspectives and points of view is what I aim to capture and display in my work."

Kielnhofer's latest works have been in the abstract form in which he brings to life with a collage of colors and a certain distance to the object. Each and every one of his paintings is individual in character and presentation.

The Largest Painting in the World

Under his guidance, 1,500 eager youngsters produced the largest children's painting in the world (3,300 m²), which was displayed at many different places in Austria. Another of his gigantic masterpieces (40,000 m²) was composed of sunflowers and other herbs that had been planted in the middle of a field of grain near the city of Enns. It could be best viewed from the sky; unfortunately, the pilot Kielnhofer hired decided to fly off on vacation before most of its "pixels" had blossomed, and the farmer had to harvest the creation before he returned.

The Time guards

Kielnhofer's "Time guards" represent the first of his works to be exhibited in the UK. Dealing with room-concepts, sculptures and installations, as well as being engaged with mystic experiences and religion, lead the artist to the engaging characters featured in "Time guards." In 2006, the first of these figures was created. Kielnhofer integrates his "Time guards" in public places such as ancient castles, old mines, main squares or parks.

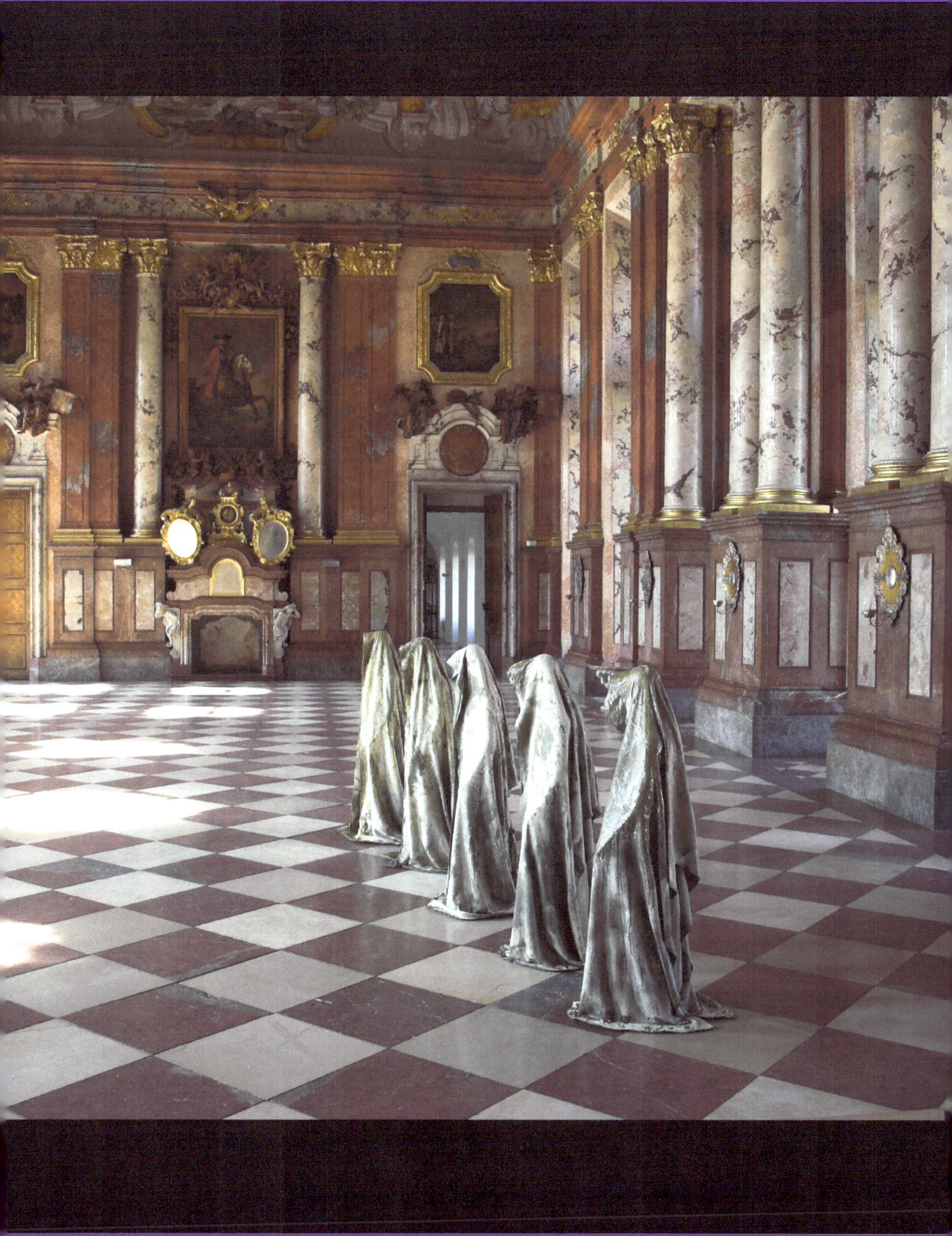

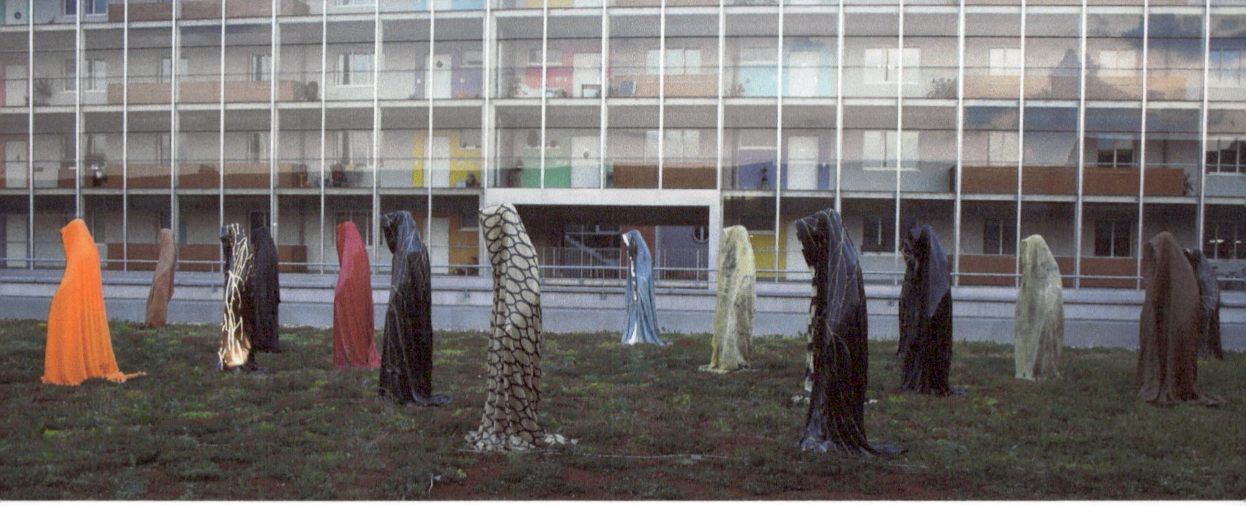

A Conversation with Manfred Kielnhofer

As a child, what did you want to become (profession-wise)?

A freelance worker.

In which town did you grow up?

Linz, an industrial town in Austria.

Do you think your background has influenced your current art and design styles? If so, what specific element in your background is most pervasive in influencing your current style?

My job as a mechanical engineer and in metalworking is the basis of my work.

What inspires you in the job of being an artist and designer?

I am following my dreams and realizing my concepts to form an object.

In which way do you consider yourself an innovative creator?

I am creating a new work. I am looking around to see if it happened before in the art world. Most times, I am too late for the shows, but sometimes I finish the work in time. This is a very hard process, but great works arise.

Do you have any other creative ambitions or dreams to which you aspire?

Sculpture, light art installations and photography.

Which basic elements of creativity did your family teach you?

My father taught me carpentry. I like the work with natural products like wood.

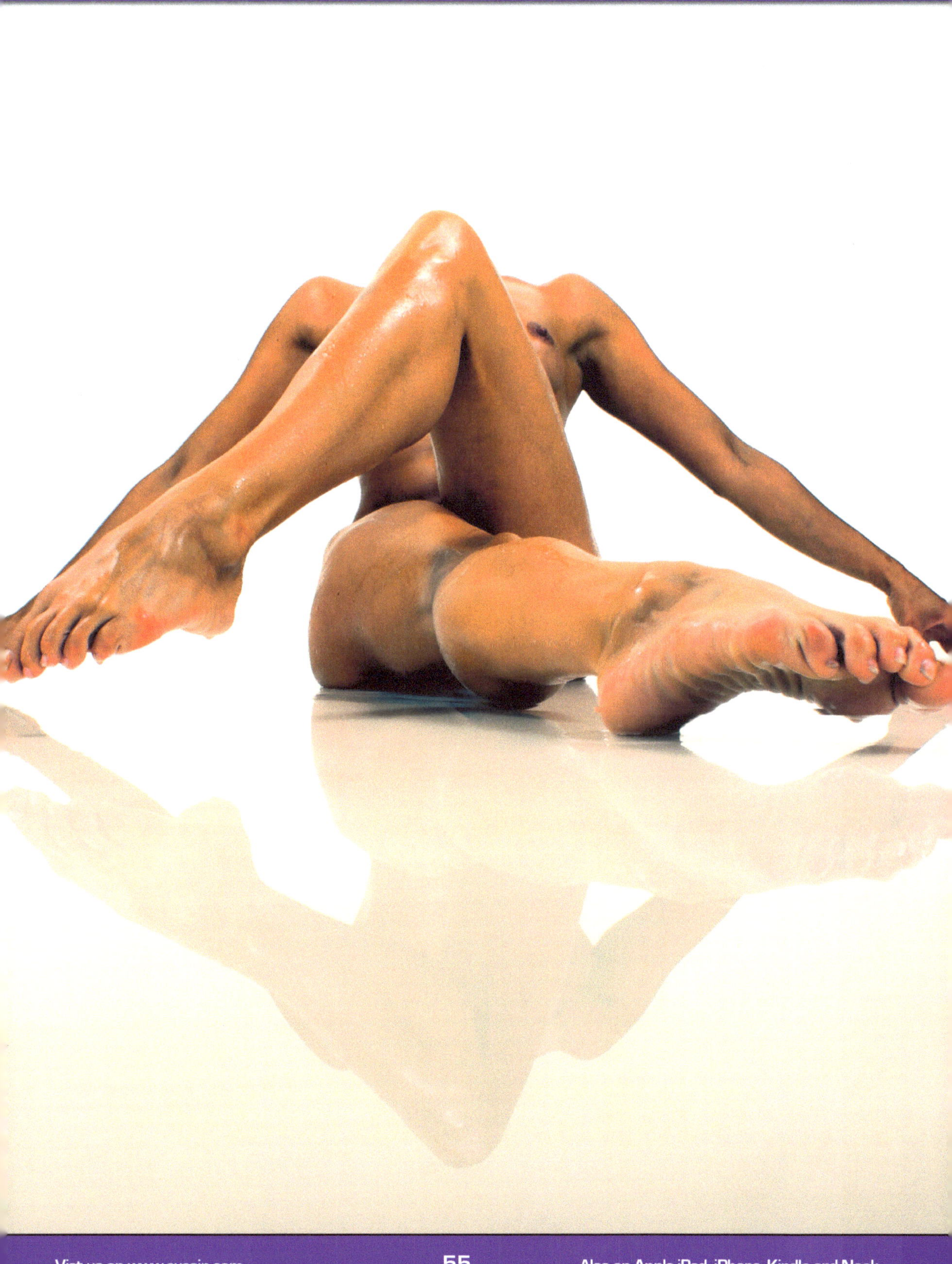

How did you get the idea for creating your art and design works?

When I am working on a concept in my head, this can take a long time, but the work itself I complete very quickly.

Do you have a favorite artist and/or designer yourself?

"The architect is an Orchestrator," according to Heidulf Gerngross. He is one of the most controversial architects in Austria. Gerngross "archive-centered" the world, uniting talented people (his "energy fields") while creating art that goes beyond the purely technical.

Are you ever afraid you will run out of inspiration and creativity in your job?

No. I have too many ideas and inspirations — enough also for a second life.

What is the most difficult thing in your job?

Advertising and promoting the works after I have made them.

What is the most fun part of your job?

To create a new sculpture.
The freedom of the art.

Do you expect your way of creating art and design pieces to change in the future?

No, I don't expect it to change. I try to change the small things, not the big things. I am working on a concept to show the pollution of the industry in my immediate surroundings — the environment-friendly paper tube chair by Manfred Kielnhofer.

Do you embrace the changes in the art industry regarding social media and technology influences?

I am using social media daily for contacts. The technical change to LED lamps will be shown in my next works.

Do you like art? Do you have any preferences for an artist and/or for creators of artistic work?

Yes... Erwin Wurm, Franz West, New Star Archistrator Heidulf Gerngross, and Architecture Biennale Venice 2002.

If so, why is that? What special quality do you like in their work or personalities?

I enjoy Wurm's and West's works. Gerngross calls his artist friends his "amigos" — for example, West, an internationally successful artist, built the "Gerngross pillar" together with the architects.

In which way do you think art and design are different and/or similar?

I am working in art and in design. Design is mostly a practical application. Art has, mostly, little to do with practical application. There are many different definitions and interpretations. In the end, it is the quality of the work that is important.

Do you aspire to collaborate in your creations with an innovative creator from another artistic discipline?

I am working in dance and theater installations for my concept photography. And work for a theater would be very interesting.

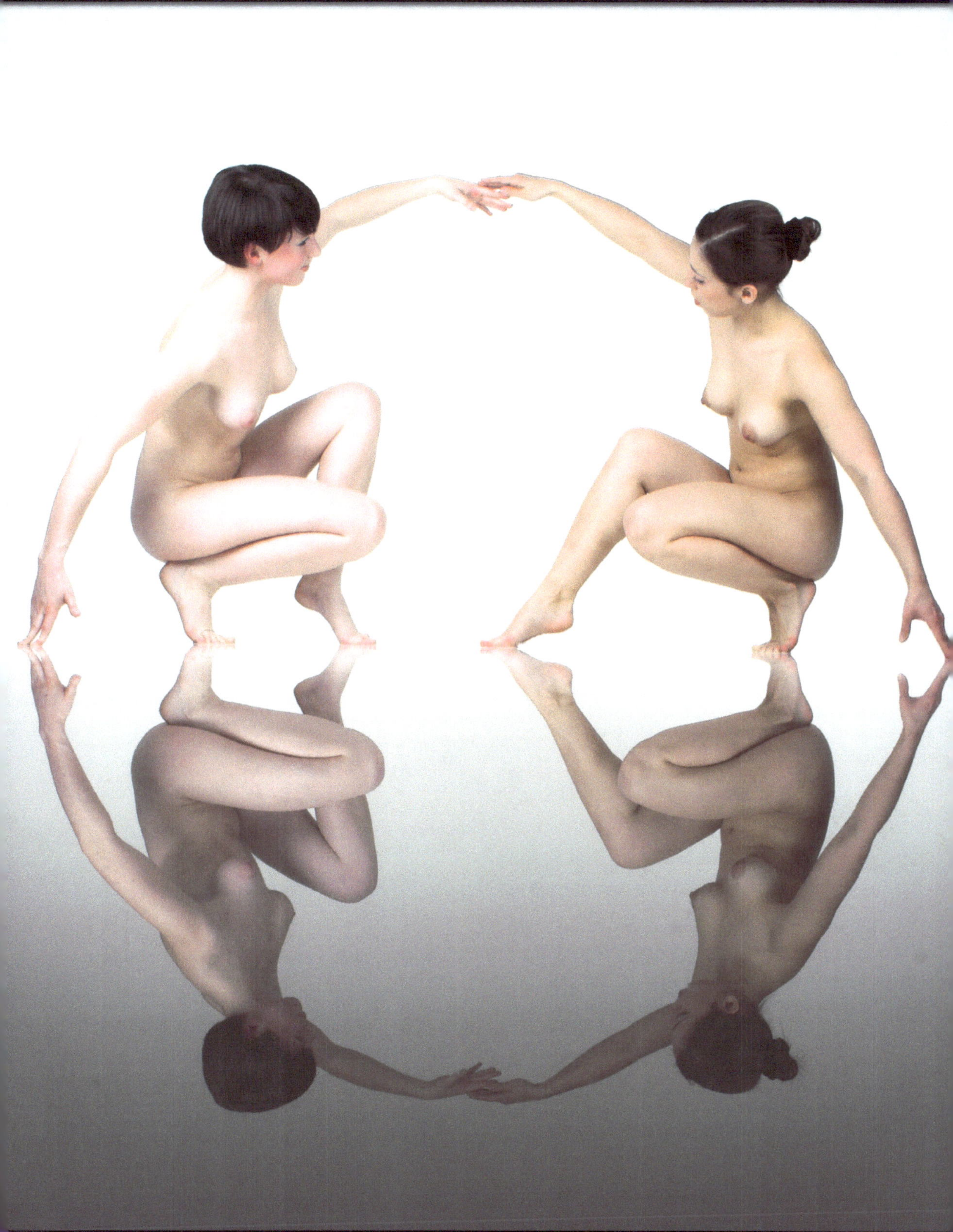

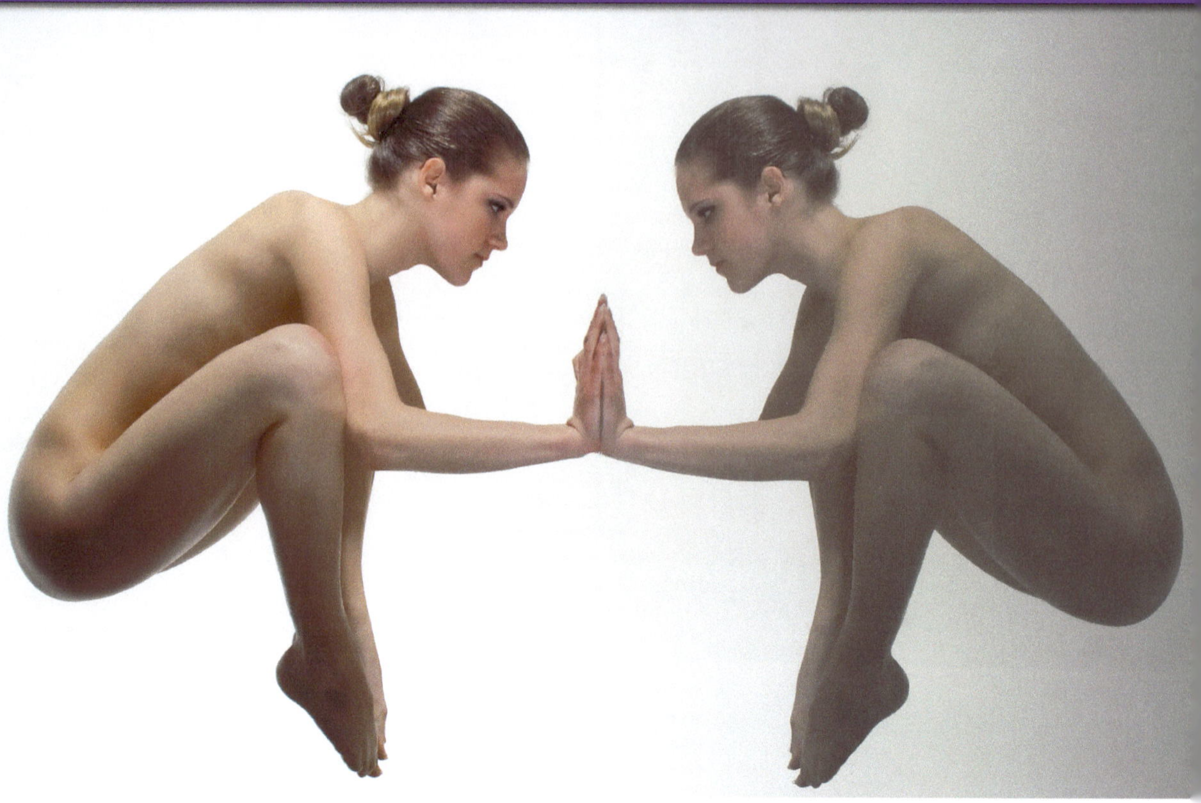

Do you have a favorite company or exciting other creator with whom you would like to work?

A light art installation for Swarovski would be interesting.

Do you follow any philosophical or psychological approach in making your art?

Museums are our new churches, as is commonly agreed. Millions of people flock to them to be uplifted, inspired, or distracted from everyday cares for an hour or two by encountering magnificent art. (http://www.eyesin.com/culture/2011/saatchi-gallery-hosting-iq-debate/)

What is your favorite hotel?

I am a mid career artist. I travel with my old camper.

What would be your ideal home?

An atelier on the Malibu beach.

Do you have any dreams for the future?

Live every day as if it was the last day of your life. Live, love, laugh — life is too short to be wasted on other less important things.

Is there anything else you would like to add to this interview?

Thank you so much for your time. See you at my next show!

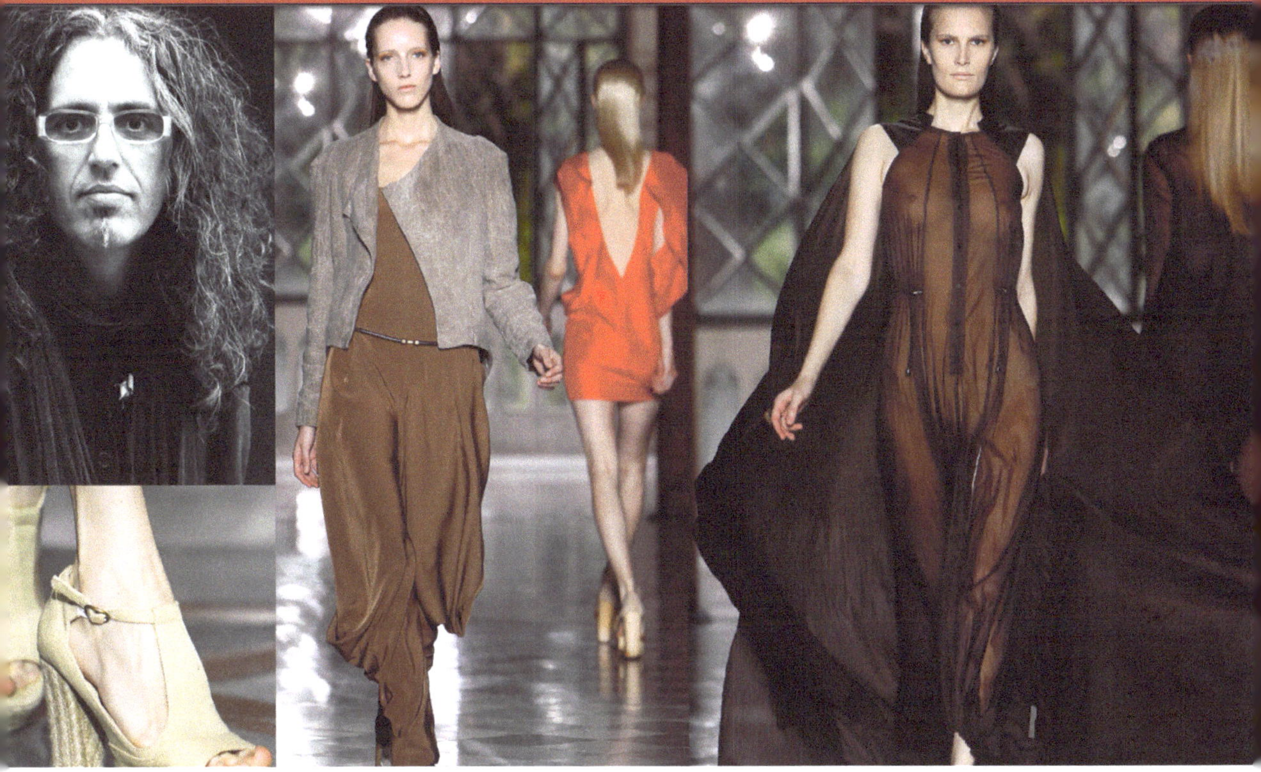

Fashion Designer Toni Francesc

Toni Francesc was born in Badalona, Barcelona, and was attracted to fashion since he was a child. His mother was a dressmaker; thus, he grew up between threads and patterns. He studied fashion design at Instituto de la Moda in Barcelona when he was eighteen and immediately after began working in the family business. In 1992 he created his own brand.

Toni Francesc first collection was presented in Mexico Fashion Week and Bread & Butter in 2007, emphasizing his fresh and dynamic style, with functional styles intended for modern, urban and sophisticated women.

Toni looks for inspiration in the streets and his people, and then he returns to his studio to create an interpretation. "Through my designs I want to communicate the moment experiences." Hence some of his most personal collections like "Feelings" or "Water's mood," sent a very human and close message.

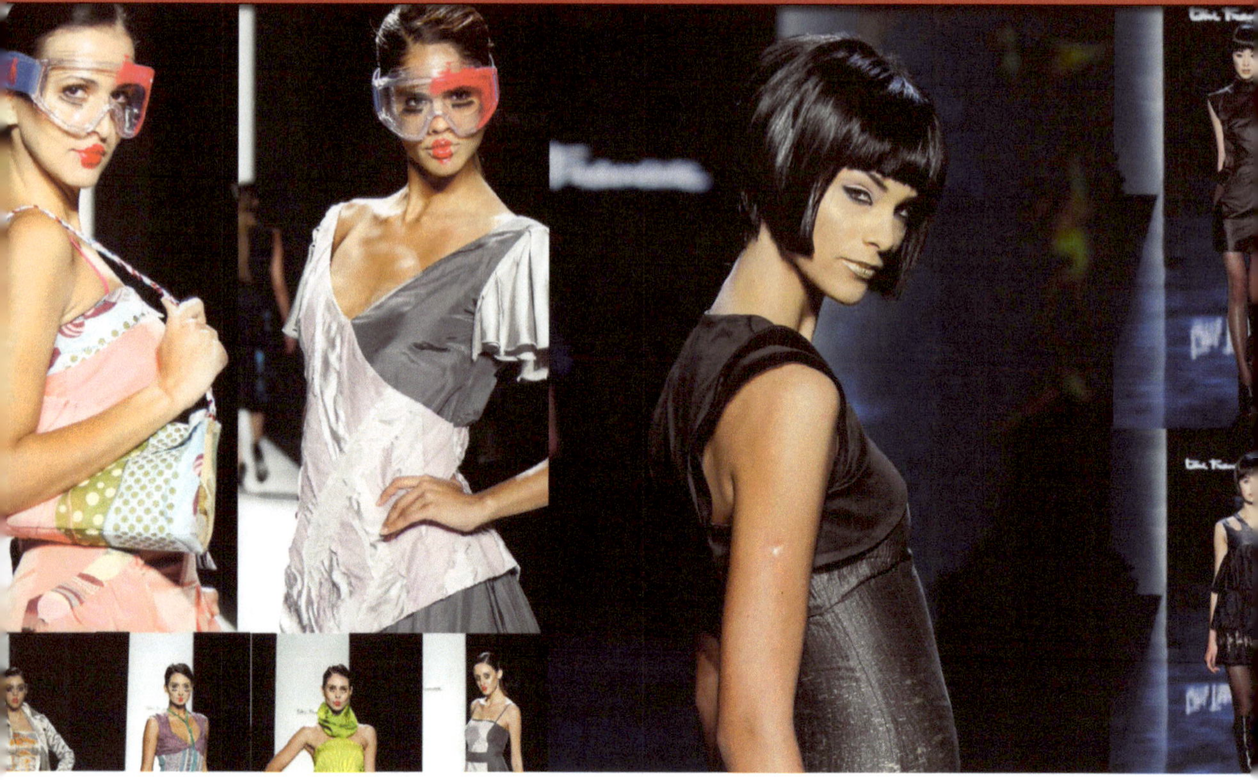

Toni bases his work on experimentation, using fabrics and patters. "I want to achieve the simplicity and the impossible at the same time, that a dress seems easy although it isn't." His style is recognized in sober colors and outstanding and defiant volumes, but enhances the most feminine side of women.
Nowadays, he presents his collections first in New York and then in Mexico Mercedes Benz Fashion Week catwalks, but he also has modeled down Cibeles Madrid Fashion Week or Russian Fashion Week catwalk. Toni's last Fashion Show was at 080 Barcelona Fashion in July 2011.His styles are sold in multi-brand boutiques and distributed through sales showroom in the most important cities of Spain, besides a permanent showroom in New York.

Toni cooperates with Mexican universities to teach fashion design and fashion business, and he took part on a discussion board in collaboration with Spain-USA Chamber of Commerce and Fashion Institute of Technology (FIT) in NewYork in September 2010.

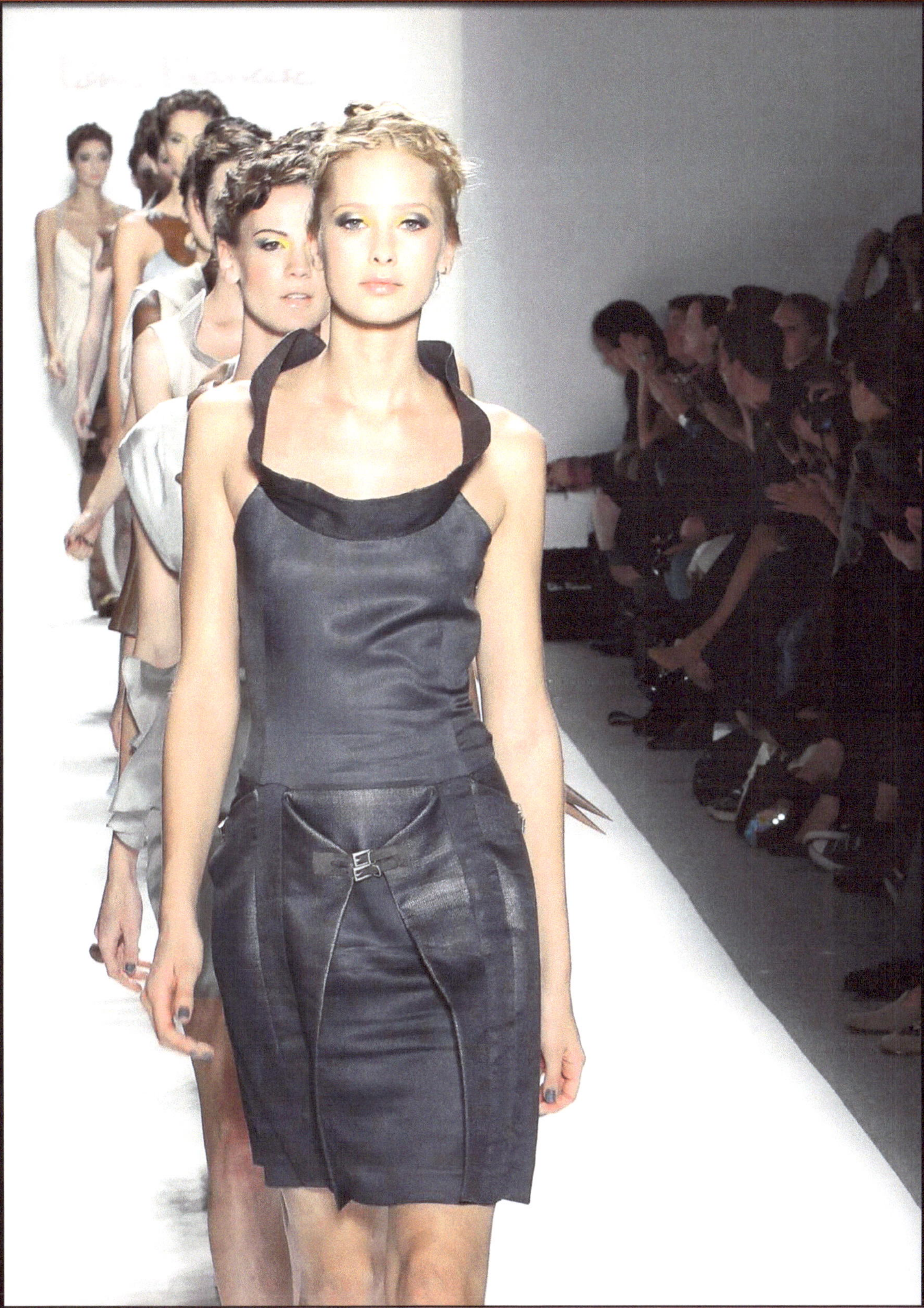

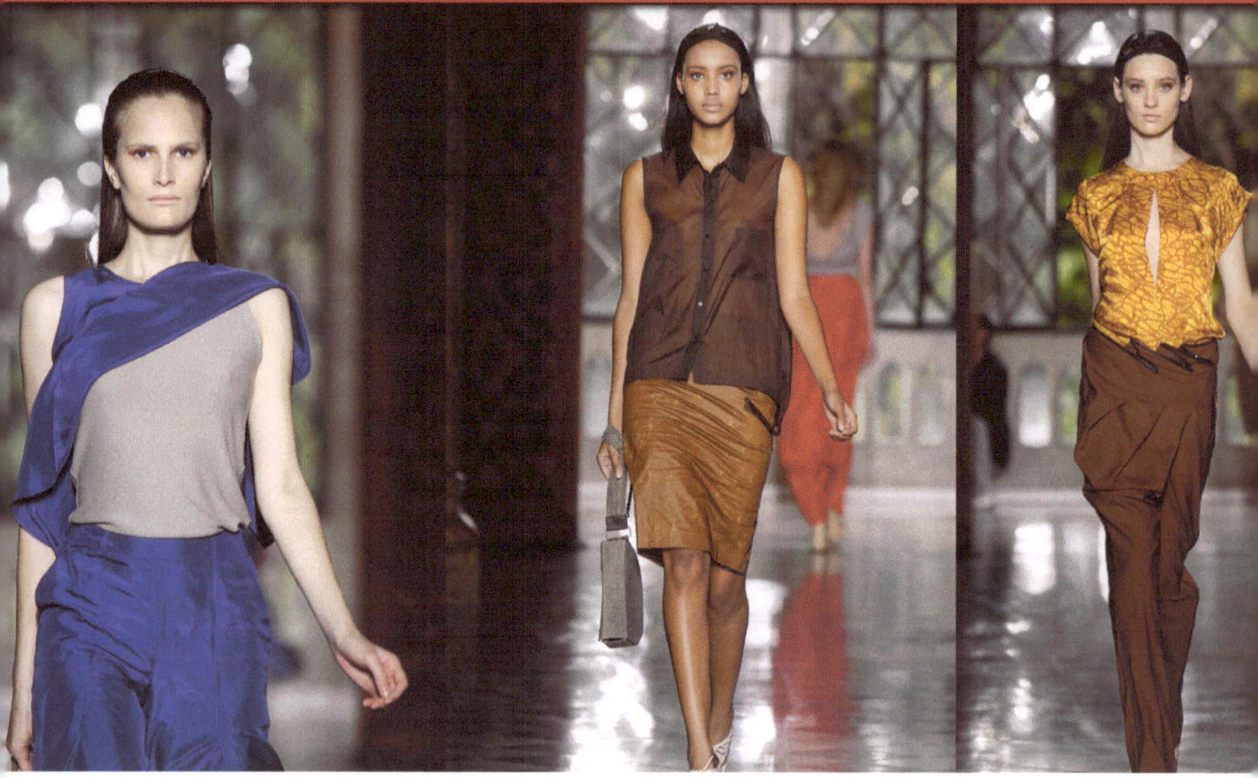

A Conversation with Toni Francesc

As a child, what did you want to become (profession-wise)?

I used to draw houses and buildings, but I also liked playing with buttons and fabrics; I guess I would have been an architect or a designer but it was something I was not sure about. Finally I became a designer, so my playground was a clear influence.

In which town did you grow up?

I live since ever in Badalona, but I studied in Barcelona, so I grew up between these two cities.

Do you think your background has influenced your current fashion design style? If so, what specific element in your background is most pervasive in influencing your current fashion design writing style?

Not in my design style. I have personally been evolving, season to season, through the process of learning and experimentation.

What inspires you in the job of being a fashion designer?

Human beings, their behavior and their relationship with nature.

In which way do you consider yourself an innovative creator?

I innovate with patterns to treat in a different way the female body and I also investigate in new materials and processes, specially interested in improving body protection, design, pattern and new technological fabrics

Do you have any other creative ambitions or dreams to which you aspire?

I like many things, but I am a very realistic person. I think that each person must work to make his dreams become true. At this moment, I am working to open my first store, this is one of my dreams that will be a reality in a very short time.

Which basic elements of creativity did your family teach you?

I think creativity is something innate, but probably I learned playing with textile raw materials since I was a child.

How did you get the idea for your fashion designs?

I seek the inspiration in moments of my real life, which suggest me the basic idea to develop a theme and then I start my research on it. For instance, the inspiration for my SS2010 Collection called "Water's mood" came out in a pretty hard time in my life due to the illness of my father. That made me think about the reasons for everything, I thought that we are mainly made of water and started working on the different moods of water and relating them with our human moods.

Another example is "Artificial Life," my Fall 2010 collection; Some friends had dinner together, but at one moment I observed that all of us were dedicated to our mobile phones, writing to other people. The situation was so absurd, technology created distance between us. My inspiration was a critical view on technology, actually affecting our personal relationships.

Do you have a favorite fashion designer yourself?

I've always liked Cristobal Balenciaga, he took care of any detail, I admire the meticulous and precious patterns, avoiding any excess and developing a timeless style. His vision of fashion has been inspiring for my work.

Are you ever afraid you will run out of inspiration and creativity in your job?

I have always gaps referring to inspiration, but I know inspiration will come back, so I must keep on working, so that inspiration finds me there when coming back.

What is the most difficult thing in your job?

Nothing is easy in my job, personal relationship with the work team, selection of fabrics, testing the fabrics reaction to a particular design, provide shape and content to the designs through the pattern. Coming from an initial idea, work takes you to a completely different and opposite result, so you must go back and restart.

What is the most fun part of your job?

Within the working routine, everyday is completely different from the rest, new situations, always something new is uncontrolled and makes the work quite fun.

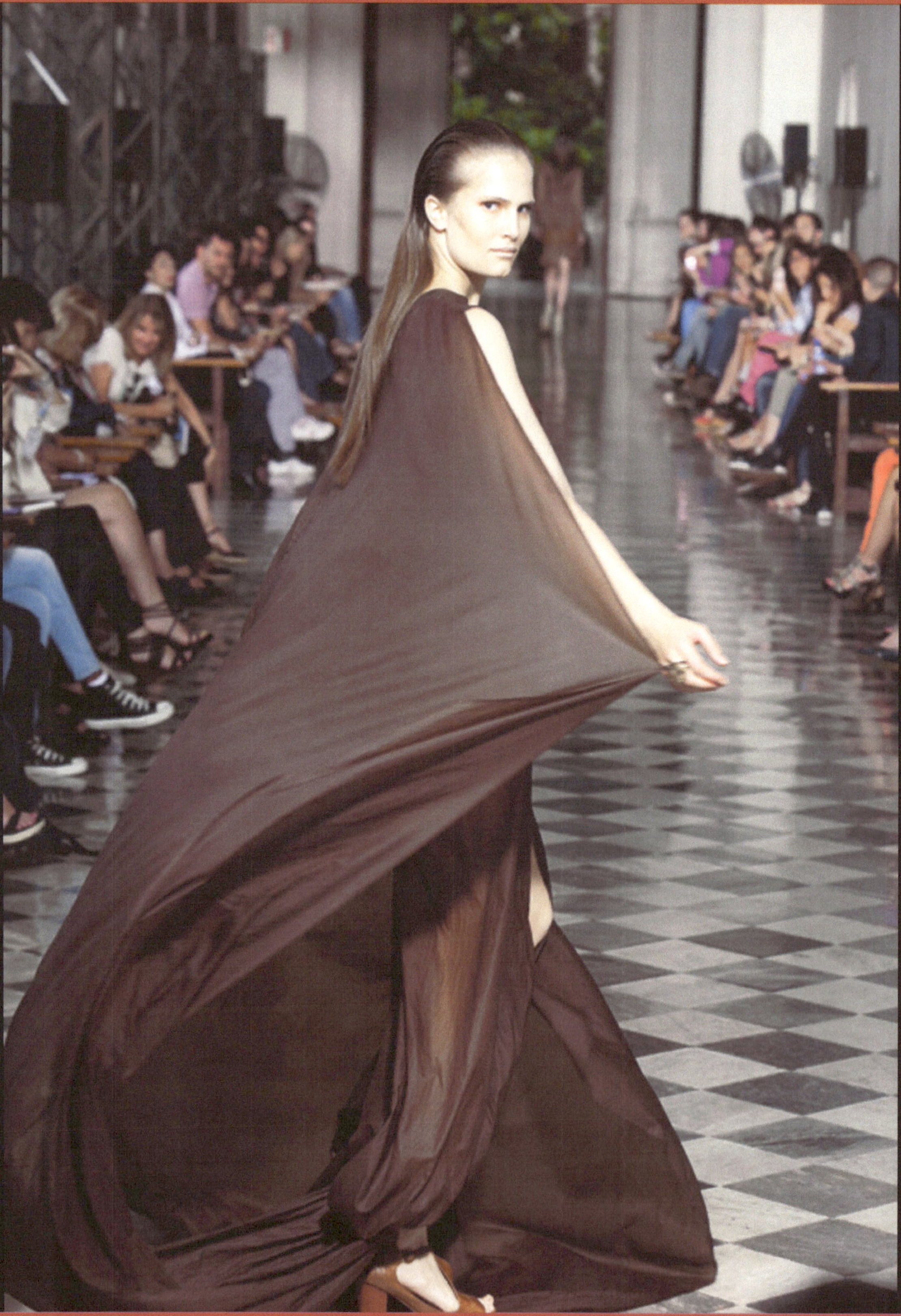

Do you expect your way of creating fashions to change in the future?

For sure I will evolve and grow, but not with radical changes, but growing together with the woman I have in mind for my designs.

Do you embrace the changes in the fashion industry regarding social media and technology influences?

I'm adapting quite well and I think they help me getting closer to reality

Do you like art? Do you have any preferences for an artist? And/or for creators of artistic work? (Creators can also be chefs, designers, photographers, authors or inventors.)

I love art and admire many artists from different disciplines, but I would highlight two specially talented and close artists, I find their work absolutely stunning and they were ahead of their time: In Architecture and design Antoni Gaudí, in Painting and Sculpture Salvador Dalí. In architecture and design Antoni Gaudí, and Salvador Dali in painting and sculpture

If so, why is that? What special quality do you like in their work or personalities?

Antoni Gaudi was a very simple, hardworking and deeply religious man but his great value lies in his work, the vision of how to shape a building, a furniture, any complement or lighting, he was inspired by the laws of nature. His work is spectacular, and the best is that I have the privilege of walking regularly in front of one of his buildings in Barcelona and every time I discover a new detail that I did not realize before. They inspired me for my SS2011 collection "Urban forest." Salvador Dali, an eccentric character emotionally influenced by his muse and wife Gala, whom he devoted much of his work. I highlight his treatment of the human figure, use of color, the magic of making an unreal scenery become like real. My collection "Artificial Life" had some abstract printings inspired in his work.

Could we feature your favorite photographer, author, artist, designer, architect, filmmaker, etc. in our publication and/or online?

Yes, I have no problem with my preferences being known.

In which way do you think fashion design and art are different and /or similar?

I think they are closely related, they both need creativity to create a piece, a movie, a song, etc ... In fashion design, there is a basic difference to other creative disciplines is that we are compatible with industry and our pieces get movement and life when people wear them.

Do you aspire to collaborate in your creations with an artist from another artistic discipline?

I would like to cooperate with painting artists, integrating clothes in a canvas to conform a whole in color, form and content.

Do you have a favorite company or exciting other creator with whom you would like to work?

I would like working for Channel or Dior's house, I know I could adapt my work to their kind of business and to the style required by them, but this is utopia, what I really care every day is about my work in Toni Francesc, where I feel happy, I can enjoy my work and I have less pressure.

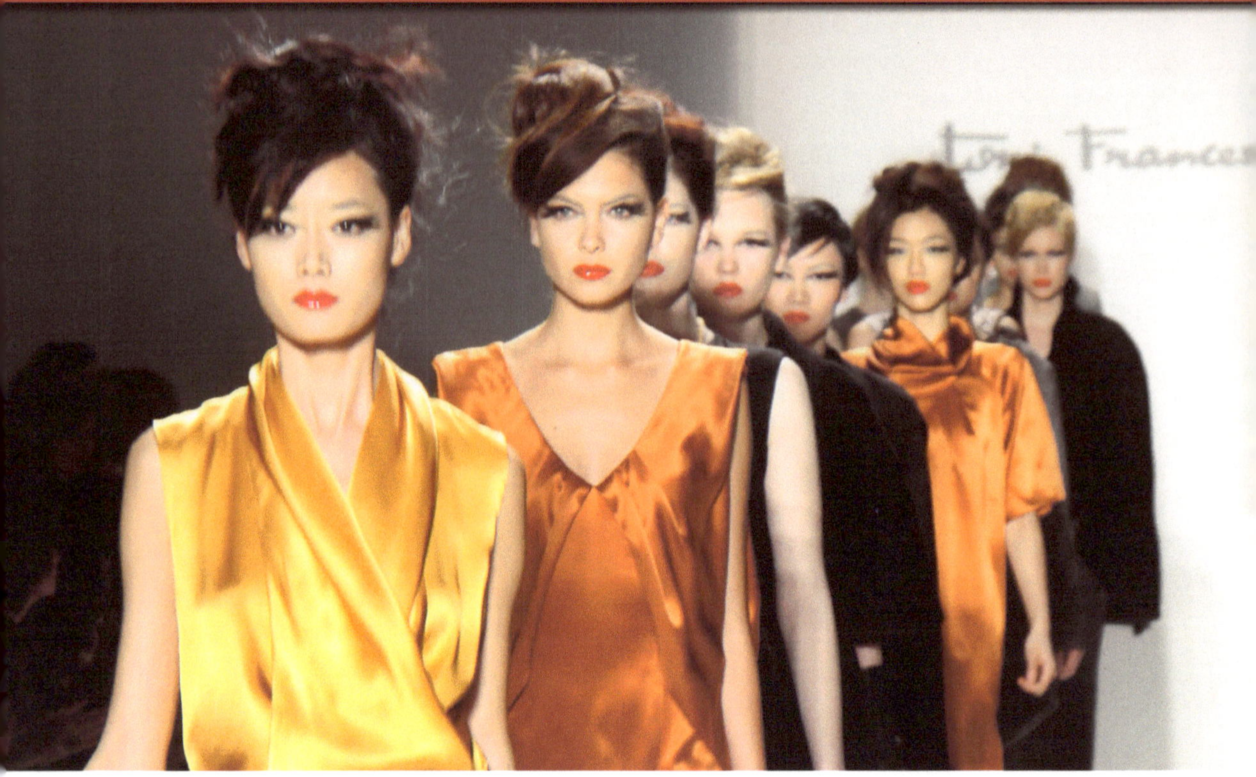

Do you follow any philosophical or psychological approach in making your fashion designs?

No, my approach is absolutely based in my personal experiences, inspiring collections such as "Feelings" or "Water's Mood".

What is your favorite building in the world?

The Sagrada Familia in Barcelona.

What is your favorite hotel?

The W-Hotel, a new generation building also in Barcelona, known as Hotel Vela; I like the design, modernity, location in front of the sea that offers a very nice view of sunrise, even though I would change one detail: the background music is too loud. (http://www.w-barcelona.com/)

What would be your ideal home? (If more than one, please list more, and if you like, please add motivation to your dream home(s).)

"Torre Amat", is the house of my friend Natxo Amat in the Sarrià district of Barcelona. This is a modernist palace, with very high ceilings, large windows, floors painted by hand. Last year I prepared a performance for press, to present my collection "Water's mood" (http://gallery.me.com/nachoamat#100073).

Do you have any dreams for the future?

I would like my clothes to be timeless and the brand Toni Francesc to follow when I'm gone.

Is there anything else you would like to add to this interview?

Thanks for your interest and attention, it has been my pleasure to attend you.

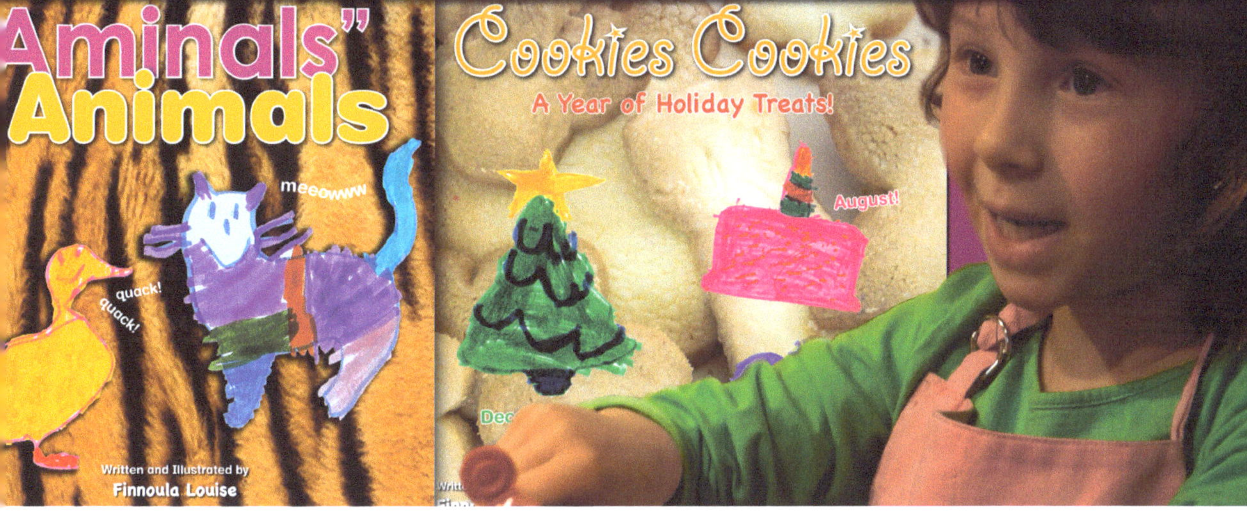

6-Year-Old Author Finnoula Louise

Finnoula Louise (age 6) steps onto the book scene taking her place among a select group of child author/illustrators published before age 18. Finnoula's love of story telling, clever imagination, and fondness for books are qualities of most authors, but it's her ability to focus on a task for long periods that is the secret ingredient to being a child author and illustrator. Miss Louise is just learning to read and write in Kindergarten, so her first title is a picture book with minimal, but poignant, text. "Animals Animals," is now available in local New Jersey bookshops and online. In this first-words book, children read animal names, the sounds they make, and fun facts, as they search for hidden animal photos. Finnoula is a recently diagnosed celiac, so this fall she takes a light-hearted look at holidays, cooking, and gluten-free recipes with "Cookies Cookies: A Year of Holiday Treats." In her spare time, Finnoula enjoys piano, karate, swimming, acting, and all manner of creative endeavors.

Finnoula's first published book, "Animals Animals," is now available in New Jersey bookstores and online at major booksellers, including Barnes & Noble and Amazon.com.

Children up to age 6 will delight as they "roar, prooot and screek" along with 12 friendly, silly animals, while exploring a whimsical world of animals as seen through the eyes of a child. In this first-words book, children can read each animal name as they search for hidden pictures and read fun facts along the way.

Children up to age 7 will enjoy Finnoula's stylized illustrations of holiday-related shapes, as well as photographs of her culinary creations—cookies of the same shapes. Uniquely sweet sentiments surprise us each month as we read how holiday shapes and cookies are connected to life, love, and family. Finnoula Louise is a celiac and cannot eat wheat or foods containing gluten. Thus, the cookies in this book are gluten free. "Cookies Cookies" is complete with recipes and cooking tips. While appropriate for all children, this title will be of special interest to those with celiac disease or other gluten-related sensitivities.

During the making of "Cookies Cookies," Finnoula not only wrote and illustrated, but also made all of the cookies featured in the book. Here she is shown measuring ingredients while she explains the process

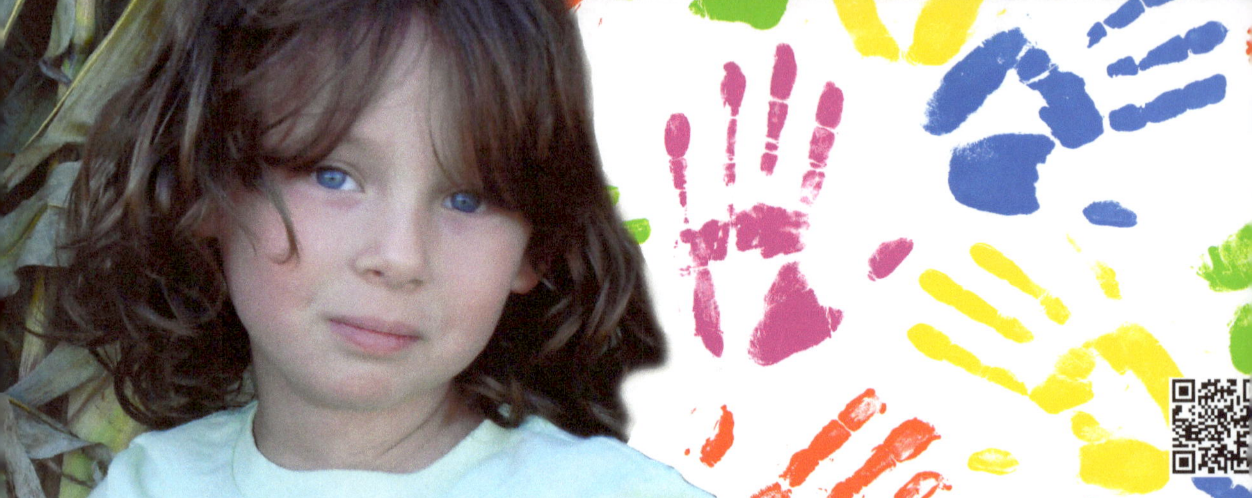

A Conversation with - Finnoula Louise (and her Mom)

What do you want to be when you grow up?

I would like to be a detective, because I like to spy on people to see what they are doing. I'm good at it. I'll be able to tell my boss (the person who hires me) when someone is doing something they shouldn't be doing.

[Mom's Comment: Apparently, this knack for spying is a source of her creative ideas. Now that I know about it, I'll have to be more careful. Lest she "spy" on me and report it back the boss.]

Where do your book ideas come from? What inspires your ideas?

Well, I got tracers [stencils] one Christmas and I started making a book out of them. That's how I got my idea for the animal book. One day we were eating cookies and I said I wanted to do a book about them. Because I'm gluten free, I wanted it to be about that. I don't know what's next, maybe something about balloons. Delia's face makes me think of things, so I could just look at her.

[Mom's Comment: Finn has been making books since she could hold a crayon and wield a stapler (age 3). At age 5, she asked if one of her books could be in the library so her friends could read it. Me being a publisher answered, "I don't see why not?"]

Do you have any other creative ambitions or dreams that you hope to reach?

I would like to build houses...be a house builder. Because I want to help make sure people have places to live. I'll put an ad in the paper for a crew to come and work with me.

[Mom's Comment: News to me.]

Are you ever afraid you will run out of inspiration and creativity [in your job]? Why or why not?

Not worried about it at all. If I am done writing books, I will start the house building.

[Mom's Comment: That's my girl!]

What is the most difficult thing about book writing?

My mom usually helps with my writing so when she is not there that is when I have trouble. Mom tells me how to spell the words. I don't need her to draw from me.

[Mom's Comment: During the development of her books, Finn is the boss. She tells her editor, designer, and publisher what she wants. They advise her as per usual such relationships. She recently had a little taste of the author-editor give-and-take experience. At a book reading, Finn turned to me and said frowning, "Mom, there is a mistake in here. I guess it's too late to fix it though." She was referring to a change the editor had suggested that we must have forgotten to run by Finn. We thought it was a minor change to make something more grammatically correct. I guess we were wrong about it being minor. Finnoula continued, ignoring the printed page by reading aloud what she had originally intended. All the while, her captivated young audience listened unaware of the alteration. Call it creative license.]

What is the most fun part about book writing?

I get to be famous! Soon you [I] can get lots of money and will be rich. When I travel to book signings, if there are little kids like me there, I make new friends when I meet people. At book signings, I get to sign my name with sharpies, and it's fun 'cause it's my name and I know it really good. [and when making books] I get to draw pictures and color them. I liked helping make the Little Valley Books logo, too. For the next one, we made cookies and a movie, and that was really fun.

[Mom's Comment: Finn has just finished kindergarten, so the world of reading and writing on her own is just opening up to her. It's interesting to witness the changes in how she views her books and writings now that she can actually decode the written word.]

Which elements of your creativity can you attribute to your family?

Well, I get a lot of it from my brain, and my sister makes me think of stories just by looking at her.

[Mom's Comment: Cordelia (Delia) is Finn's two-year-old younger sister.]

Who is your favorite author(s)?

Mo Smells Christmas is my favorite book, so whoever wrote that book is my favorite. [Margaret Hyde; A Sensational Journey (Mo's Nose) series] (Some other favorite books are pulled off the shelf as we talk.) This used to be my favorite, but now it's Delia's. (Hungry Caterpillar by Erik Carle)Me and Delia laugh so hard when we do the moves like the dogs in this book (Doggie Do! by Dar Hosta). I've read a lot of these books. I love fairies. (Rainbow Magic Fairies series by Daisy Meadows) Oh, how about the author I met and she signed a copy of her book Where Did Mommy's Superpowers Go? (Jenifer Gershman) Her son really likes my book, which is cool. And the one who gave me a signed copy of her book Red Penguin and the Missing Sushi (Eileen Wacker; Fujimini Adventure Series). Oh, and the nice lady who gave me a stuffed bee when I fell, and she signed a copy of her book Ruby Lee the Bumble Bee. (Dawn Matheson; A Bee's Bit Of Wisdom series)

[Mom's Comment: While at BEA 2011, we were in the Mom's Choice Awards booth and Finn fell. Dawn offered her a prize from the raffle box to dry her tears. Unknowingly, Finn chose Dawn's Ruby Lee Bee and Dawn exclaimed, "of all the things here, you just picked out my bee!" I think Finn must have sixth sense about people. The Ruby Lee Bee now accompanies us on book signings where it is placed on the table along with Finnoula's other animal mascots.]

Do you like art?

Yes, I like art. I like pottery. I get to use my hands and it's fun 'cause I get to design and paint it however I want.

[Mom's Comment: We have three large bins full of "art." I'm not allowed to throw any of it out.]

Is there anything else you would like to add to this interview? What tips would you give to other kids who want to be authors?

Well, a tip I would give is to make sure you are with a grown up who can help you write the words! Mom does that for me. Dad's can help if they are home. He [my dad] helped me a little bit.

[Mom's Comment: Dad's helping is limited because he paraphrases rather than transcribes. Finn asks for us to read it back to "check" our work.]

I'm told that you've considered being an actress as a career. Is this true?

Well, I already am one because I was in "Pirates of Penzance" and "Midsummer Nights Dream." I would like to be in a video on the Internet and I want to be on TV someday. I could be in a toy or movie preview, or commercials. Hmm, could anyone make their own TV show? Because if they [TV people] said 'yes' to my idea. I would put an ad in the paper. I would have my own little helpers and put out a sign "Finnoula's Kid Show—Who Wants to be In It?"

What do you think would be a good TV idea?

Sort of like the Spy Kids movie. My show would be called Spy Kids Forever. There are only two adults in the show, one is the mom and the other is a bad guy. We [the kids] spy on the bad guy and he has bombs everywhere. Spy Kids take them and throw them in the water so he [bad guy] can't get them. We go under the water and light [diffuse] them. We swim out, and go behind a building and watch them explode. We get rid of the other bombs. Then, a Loch Ness monster corners us. We find even more bombs, light them, put them in his mouth, and he explodes. We take the pieces and make sushi. Then we go to the mom and we say "Spy Kids, reunite!" and then we all have the sushi for dinner. At this point, the picture on the TV would get smaller and smaller, on my face and then it shuts closed. At the end, we always have sushi from the Loch Ness monster.

[Mom's Comment: With mouth agape, I listen to this story but can't help commenting, "It sounds kind of dangerous for kids to be working with bombs." Her terse response, "They not real bombs, because it's TV. It would just be guys with fireworks on a hidden dock somewhere. It's fine, Mom." I guess I wouldn't be a very good stage mom. Better stick to author mom.]

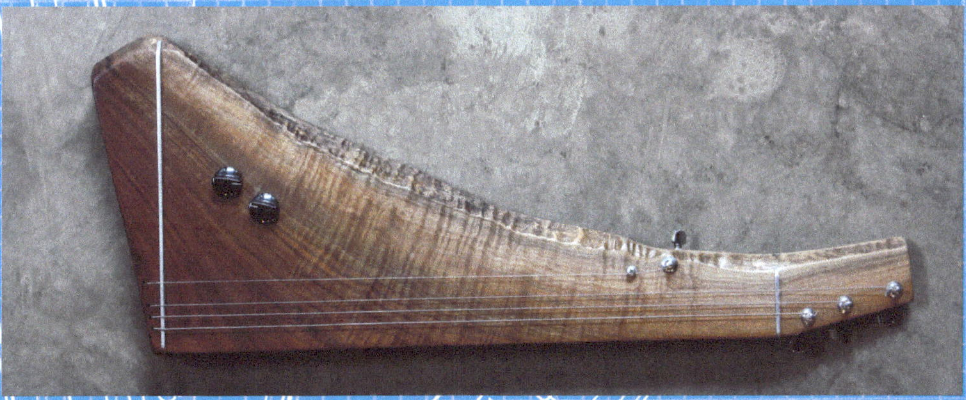

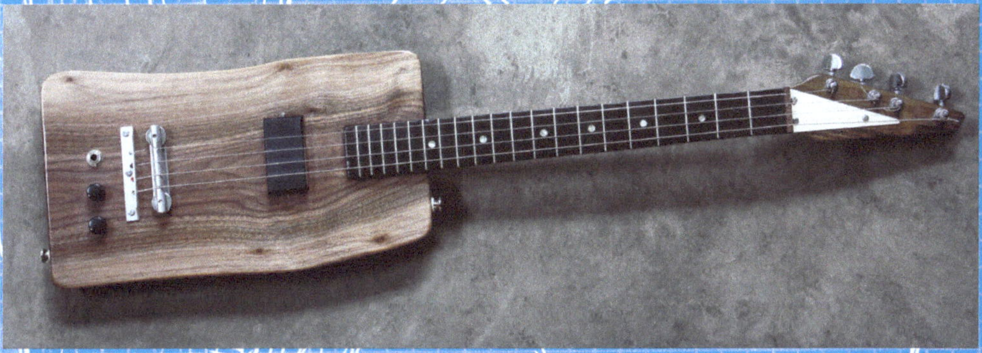

Musician / Designer Edward Potokar

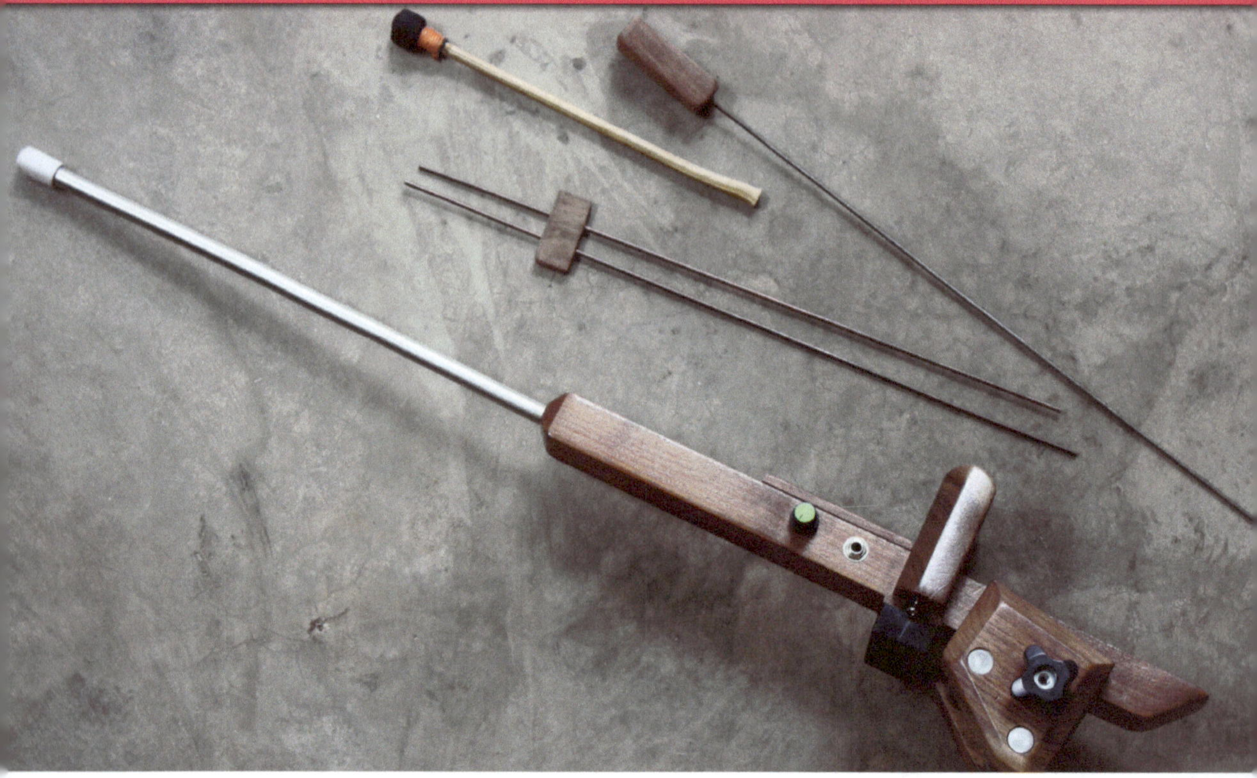

A Conversation with Edward Potokar

As a child, what did you want to become (profession-wise)?

An artist.

In which town did you grow up?

Cleveland, Ohio.

What specific element in your background has influenced your current music style?

My father as a jazz/polka drummer was a huge influence. We always had music playing in our house. Mother played flute. My sister played piano. My brother played the trumpet. There was always a party with people jamming.

What inspires you in the job of being a musician?

Making sounds I haven't heard before.

In which way do you consider yourself an innovative creator?

I love the concept of making something out of nothing.

What other creative ambitions or dreams do you have?

I would like to do more astronomy. There seems to be so many answers out there.

Which basic elements of creativity did your family teach you?

Don't do what every other person is doing. Try something off beat. My mother told me I could be whatever I wanted to be.

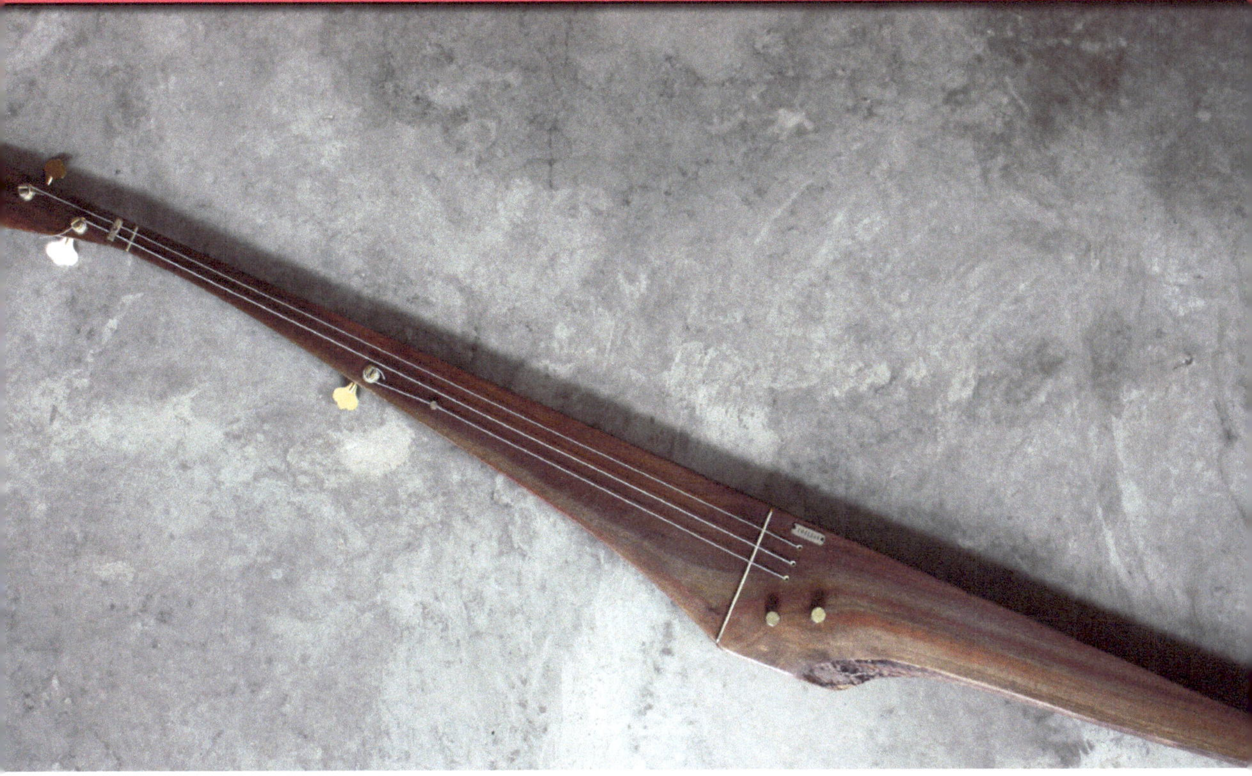

How did you get the idea for creating this music?

Making the instruments make the ideas.

Do you have a favorite musician yourself?

So many..... Kraftwerk, Oscar Peterson, Wendy Carlos, Peggy Lee, Devo, Bowie, come to mind.

Are you ever afraid you will run out of inspiration and creativity?

No, time is what I most fear of running out of.

What is the most difficult thing in your job?

Promoting what I am doing and getting the info out there.

What's the best part of your job?

Putting things together late at night and turning something on for the first time.

Do you expect your style of creating music to change?

It always does so more of the same!

Do you embrace the technological changes in the music industry, like social media?

I do on some level. On another level I think one can get lost in the sauce and not be productive.

Who are other artists you like?

Tim Hawkinson, Man Ray, Alexander McQueen, Andy Goldsworthy, Calder, Dali, Scott Williams, Harry Partch, Andrew Wyeth,Tinguely. What's not to like?

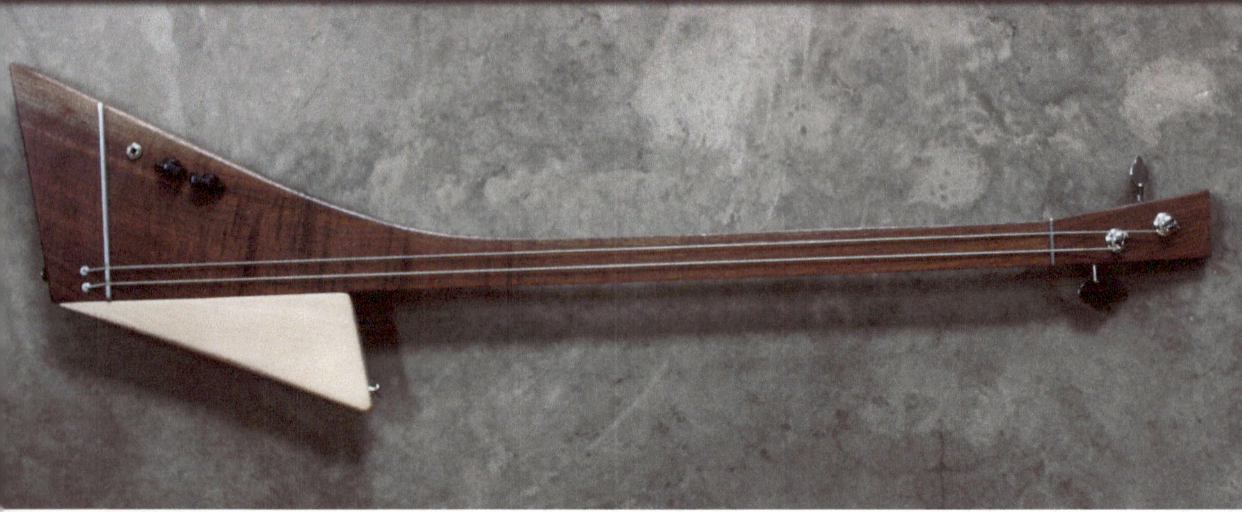

What special quality do you like in their work or personalities?

Craftsmanship, completeness, follow through, the rest is subjective.

Do you think music, art and design are different or similar?

They are all the same except live music is of the moment and then gone forever.

Would you collaborate with an artist from another discipline?

I love multimedia and what other visual/audio artists can bring to the pot. Collaboration is a blast!

Which artist you would like to work with?

That would Be John Houshmand and we are working together on out new Sound Wall project.

Do you follow any philosophical approach in making your music?

Not to loud; don't play too much; If you don't know what to do don't do anything; and, go get a beer.

What is your favorite building?

It would be my house in upstate New York. Not because of what it is but because of how I feel there. For now I enjoy the comfort, seclusion, security, and resources I have there. I love to
travel and I love to come home.

What is your favorite hotel?

I don't generally like hotels. Sleeping where other people have been is weird.

What would be your ideal home?

My ideal home could be the next one I design and build with my wife. I have learned so much since the last one. Maybe it will be in another country.

What are you future dreams?

Not so much a dream ... more like a hope. If you can't make things better then don't make it worse. I would like to learn Spanish.

Is there anything else you would like to add to this interview?

I crave the sublime moments when time stops and I am not aware of my surroundings ... in other words "art."

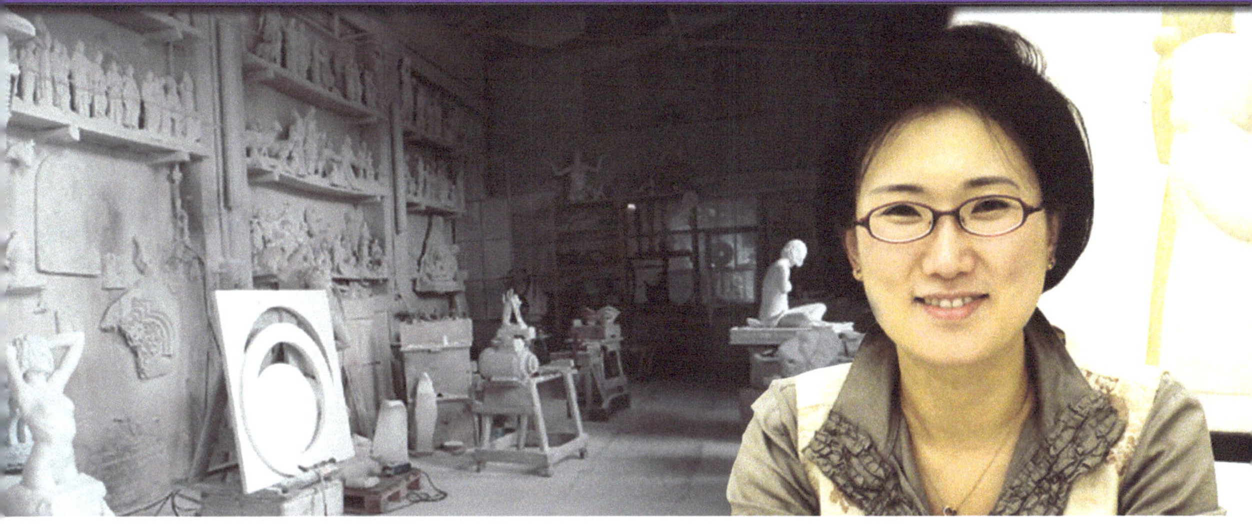

Artist Ming-jung Park

"The Human Body as a Vision of Daily Life and Reality"

Since the modern times, sculptors have taken the human body as a motif for expressing the law of nature, human spirit and emotion. Sculptures of the human body have evolved from the traditional role of serving a purpose such as a means to create well-known figures in the form of statues. Sculptures capture the vision presented by the creators, their take on reality. Sculptors imbue their thoughts and emotions into their art work as a way to express and reaffirm their existence.

Min-jung Park is no exception. Like most people who constantly remind themselves of their existence through daily experiences, Min-jung Park does the same through the emotions from significant and memorable experiences of everyday encounters. Park, however, resorts to the expression of the human body. Park's sculptures convert a very personal experience into something universal that can touch all audiences.

Park's works of art do not demand the audience to overstretch their imagination. She intentionally avoids dramatic movements, fierce facial expressions or exaggerated rhetorics but relies on inner strength to convey her message. The simple postures symbolize the state of emotion. Seemingly ordinary faces that appear anything but extreme nonetheless display the dynamic movement of the spirit and the energy of the soul. The expression on the faces are intentionally watered down and impersonal, which in turn represents 'us' as anonymous beings.

Just as emotion is the basis of life, so is the harmony of texture from the carved stone, the joyous interaction of surfaces, and the light and shadow resulting in the dynamic movement of her works. Min-jung Park cherishes the hand, among other parts of the human body. The hand represents her life, her way of living. It is also an important medium that symbolizes her self-perception and state of mind. The hand in her works is an expression that beckons one's emotion to wake up and appreciate the essence of the meaning and symbols in our everyday lives.

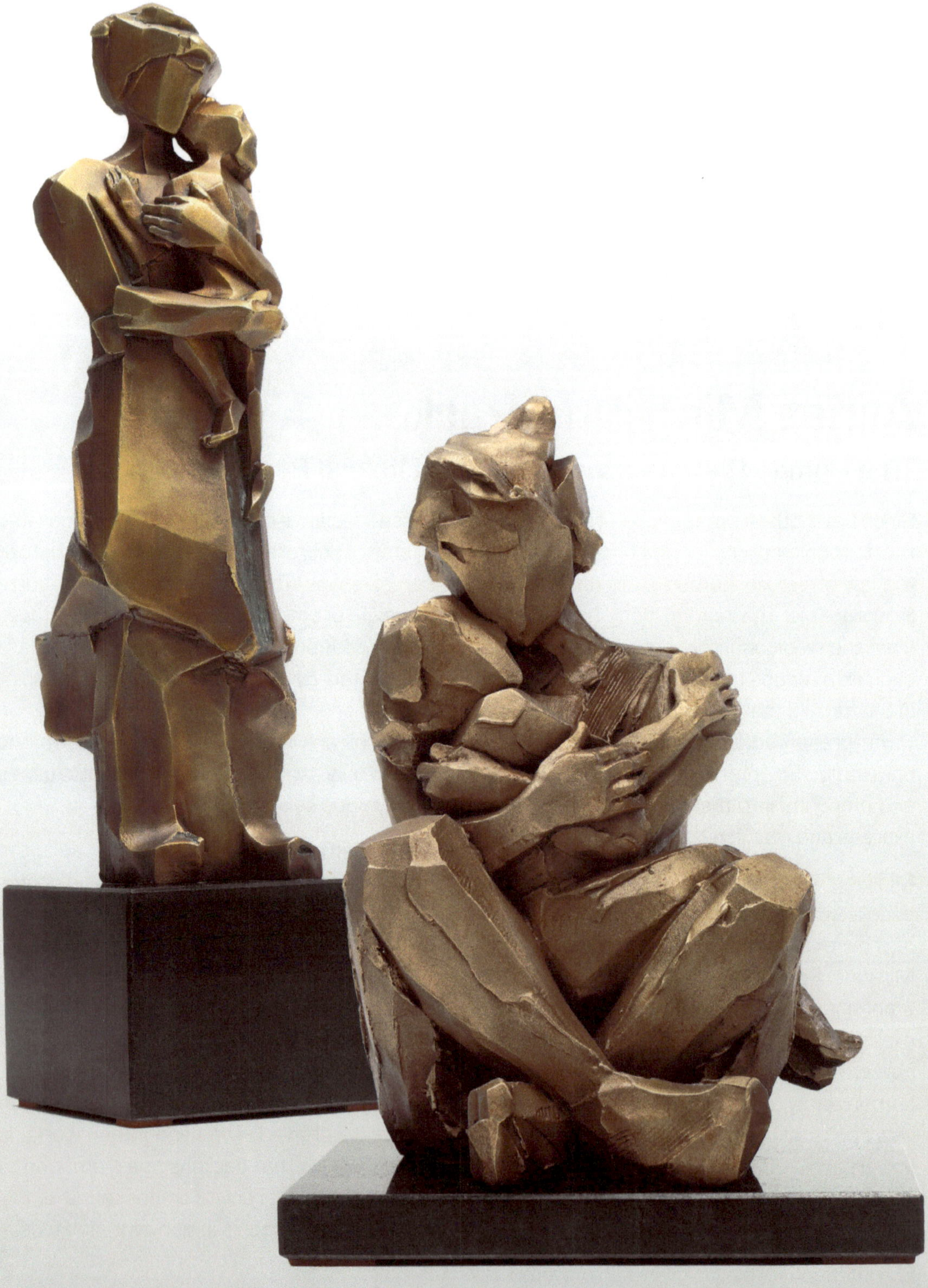

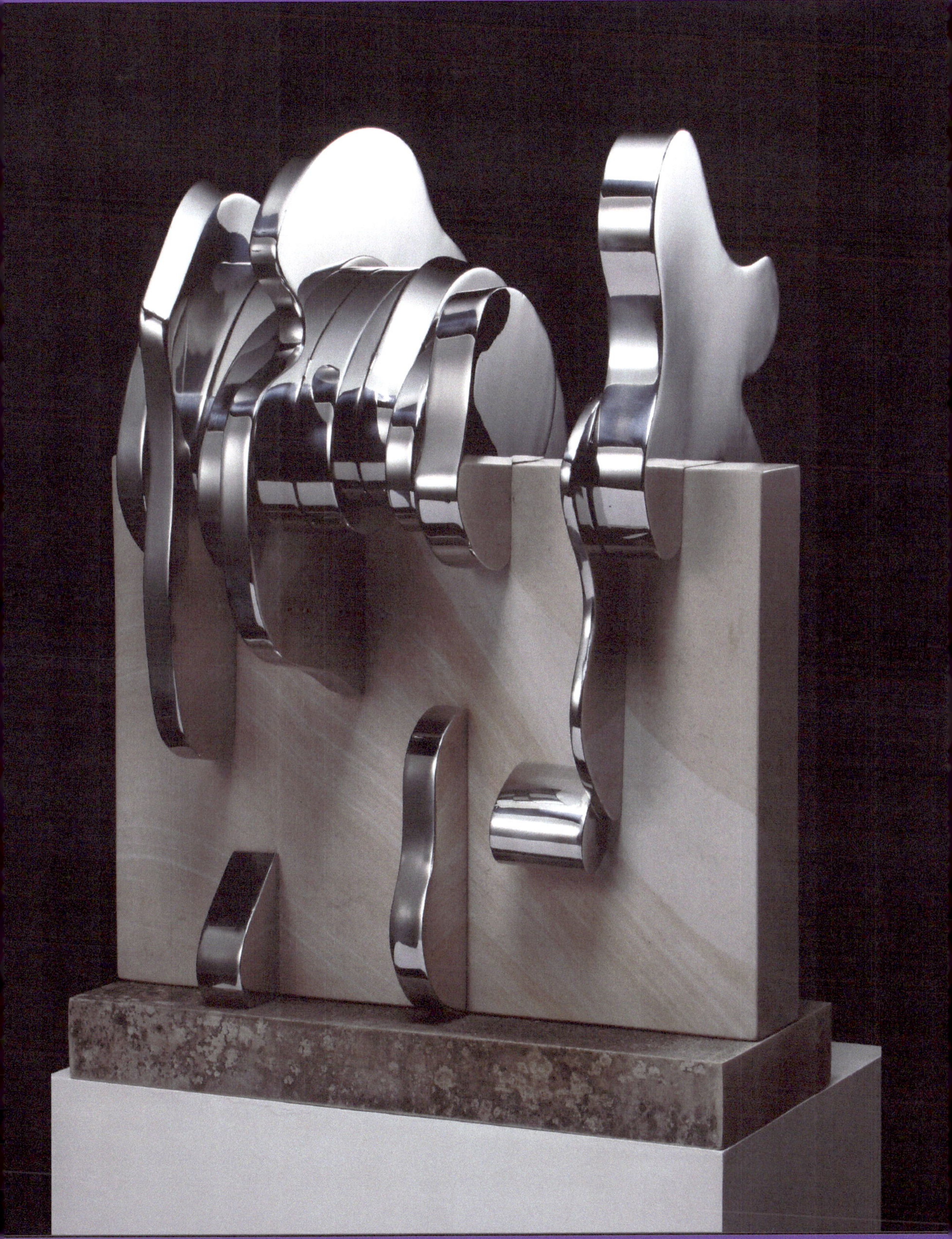

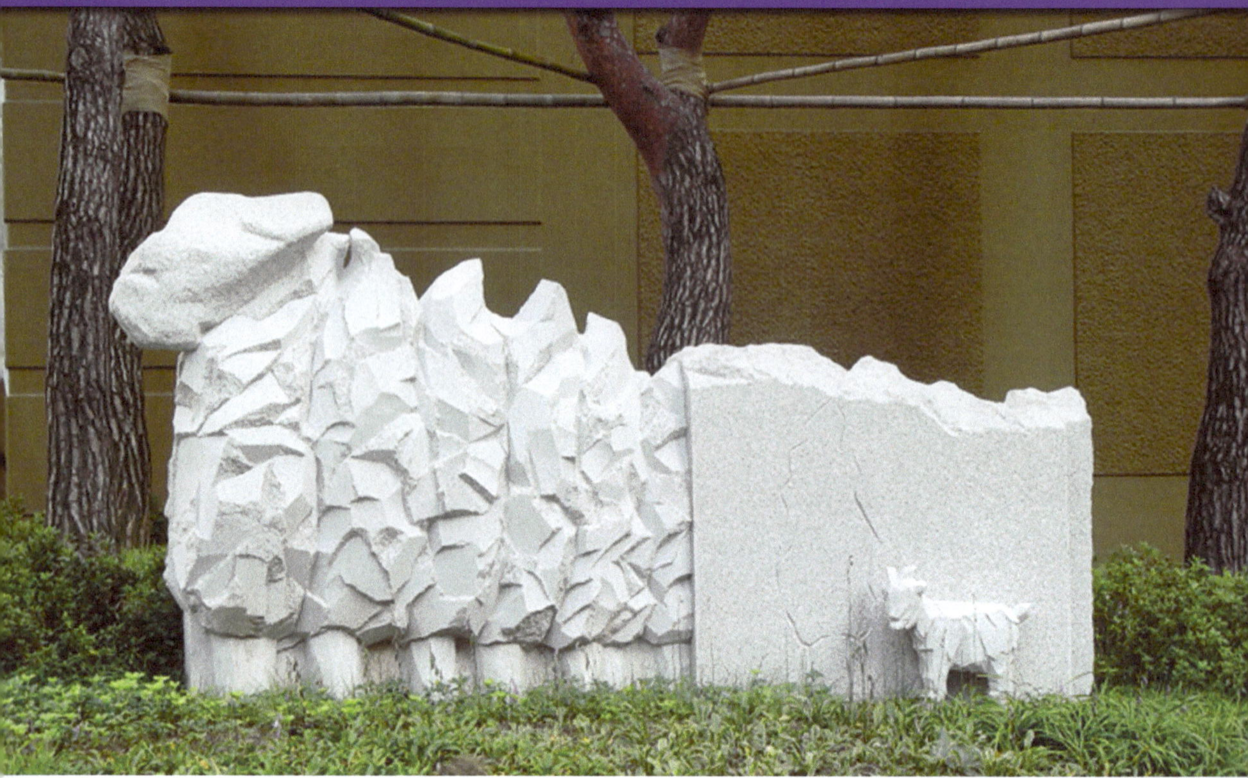

Particularly interesting is the imagination her works, which arouse from the audience. The first things that occupy one's mind at the sight of her work are the processes of the creation, and her labor and tools involved in the completion of her works. They pass through like a story line – the struggle between the artist and the material, the tension felt by the artist who was well aware that the material, once cut or carved. The material cannot be restored to its original shape, and the resistance of the lifeless mass at each touch of the chisel, the conflict between the artist and the tool caused by the sensitivity are required to breathe life into one's creation.

The touch of her works that signals the 'completion of the unfinished' resonates strong and wide, representing her view of sculptures as both a re-creation of the human spirit and emotion as well as an independent figure. The audience, as a result, are allowed to go beyond the story conveyed through the work and concentrate on the effect of the form of the sculpture itself. The artist, in the end, is able to achieve a sense of independence by having both the medium (sculpture) and the technique become the object of aesthetic appreciation. The potency exuding from the form and meaning leads to the same road.

The human body, expressed by Min-jung Park, holds numerous surfaces full of life. It is the symbol of her ability to capture life and spirit under all circumstances, since no aspect of life is without meaning. Through her works and the surfaces of her sculptures, Min-jung Park successfully calls upon us to wake up and plunge into the essence of the spirit and emotion.

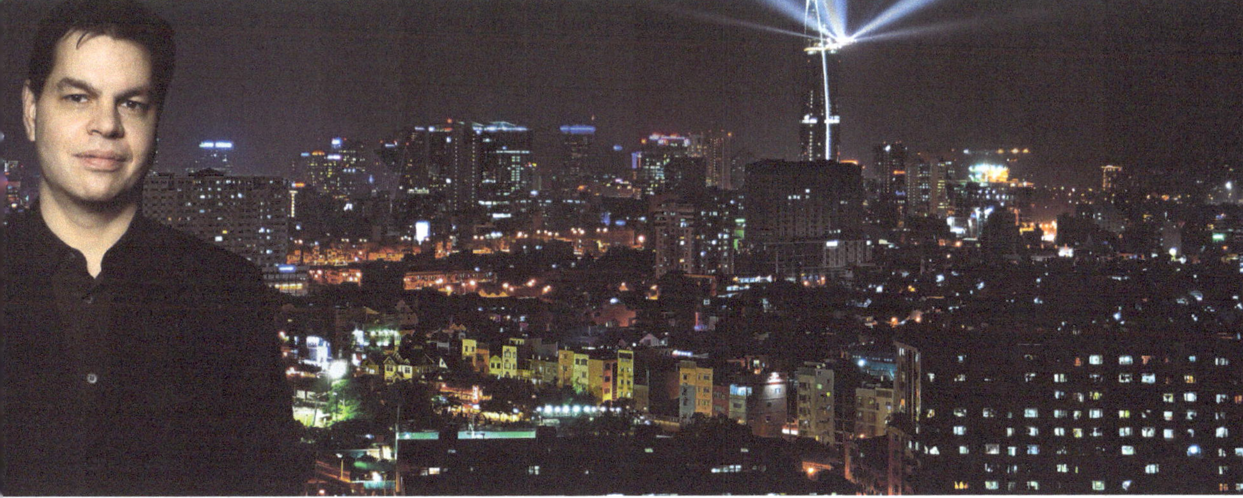

Architect Carlos Zapata

Carlos Zapata's interest in design can be traced to his childhood, where his parents raised his family in different countries throughout Latin America. As a member of UNESCO, Carlos' father was responsible for opening elementary schools in Venezuela, Mexico and Ecuador. Living in different countries opened Carlos' mind, creating an awareness of the nuances that make a place special.

Carlos was born in Venezuela but moved to Mexico when he was 2 years old. The family lived in Mexico for several years before relocating to Quito, Ecuador, where the family stayed until Carlos came to the US for college. The Zapata household was always filled with art; Carlos' mother opened her own art gallery in Quito where she discovered and featured numerous local artists as well as international artists. Both of Carlos' parents are avid collectors of historical and religious art as well as contemporary, and Carlos grew up in an environment rich with expression. Carlos' father is a devoted music aficionado whose tastes range from classical to opera to jazz.

At the age of 17, Carlos came to the United States for preparatory school at Northfield Mt. Hermon in Massachusetts. Once here, Carlos decided to complete his education in the US. Carlos only decided to pursue architecture at the suggestion of one of his art professors and Carlos found himself at Pratt Institute in Brooklyn, one of the country's leading design schools. Here, Carlos excelled at architectural design, and upon completing his degree, he was approached by a senior associate at a large firm in NYC. Carlos was asked to join the firm as a design associate. While working at various firms in New York City, Carlos also completed his master's degree at Columbia University.

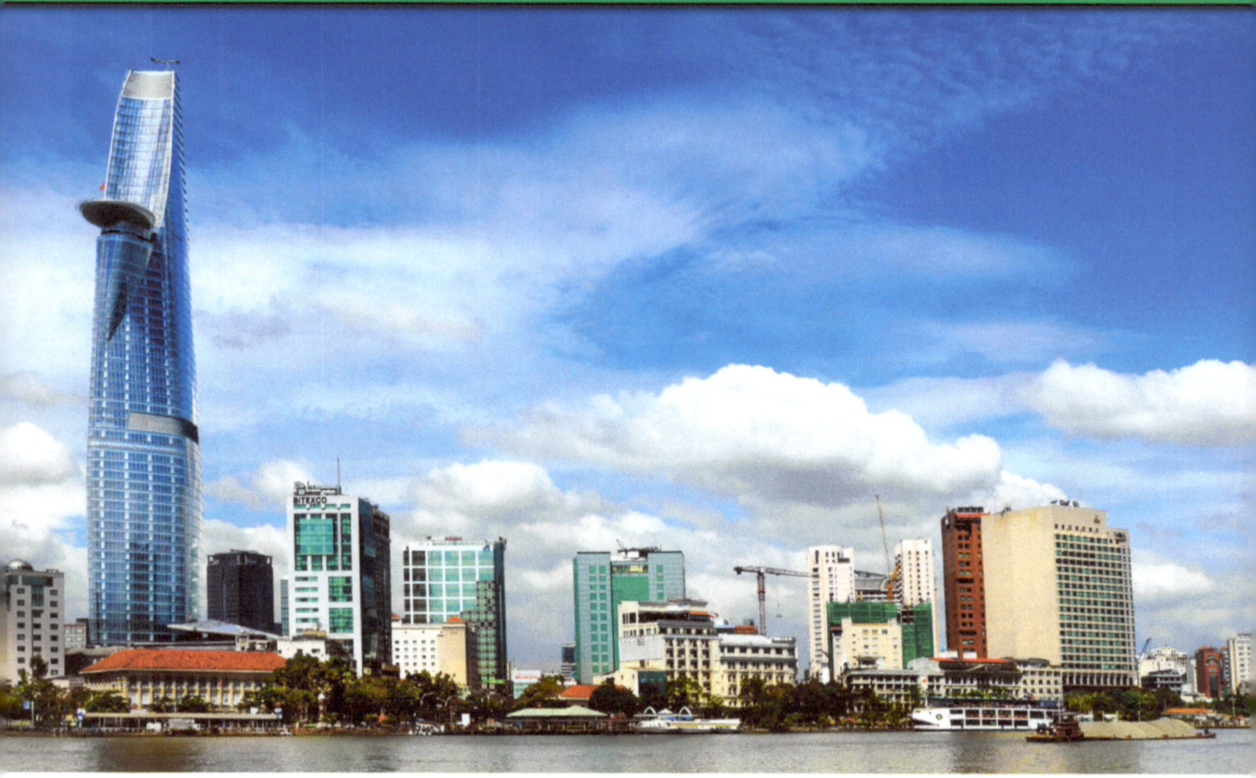

Before starting his own firm, Carlos Zapata Design Studio, Carlos most notably served as Design Director of Ellerbe Becket / New York. Here he led a team of young designers to win design awards in 5 consecutive years from the New York Chapter of the American Institute of Architects, on a variety of projects ranging from a new terminal at JFK International Airport to a high-rise tower at Manhattan's South Ferry Terminal. His experience at Ellerbe Becket was extremely positive and allowed Carlos to contemplate diverse project typologies, which was extremely beneficial when, in 1992, Carlos decided to leave the corporate architecture world and open his own firm. With a commission for a new 6,000 square foot house on the beach in Miami and a corporate interiors project in a mid-rise office building in downtown Miami, Carlos moved to Miami Beach and opened his own firm. The interior design project for the investment firm, JPBT Advisors, was the first completed project of Carlos Zapata Design Studio. It was featured as the cover story of Architectural Record and won Carlos his first National AIA award.

Other projects followed for Carlos' studio, and he then met his former partner, Benjamin Wood. Ben was looking for designers to collaborate on his renovation and rehabilitation of Miami Beach's historic Lincoln Road. Shortly after meeting, Ben asked Carlos to work with him on a competition to design a new stadium for the Chicago Bears, one of the founding teams of American football.

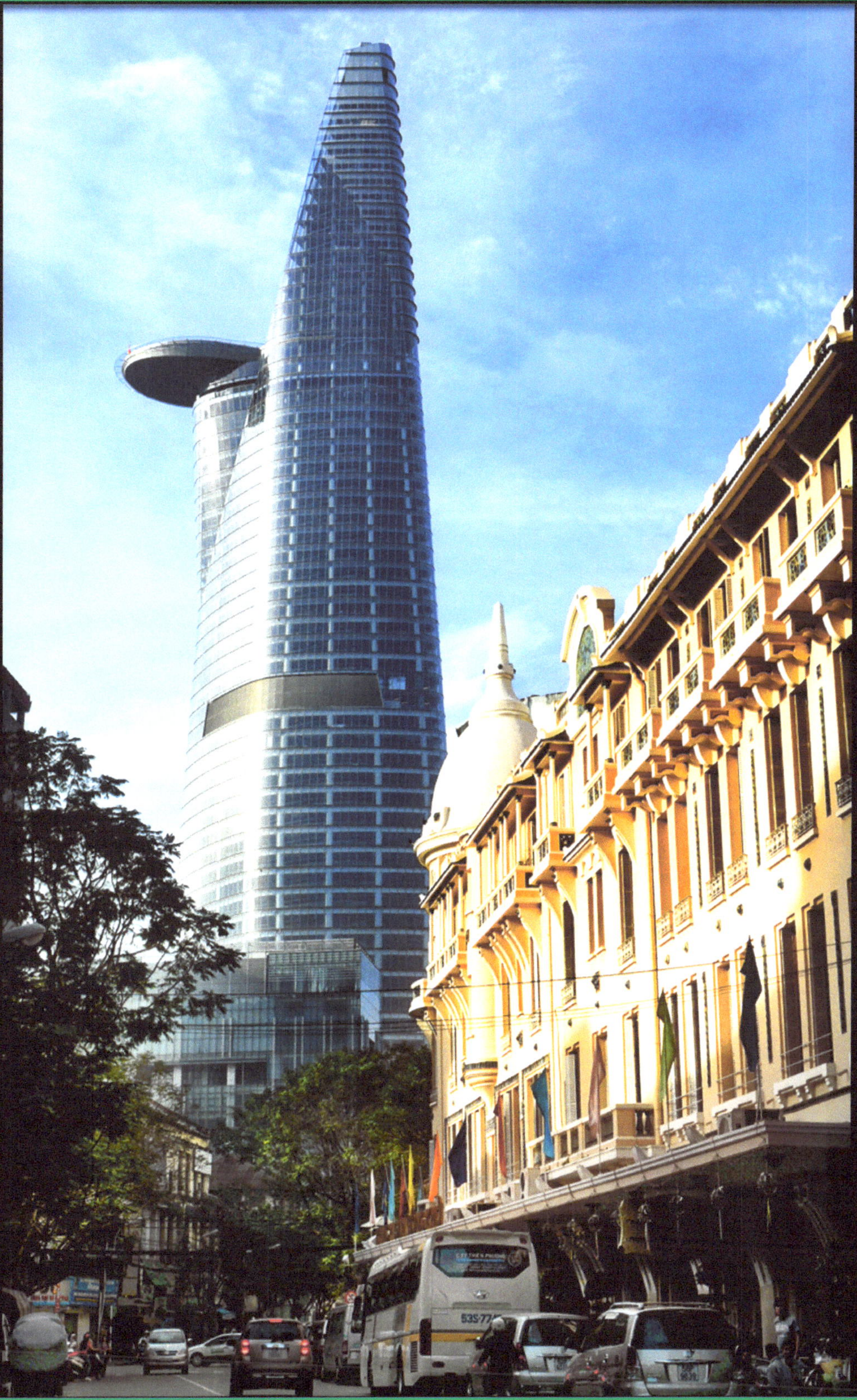

Carlos brought a small team up to Ben's office in Cambridge, Massachusetts, and their design won the commission. After designing several schemes for the new stadium in various locations in and around Chicago, Ben and Carlos realized that if they changed the paradigm of the typical football stadium, they could shrink the footprint and build a new stadium in Soldier Field, where the existing stadium stood. This asymmetrical solution has become a landmark in Chicago, where its design maximizes the views of both Lake Michigan and downtown Chicago, and also offers fans one of the best experiences in professional sports.

During the eight years of Wood + Zapata, Carlos designed such varied projects as Concourse J, a 14-gate international concourse at Miami International Airport, Publix Supermarket, which has become a modern architectural icon in the historic South Beach section of Miami Hamilton Square, a 9-story market and parking garage in Philadelphia, and Xintiandi, the award-winning restoration, renovation and new construction of 2 historic city blocks in the French Concession of Shanghai.

In 2003, Carlos and Ben decided to evolve Wood + Zapata into two separate companies and Carlos moved Carlos Zapata Studio back to his original base of New York City. Since 2003, Carlos has designed such notable projects as the 450-room JW Marriott Hotel in Hanoi; the 22-story Cooper Square Hotel in New York City's exciting Bowery neighborhood; and the 3800-room Fontainebleau Hotel and Casino in Las Vegas.

The work of Carlos Zapata Studio has won numerous design awards and been featured in books and magazines around the world. Carlos himself has received several prestigious awards, including being named by Time Magazine as "Someone to Watch" at the beginning of his career as well as being selected as one of Interior Design Magazine's "30 Under 30" as well as their "40 Under 40". One of Carlos' most notable projects is the 68-story Bitexco Financial Tower in Ho Chi Minh City, which celebrated its grand opening on October 31, 2010. This building is extremely important to Carlos, both for its design and for what it represents.

Working closely with Mr. Vu Quang Hoi, the Chairman of Bitexco Companies, Carlos designed a building that is meant to be an icon representing Vietnam as a sophisticated and important participant in the global arena, both architecturally and financially. The thoroughly modern expression of the lotus bud, Carlos' design inspiration for the building's shape and façade treatment, represents Vietnam's rich cultural heritage, which is now being translated into the 21st century and into the future.

Carlos' newest project is a luxury development located at 39-41 West 23rd Street in New York City. Starting next summer, what was once a parking lot will be transformed into a dramatic new building of iconic design.

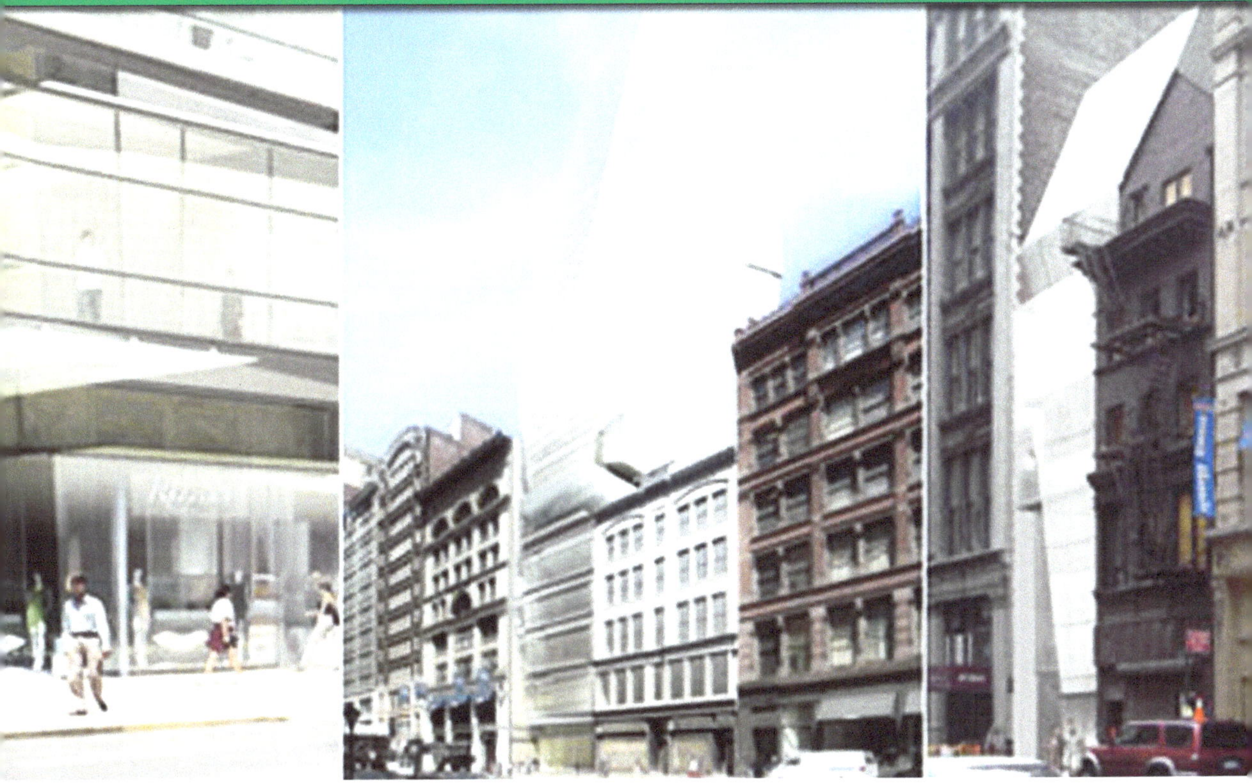

A 97,000 square-foot, 22-story building will sit on the 23rd Street side of the property, and a small ancillary amenity structure will occupy the 24th Street side. The ground floor and cellar are reserved for retail space. The upper floors will consist of approximately 38 condominium residences, each with stylish gourmet kitchens with state-of-the-art appliances and stone counter tops, contemporary bathrooms, high-end fixtures and hardwood floors. The building's modern façade designed with large amounts of glass will maximize views and light, giving the upper floors panoramic vistas of Chelsea and the Flatiron District.

The new development is designed to deliver meaningful sustainability in terms of energy efficiency, quality of life and health benefits for the residents, cost savings and other benefits that result from the creation of a high performance building.

"This property will be 'green' from the inside out," noted Barbara van Beuren, co-founder of the building's developer, Anbau Enterprises. "We are creating a building that pushes the envelope of sustainability, and offers home owners true health benefits and energy cost savings," she said. "We will integrate state-of-the-art building systems and technology, materials and finishes that have eco-conscious properties, and take into consideration issues like sound attenuation and other quality-of-life aspects."

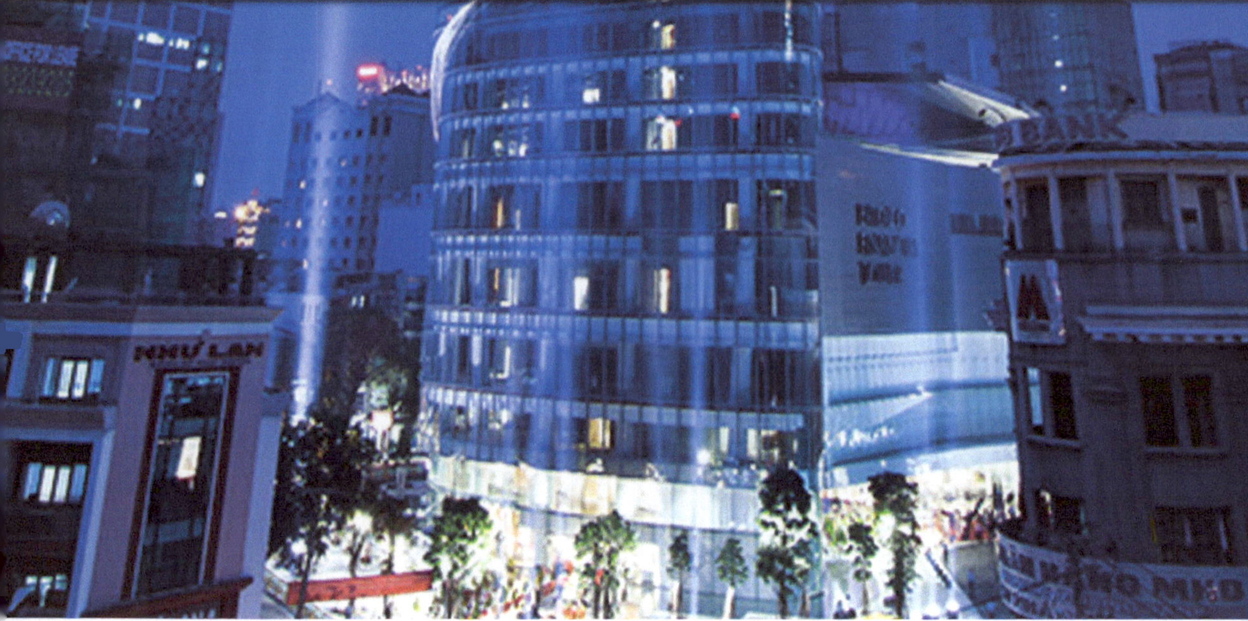

A Conversation with Carlos Zapata

As a child, what did you want to become (profession-wise)?

As a child, I considered becoming a doctor as well as an artist. I started painting at a very early age. The doctor idea faded out of my mind quite quickly.

In which town did you grow up?

Several, since my father worked for the United Nations and part of his profession involved opening schools in rural areas of Latin America. I was born in Rubio, Venezuela where we lived until I was 2 and a half years old. My parents then moved to a small town in Mexico, called Patzcuaro, and then my family moved to Quito, Ecuador where we lived until I was 16, when I came to the US.

Do you think your background has influenced your current architectural style? If so, what specific element in your background is most pervasive in influencing your current architectural style?

I would say yes. My parents owned an art gallery, which was certainly influential in terms of awareness of art. I have also found that Latin America embraces modern architecture more than the US. Also, my family traveled quite a bit and later on, I picked up the travel habit and continued to travel on my own.

What inspires you in the job of being an architect?

The challenge of developing something new, for instance a three-dimensional structure that evolves through you from pure data is inspiring. Also, beautiful proportions, finding the appropriate structural resolutions, responding to light and color.

In which way do you consider yourself an innovative creator?

In the way that I use structure to express and capture movement in static objects, including architecture.

Do you have any other creative ambitions or dreams to which you aspire?

I aspire to make all sorts of design objects, not necessarily only architecture.

Which basic elements of creativity did your family teach you?

My parents taught me appreciation of art through their interest in art forms of all types, including music, theater and dance. My father is a true enthusiast of classical music and jazz.

How did you get the idea for creating this architectural design?

The building on 23rd Street presented a fantastic opportunity to design a truly modern piece of architecture in my favorite city in the world. I simply wanted to take the evolution of style in the area one step further. The answer was to produce an asymmetrical iconic form, simple enough to blend with the sky and complex enough to effortlessly lean back towards the north,expand towards the east, in an effort to respond to very specific elements of its immediate area.

Do you have a favorite architect yourself?

I have always admired the work of Carlo Scarpa for his attention to detail, color and articulation. As for current practitioners, I very much appreciate the work of Renzo Piano.

Are you ever afraid you will run out of inspiration and creativity in your job?

No, sometimes I am afraid clients run out of inspiration.

What is the most difficult thing in your job?

One of the most difficult things is trying to communicate the value of certain elements which are not understandable solely in economic terms.

What is the most fun part of your job?

Seeing your projects being built and then getting to experience them once they're done.

Do you expect your way of creating architecture to change in the future?

Every project is different and benefits from technology and cultural knowledge in different ways. Both knowledge and technology are progressing exponentially and my interest lies in knowing how to apply new findings to the creation of architecture. So yes, I expect my way of creating architecture will keep developing with time.

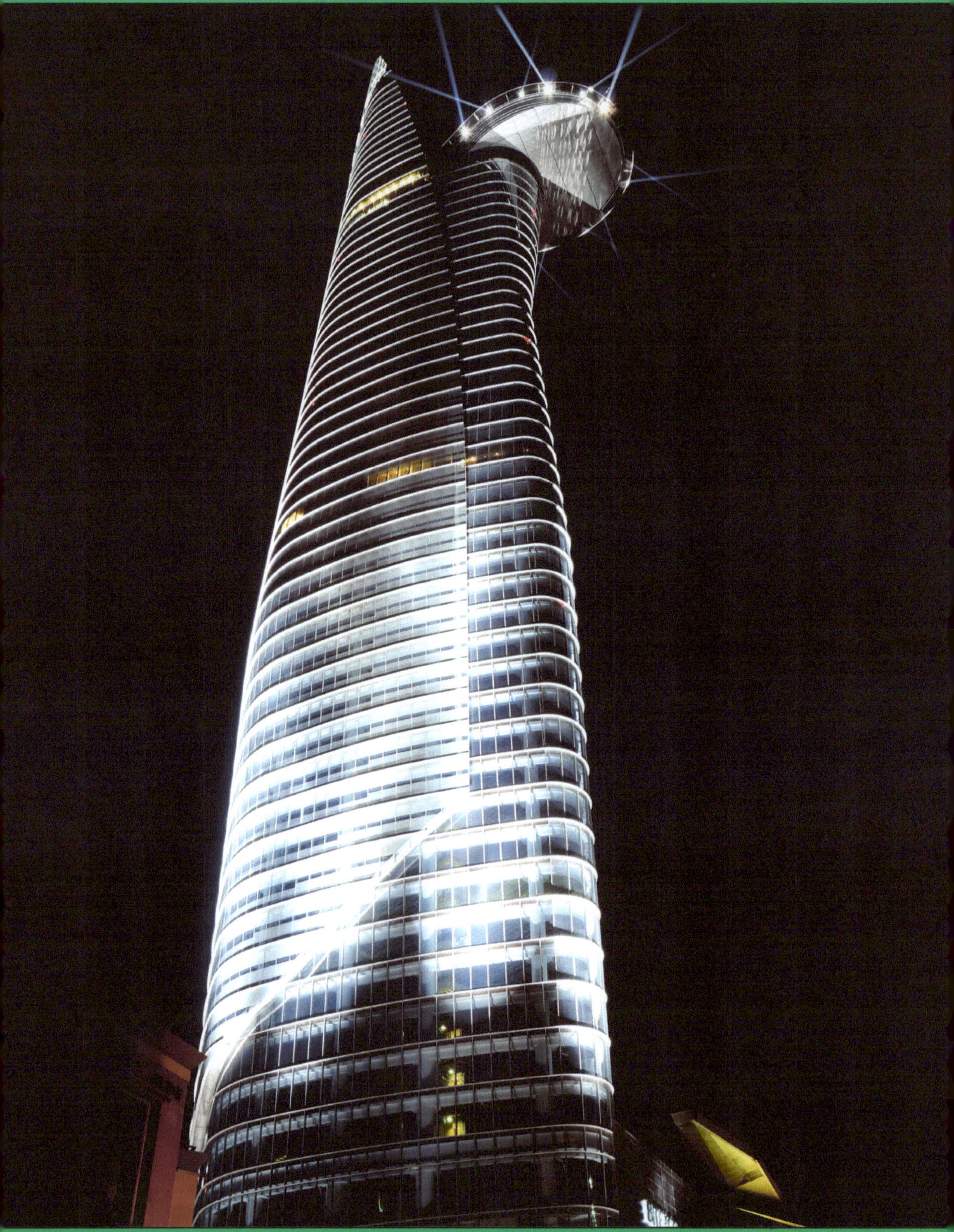

Do you embrace the changes in the architectural industry regarding social media and technology influences?

I completely embrace changes in technology especially when it comes to building materials and systems.

What do you consider to be your greatest masterpiece?

I don't believe in masterpieces but I do believe in good buildings. And since I work in different types of buildings regularly, that makes it difficult for me to compare one project to another. That said, I enjoy the expressive quality of Soldier Field, and I enjoy how the Financial Tower of Ho Chi Minh City has contributed to the skyline of the city. I am very much looking forward to seeing 23rd Street completed and inhabited.

Do you like art? Do you have any preferences for an artist? And/or for creators of artistic work?

I love art and enjoy the work of different artists. Some of my favorites are Roberto Matta, Lucio Fontana, Arnaldo Pomodoro, and Yoshitomo Nara. In fashion, I love Jil Sander and Yojii Yamamoto. I love the design of machines, and very much appreciate the design of Carlo Rivaboats from the 1960's, Ducati motorcycles and in cars, Aston Martins.

If so, why is that? What special quality do you like in their work or personalities?

About Nara, I love his sense of humor. About Fontana, I love the minimal simplicity of his work and about Matta, I love the blurring of realities present in his work. About Pomodoro, I love the strictness of his eroded forms.

Could we feature your favorite photographer, author, artist, designer, architect, filmmaker, etc. in our publication and/or online?

Of course.

In which way do you think architecture, art and design are different and/or similar?

I think architecture and design are very similar because they deal with how they are used. They are also similar to art it that they can be borne of or evoke emotional reactions but art itself, whether painting, sculpture or photography, does not need to be used and that's a big difference.

Do you aspire to collaborate in your creations with an artist from another artistic discipline?

Yes, it would be a very wonderful experience to collaborate with an artist from an other discipline.

Do you have a favorite company or exciting other creator with whom you would like to work?

Not at the moment.

Do you follow any philosophical or psychological approach in making your architectural designs?

My philosophy is very simple: I subscribe to modernism, which looks at art and architecture as an exploration that has no end to it.

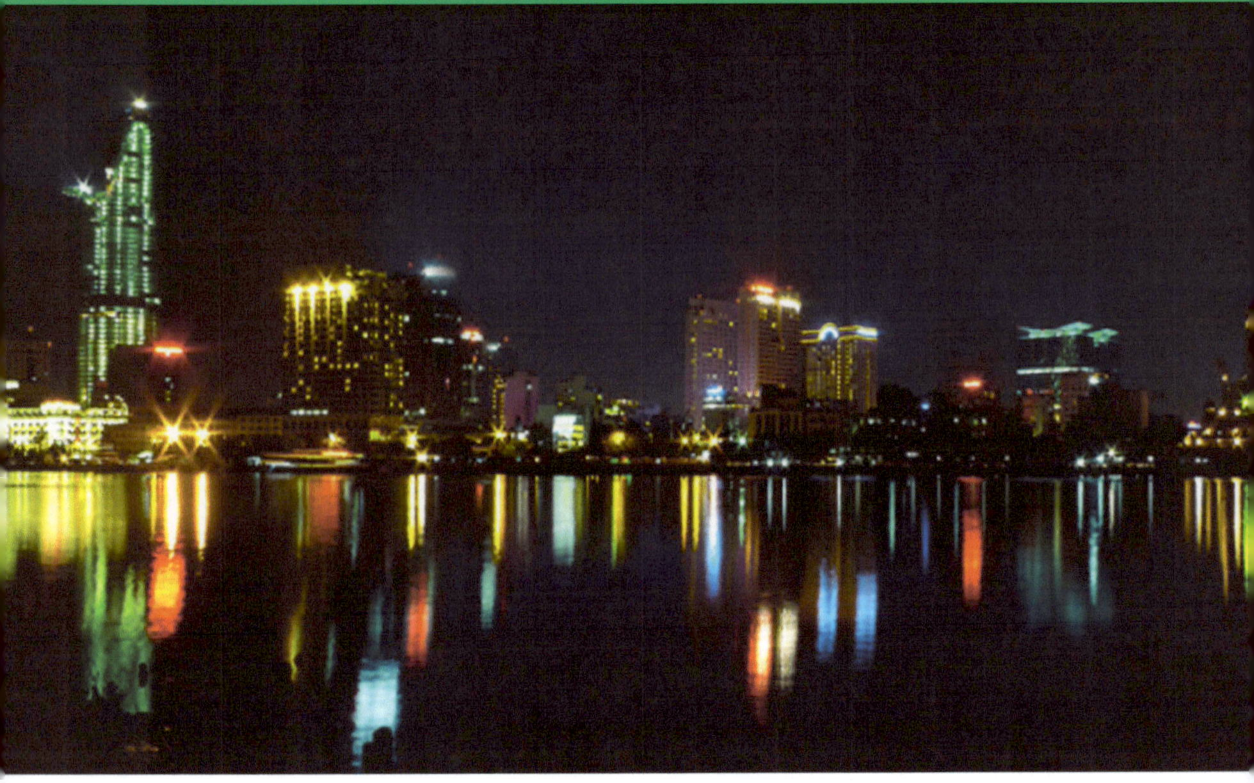

What is your favorite building in the world? (If more than one, please list more, and if you like, please add motivation to your favorite(s).)

I don't have one specific favorite but I greatly admire buildings and places of very different eras, I love Machu Pichu, Angkor Wat in Cambodia, I love Gothic cathedrals, the top of the Chrysler Building, Frank Lloyd Wright's Guggenheim, Renzo Piano's Marie Tjibaou Cultural Center in New Caledonia, and Utzon's Sydney Opera House.

What is your favorite hotel? (If more than one, please list more, and if you like, please add motivation to your favorite(s).)

I love the Metropole in Hanoi, Pershing Hall in Paris, the Bulgari Hotel in Milan, the Villa d'Este in Lake Como and Aman resorts, just about anywhere.

What would be your ideal home? (If more than one, please list more, and if you like, please add motivation to your dream home(s).)

It would have to be a beautiful modern house designed by me in Lake Como, with a dock for my 1965 Riva Ariston, and a penthouse on top of one of my buildings in New York City.

Do you have any dreams for the future?

My dream is to work for the simple pleasure of working only.

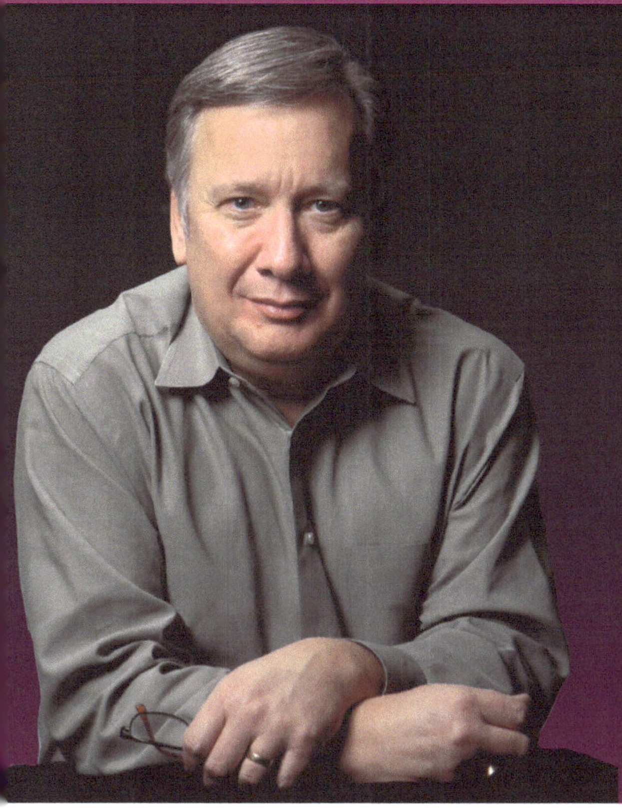

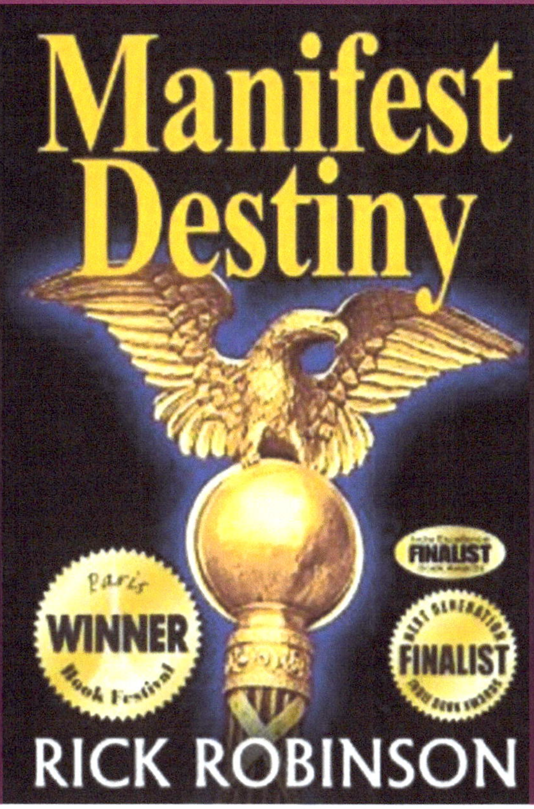

Manifest Destiny
RICK ROBINSON

Author Rick Robinson & Manifest Destiny

Rick Robinson has spent more than 30 years in politics and law, including a stint on Capitol Hill as legislative director/chief counsel to then-Congressman Jim Bunning (R–KY). He has been active in all levels of politics, from advising candidates on the national level to walking door-to-door in city council races. He even ran for the United States Congress in 1998.

A graduate of Eastern Kentucky University and Salmon P. Chase College of Law, Robinson currently practices law in Ft. Mitchell, Kentucky, with the law firm of Graydon Head & Ritchey LLP. He and his wife, Linda, live in Ft. Mitchell, Kentucky, with their three children, Josh, Zach and MacKenzie. Robinson has also achieved wide success as an author. His first book, "The Maximum Contribution," was named Award Winning Finalist in the 2008 Next Generation Indie Books Awards in the genré of political fiction. It also won an Honorable Mention at the 2008 Hollywood Book Festival. His book, "Sniper Bid," was released on Election Day 2009 and opened on Amazon's Top 100 Best Seller list at #46 for political fiction. "Sniper Bid" went on to win five national awards: Finalist USA Book News Best Books of 2009; Finalist Best Indie Novel Next Generation Indie Books Awards; Runner-up at the 2009 Nashville Book Festival; Honorable Mentions at the 2008 New England Book Festival; 2009 Hollywood Book Festival. Throughout 2009 both books appeared on Amazon's Top 100 Best Seller List on the same day.

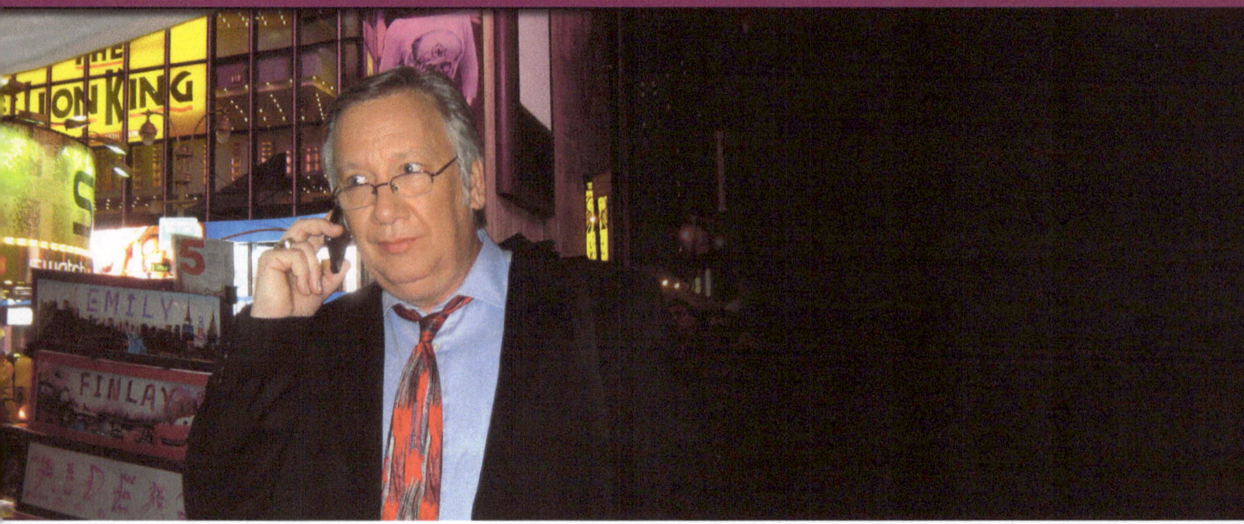

Robinson's latest book, "Manifest Destiny" (released on May 1, 2010) was named the Best Independent Book in America in the 2010 DIY Book Festival, which honors independent works of merit. According to the press release issued by the festival, "Robinson's third novel sees the worlds of politics and law collide in a high-tension drama of international intrigue. The author's 30 years of political and legal experience is evidence throughout the page-turning novel. Combined with Robinson's savvy promotion and use of social media, the work captured the imagination of the judges for the ninth annual competition."

"Manifest Destiny" was also recognized as the Best Fiction winner in the prestigious New York Book Festival competition and Best Fiction at the Paris Book Festival, as well as being named a Finalist for Best Fiction Indie Next Generation Book Awards, Finalist for Best Thriller Indie Excellence Book Awards, Honorable Mention for Best Fiction at the San Francisco Book Festival, and an Honorable Mention at the Beach Book Festival.

"I am humbled by the national acclaim and honors," Robinson said. "Manifest Destiny" centers on fictional U.S. Rep. Richard Thompson as he investigates the kidnapping of one of his staffers by Communist rebels in Romania. In the process, he becomes embroiled in a high-stakes game of cat and mouse, with the control of Eastern Europe hanging in the balance.

"The part of the story that takes place in Romania includes fictionalized versions of actual events that occurred during and after the Ceausescu regime," Robinson said. "While doing research, I spent time with American election observers who were the first in Romania following the execution of Ceausescu and his wife."

In early 2011, Robinson's book was acquired by Los Angeles-based producer Peter R.J. Deyell (Road to Nowhere) in a six-figure agreement, with Academy Award-nominated screenwriter Quinn Redeker (The Deer Hunter) attached to write. Deyell and his team are currently in the early stages of developing "Manifest Destiny" into a motion picture with a tentative release date of 2012.

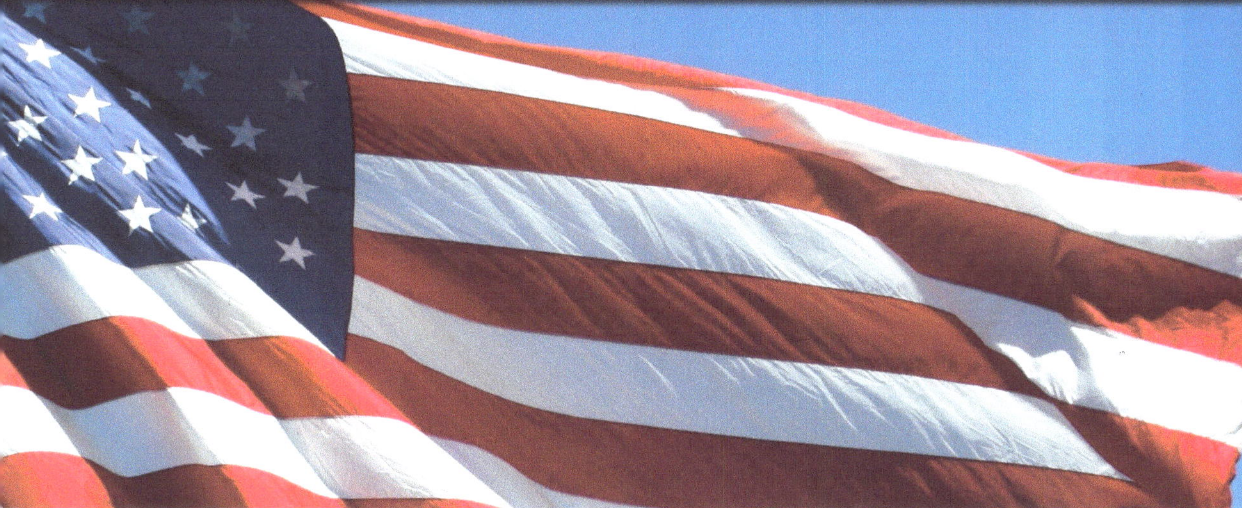

A Conversation with Author Rick Robinson

In which town did you grow up?

I grew up in the small Ohio River town of Ludlow, Kentucky, the third generation to graduate from the same high school.

As a child, what did you want to become (Profession-wise)?

From a very early age, I wanted to be an attorney. I enjoyed writing, but I never thought that it would end up as a career path for me.

Do you think your background has influenced your current book writing style? If so, what specific element in your background is most pervasive in influencing your current book writing style?

Growing up in a small town definitely influences my writing. The main character in my series, Richard Thompson, actually hails from Ludlow. More importantly, Thompson has small town values and constantly fights to remain true to his beliefs — not an easy task in a town like Washington, D.C.

What inspires you in the job of being an author?

My family is my ultimate inspiration. I want to make them proud of what I put down on paper. When I am in writing mode, I listen to a wide variety of music to get my muse on. I have a special mix of Warren Zevon, Meat Loaf, John Prine and The Pogues looped on my computer that always gets me in the mood.

In which way do you consider yourself an innovative creator?

I bring a different voice to political thrillers. Most authors try to stay away from politics. I've spent 30 years in politics. I want my characters to be real, and in order to do so they have to occasionally express political opinions.

Do you have any other creative ambitions or dreams to which you aspire?

I play a little guitar ... very little. Every other week, I have a bunch of players over to my house to play and sing. We call ourselves The Cheater Glasses and our sessions involve a both of bourbon and Guinness.

I'd love to become good enough on the ax to have The Cheater Glasses perform an original song for the closing credits on a big screen adaptation of one of my books.

Which basic elements of creativity did your family teach you?

I grew up in a small town, and my parents taught me that, in whatever I did, I should revel in my small-town roots. I think that my small-town upbringing comes through in my writing.

How did you get the idea for writing Manifest Destiny?

I came up with the idea for Manifest Destiny when I was watching a special on C-SPAN regarding the United States Capitol. There was a short segment on "The Mace" — the ceremonial facie used in the United States House of Representatives. In that segment, I learned that the original mace went missing after the British gained control of Washington during the War of 1812. I suddenly wondered what would happen if the mace used today was stolen. From that emerged the Prologue and first chapter of the book.

Do you have a favorite author yourself?

I became inspired to write in high school when I got to meet the great Jesse Stuart. His books of mountain life are exceptional. My favorite thriller author is Harlan Coben. On the non-fiction side, I've read everything ever written by P.J. O'Rourke.

Are you ever afraid you will run out of inspiration and creativity in your job?

No. Politics and politicians are so rife with flaws that there are more story lines out there than time I have left on Earth to write.

What is the most difficult thing in your job?

Writing is like any other job, and writers usually try to figure out ways to get out of writing. I try to discipline myself to writing every day, but there is always a distraction calling my name.

What is the most fun part of your job?

I absolutely love going to book shows and teaching at writers workshops. Meeting aspiring writers and assisting in their efforts is very cool. There is nothing like being at a show and having someone come up and say they really like your work.

Do you expect your way of creating books to change in the future?

No — although I have been toying with the idea of trying some voice-recognition software to play with first drafts.

Do you embrace the changes in the writing industry regarding social media and technology influences?

Absolutely! I sincerely believe that Harry Potter and electronic readers will save publishing. Both have young people reading again.

Do you like art? Do you have any preferences for an artist? And/or for creators of artistic work?

When I was in law school, my roommate was post-modern artist Kevin Kelly. His work currently is hanging in the Breitling watch store in New York City. He has done the first drafts for the covers of each of my books. I have known Kevin since we were kids. He has really made me appreciate different forms of art. I have a lot of his art in my home and office. He's a great creative talent. He can't wait to show me a new painting, and he is a sample reader for my manuscripts.

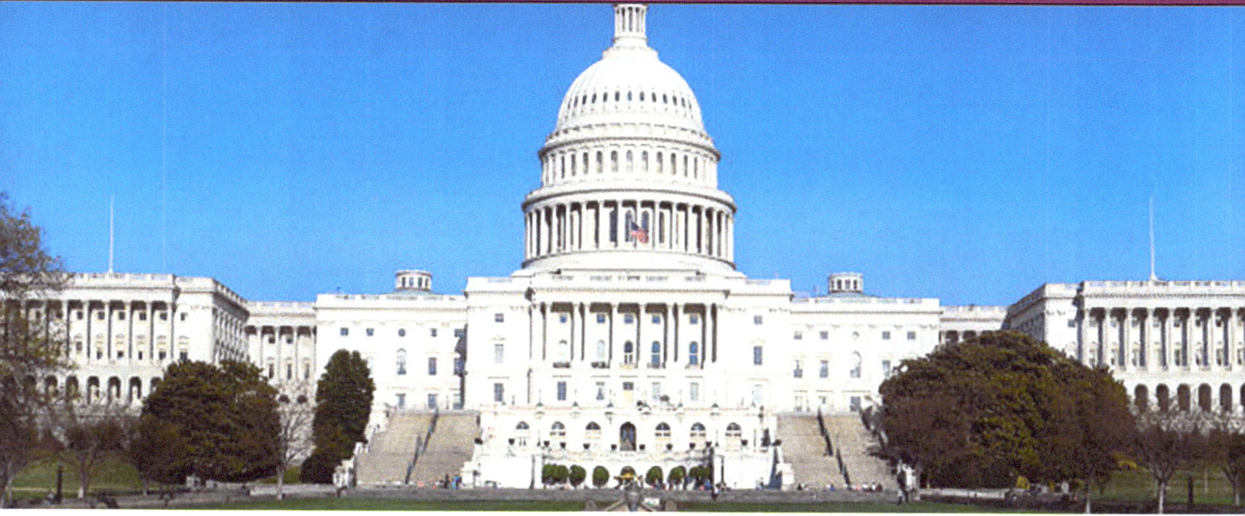

Could we feature your favorite photographer, author, artist, designer, architect, filmmaker, etc. in our publication and/or online?

I'd be glad to put you in touch with Kevin. His website is www.kevintkelly.com.

In which way do you think writing, art and design are different and/or similar?

The beauty of any creative process is that your only limit is your own imagination. I have found that nearly ever artist or writer has those moments when they are in such a strong creative zone that they never want it to end. Visual artists talk about it all the time. I get a great deal of satisfaction when I have one of those days.

Do you aspire to collaborate in your creations with an artist from another artistic discipline?

I'd love to create a graphic novel someday with Kevin. We tried to do a comic strip together when we were in college and had too much fun.

Do you have a favorite company or exciting other creator with whom you would like to work?

I am co-writing a sports thriller right now with my friend Dennis Hetzel. Writing together is hard because you have to balance two styles. But we're come up with a great story line and are having fun.

Do you follow any philosophical or psychological approach in writing your books?

No, but my characters all have quirks and philosophical beliefs that cause them to act the way they do.

What is your favorite building in the world?

The United States Capitol ... the beacon of freedom and democracy around the world.

What is your favorite hotel?

My wife and I spent our 25th anniversary at Ashford Castle in Ireland. It was such a great experience that I wrote Ashford Castle into my next book.

What would be your ideal home?

A 50-foot, live-aboard sailboat docked in Key West.

Do you have any dreams for the future?

A small writer's flat in the Village would be nice.

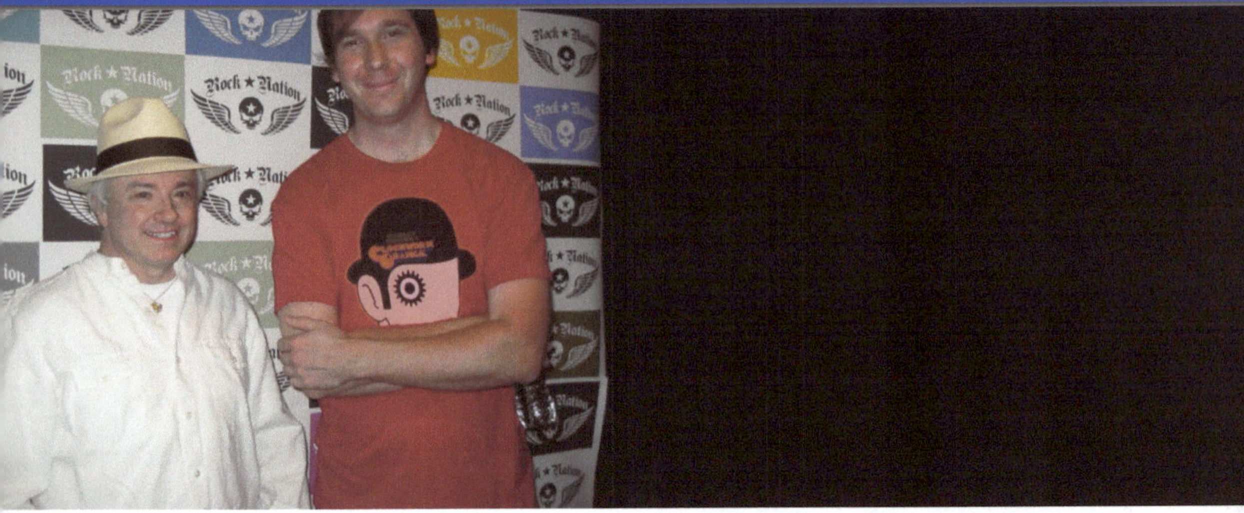

American Filmmaker Peter R.J. Deyell

Peter R.J. Deyell is an American filmmaker, with a diverse background in movies, television, radio and theater, including acting, writing, directing and producing.

Upon acquiring the rights in early 2011 to Rick Robinson's "Manifest Destiny," Deyell was quoted as saying, "Manifest Destiny" is so good, I read it in two sittings. It's an international thriller in the truest sense. The characters are multidimensional and the story is absolutely chilling and believable."

Born in Brooklyn, New York, Deyell began his career in show business as a child, when he auditioned for the role of Tiny Tim, in an NBC musical version of "A Christmas Carol," starring Basil Rathbone as Scrooge. Deyell did not get the part, but Rathbone was so impressed with the youngster that he put him in touch with a talent agent. That introduction eventually led to roles for Deyell on the New York stage with the likes of Steve Allen, Eve Arden, Danny Kaye, Bob Hope, Ethel Merman, Edward Mulhare, Mary Martin, Victor Borge, Robert Q. Lewis, Pat Boone, Patrice Munsel, Jimmy Rogers and Jack Sterling.

During the last phase of live television in the late-1950s, Deyell performed on the NBC series Frontiers of Faith. He appeared in many TV commercials and skits on the NBC broadcast of "The Patti Page Show." He also played the son in the live television series "Sid Caesar Invites You," which starred Sid Caesar and Imogene Coca, and was written by Carl Reiner, Mel Brooks and Neil Simon.

Deyell's first feature film as an actor was Paramount Pictures' "That Kind of Woman" with Tab Hunter and Sophia Loren, produced by Carlo Ponti and directed by Sidney Lumet. On NBC's "Shirley Temple's Storybook" series, Deyell performed in productions of Kim, "The Prince and the Pauper," and "Madeline." As a young adult, he portrayed Peter on the TV series "Mr. Novak" starring James Franciscus. He had his first screen kiss in the Sam Katzman feature of the Hank Williams biopic "Your Cheatin' Heart," which co-starred George Hamilton and Susan Oliver. He also had a recurring role as the character Mr. Muscles on the Emmy Award-winning TV series "Dusty's Attic" (aka Dusty's Tree house).

When Deyell was a teenager, he moved with his family to Los Angeles and began working on an independent film with a group of friends. A story about the project in The Hollywood Reporter caught the attention of a young director named Steven Spielberg. Spielberg contacted Deyell, and hired him as assistant director on a short film that Spielberg was directing, "Slipstream," starring Tony Bill. "Slipstream" was never completed, but through that association, Deyell introduced Spielberg to cinematographer Allen Daviau, who later teamed up with Spielberg to shoot several critically acclaimed films, such as "E.T. the Extra-Terrestrial," "The Color Purple," "Twilight Zone: The Movie," "Indiana Jones and the Temple of Doom" and others.

Deyell continued acting and was signed as a contract player at 20th Century Fox Television. While there, he shot a test pilot for the original TV series "Batman," in which he auditioned for the role of Robin, with Lyle Waggoner as Batman. Unfortunately for Deyell, the role of Robin went to actor Burt Ward, although Deyell's screen test can still be seen in the documentaries "Holy Batmania" and "Hollywood Screen Tests:" Take One produced by Kevin Burns. Later, Deyell was cast in the recurring role of the delivery boy on the long-running prime time soap opera Santa Barbara. He also appeared on the hit TV series Newhart. Deyell's acting career was temporarily interrupted when he served in the U.S. Coast Guard Reserve, eventually working his way up to the rank of First Class Petty Officer. He later accepted a commission and served with distinction as a U.S. Coast Guard Reserve Officer. Deyell is a life member of the Reserve Officers Association.

In his 20s, Deyell began to transition from acting to production jobs behind the camera, including positions in make-up, assistant directing and directing. At age 20, he was the youngest vice president of production in motion picture history at Cinevest International, one of several production companies at General Service Studios in Hollywood. There, he was responsible for up to five feature films in development and production simultaneously.

Deyell's first experimental film, "The Diabolical Destiny," starred Elizabeth Baur (Ironside) Jonathan West (director of photography for Star Trek: The Next Generation) and Janice Fisher (writer of Lost Boys).

For Deyell's first feature film, he produced, adapted and directed Elaine May's "Not Enough Rope" starring Zalman King (Red Shoe Diaries), Florence Lake (Lassie), and Sandy Brown (General Hospital). Other feature films included "Zoo Ship," "The Ghost Dance," and the documentary "Meet John Wooden." Deyell directed "Lucky Angel," a film starring Betsy Monroe (Mrs. Doubtfire), Robert Abrams (Hot Springs Hotel) and Ted Kurtz (Howard the Duck), which was released theatrically in Europe. As a writer, producer and director, Deyell has worked on over 100 commercials and music videos with musical artists such as The Commodores, WAR, Electric Light Orchestra, Paul Anka,

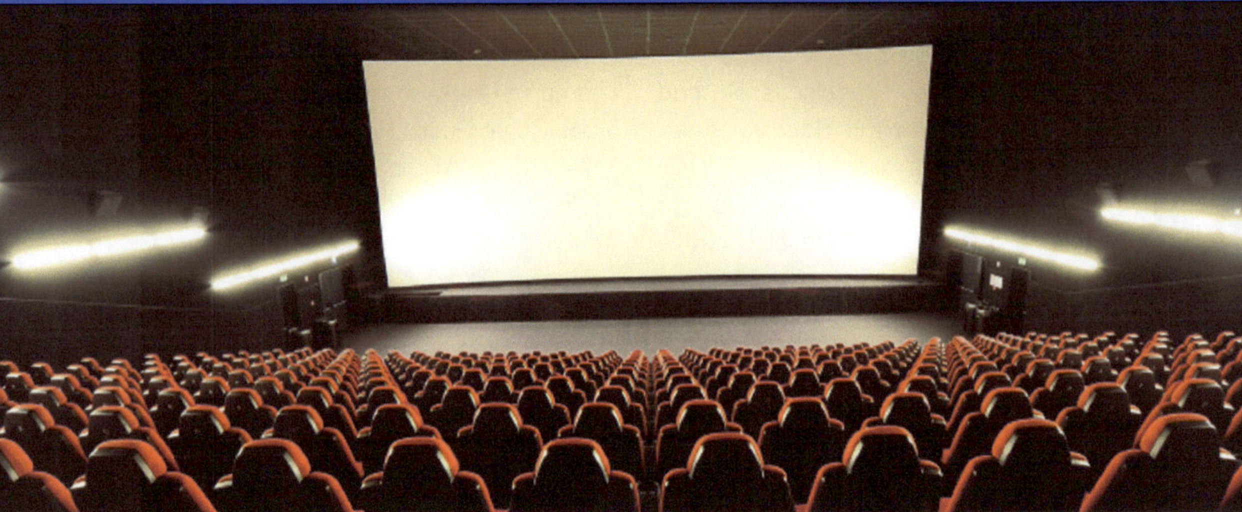

Ringo Starr, Stevie Wonder, Smoky Robinson, Michael Jackson, Rufus, Chaka Kahn and Helen Reddy. His network television credits include Chips, Hunter, Remington Steele, and Matlock. Additionally, Deyell has sold a total of 13 screenplays.

Deyell's latest works include "Manifest Destiny" (2012, producer), "Meet John Wooden" (2011, documentary) (co-executive producer), and Road to Nowhere (2010, co-producer). Deyell currently serves as president of the Panamanian production company PanAm Film Works, for which he is packaging a series of horror/adventure features to be filmed in Panama. He has also been working with Panamanian officials to develop an international film school to be based in Panama City in an effort to help develop a more skilled film community in that country.

Deyell is a member of the American Federation of Television and Radio Artists (AFTRA), Screen Actors Guild (SAG), Actors Equity Association (AEA), Directors Guild of America (DGA), Writers Guild of America (WGA), Society of Stage Directors and Choreographers, and the Academy of Television Arts & Sciences. In his capacity as a member of the DGA, Deyell serves on the organization's Special Projects Committee, and he was one of the founders of The Artists Rights Foundation, along with J. Paul Getty, Jr., Steven Spielberg, Allen Daviau, Frank Pierson, Arthur Hiller, Sydney Pollack, Gene Reynolds, George Lucas and Martin Scorsese. The Artists Rights Foundation has since merged with Martin Scorsese's The Film Foundation.

Deyell is the former artistic director of Center Stage Theatre in Los Angeles, where he helmed productions of "A Funny Thing Happened on the Way to the Forum," "Anything Goes," "You're a Good Man Charlie Brown," "Once in a Lifetime," "A Shot in the Dark," and "Plaza Suite." He has been a guest lecturer/director at the American Film Institute and the American Academy of Dramatic Arts.

Deyell's projects have garnered many nominations, awards and honors, including The Walter Elias Disney Award; The Atlanta Film Festival; The Chicago Film Festival; The Bronze Eagle Award; The Bronze Halo Award; the 1995, 1996, and 1997 International ANGEL Awards (for Motion Picture Screenplay); and the 1996 International TELE Awards (Bronze Statue) for Music Video.

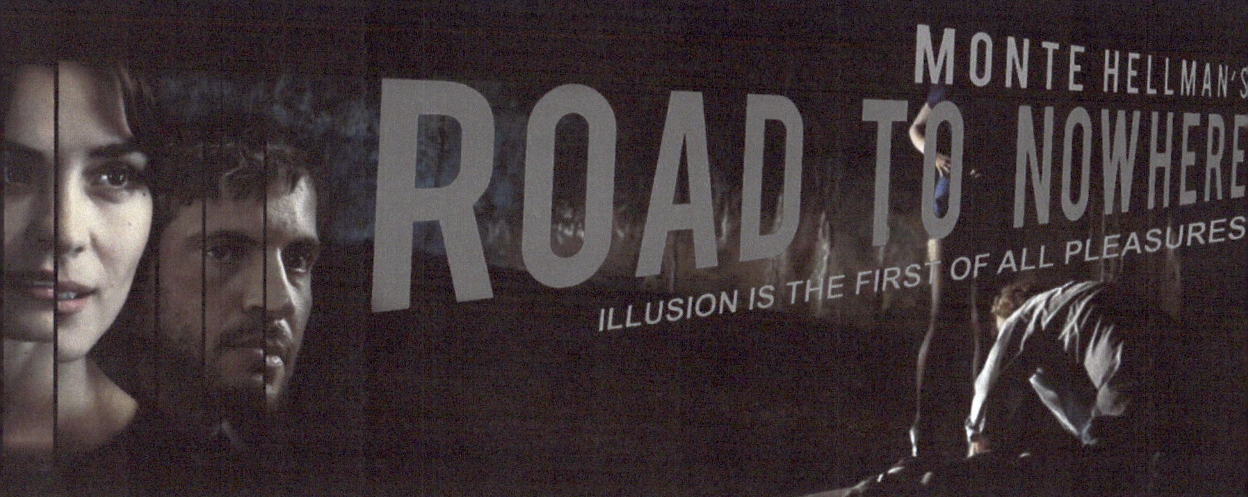

A Conversation with Peter R.J. Deyell

As a child, what did you want to become (profession-wise)?

I was enamored by cowboys in the movies and TV, so I told my mother I was going to be a cowboy. When I learned that they were actors and they could be many things, then I wanted to be an actor.

In which town did you grow up?

Brooklyn, New York City.

Do you think your background has influenced your current work style? If so, what specific element in your background is most pervasive in influencing your current work style?

If you grow up in Brooklyn, you can survive anywhere. Showbiz is a tough sport, Hollywood a tough town, but Brooklyn was great training.

What inspires you in the job of being a producer?

I was fortunate to be a child actor. Growing up in the industry, I was inspired by the great talent around me and the movies they made.

In which way do you consider yourself an innovative creator?

My ability to recognize talent and to understand their process of working. Movies deal with human emotions, and when you connect with the audience it's magic.

Do you have any other creative ambitions or dreams to which you aspire?

I will continue to write and direct. I'd love to get back to theater and direct a musical.

Which basic elements of creativity did your family teach you?

That is was okay to color outside of the lines. All trees are not green. And don't let anyone tell you what you cannot be.

Do you have a favorite producer yourself?

Yes — several. Stanley Kramer for his social consciousness. Sir David Lean who was uncredited for Lawrence of Arabia, nevertheless was the overseer of every aspect. My great friend and mentor Robert Wise for his direction and producing. And Frank Capra for everything.

Are you ever afraid you will run out of inspiration and creativity in your job?

I wake up in the morning with a smile on my face for every day is filled with excitement.

What is the most difficult thing in your job?

As Frank Capra told me years ago, that he spent more time chasing money than making movies. I found out it was true.

What is the most fun part of your job?

Making it all happen and getting to the first day of filming.

Do you expect your way of producing films to change in the future?

As technology changes, we change. Digital filmmaking is part of the evolution of the industry, and there will be many other significant changes to come. I'm currently at Sony Studios where I'm directing 3D tests getting ready to embrace that whole new world.

Do you embrace the changes in the film industry regarding social media and technology influences?

We filmed Road to Nowhere with the Canon 5D — the first feature to do so. The movies will go with any way to reach the audience. I once said, "Who will want to watch a movie on a cell phone?" Now I have 22 feature films on my iPhone — mainly classics that I watch when I have to stand in airport lines.

Do you like art? Do you have any preferences for an artist? And/or for creators of artistic work?

I like all forms of artistic expression. In fine art, I particularly like the Dutch masters. When I went to the Rijks museum in Amsterdam, where Rembrandt and his pupils are exhibited, I was captivated by their use of and manipulation of the light source. The Dutch masters used focus, light, color and shadow to illuminate their art. They captured their subjects with a heightened sense of reality. They would have made great filmmakers.

Could we feature your favorite photographer, author, artist, designer, architect, filmmaker, etc. in our publication and/or online?

My brother, David Deyell, is a famous, award-winning California-style plein-air watercolorist.

In which way do you think creating films, art and design are different and/or similar?

I believe that all art, to be great art, needs a point of focus. Great design leads the eye. Color, shape and form, dramatically placed, adds emotion. When you put that all together with sound, music, moving images, story and characters, you have movies.

Do you have a favorite company or exciting other creator with whom you would like to work?

Dreamworks and SKG Warner Bros. Both have great collaborative creative executives. Steven Spielberg, George Lucas, JJ Abrams, Francis Ford Coppola and Marty Scorsese. Don't think I need to explain these guys.

Do you follow any philosophical or psychological approach in producing films?

I look for the emotional appeal of the story. Good characters that develop a bond with the audience are a must. And everything must pay off at the end — a denouement.

What is your favorite building in the world?

The Eiffel Tower — awesome. Tall, graceful, majestic, like a huge Erector Set with more pieces than what comes in the box.

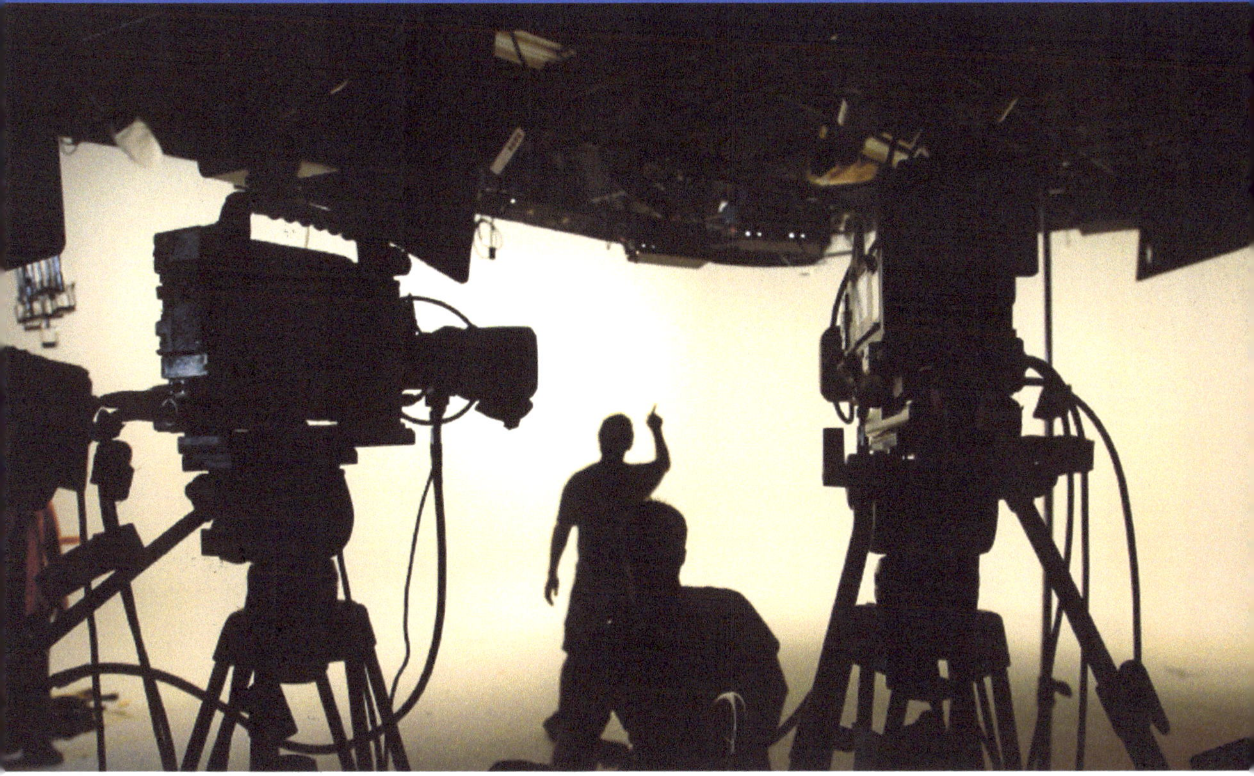

What is your favorite hotel?

Hotel Du Cap (Cap d'Antibes in the south of France); George V (Paris); Imàgo at the Spanish Steps (Rome); The Plaza (NYC); and The Savoy (London).

What would be your ideal home?

I could live anywhere. Every time I travel, I say to myself, "I could live here." The ideal home would be a comfortable respite influenced by the country it was in.

Do you have any dreams for the future?

Too many to mention.

Is there anything else you would like to add to this interview?

If you are a fan of the movies, if you like the entertainment we provide, please don't steal. Internet theft is destroying the movies. Every time someone downloads or streams an illegal copy of a movie, it hurts all of us who love the movies. When it becomes unprofitable for producers to make movies, the distributors to distribute, the theaters to exhibit, then the great films will die like dinosaurs. This is not evolution. Internet theft, illegal streaming and counterfeiting will kill the movies you and I love.

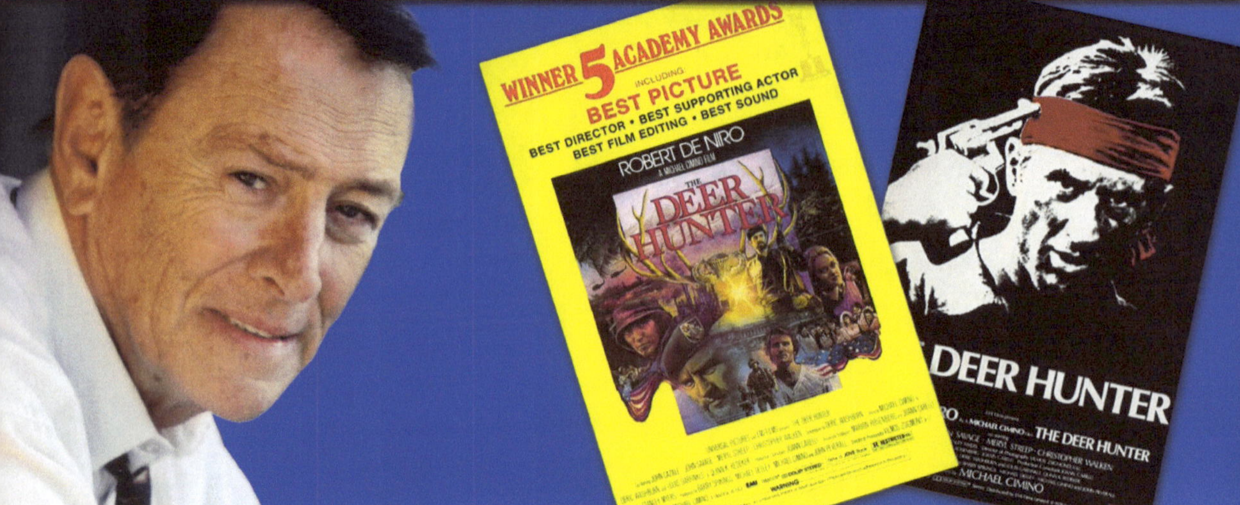

Screenwriter Quinn Redeker

Born May 2, 1936, in Woodstock, Illinois, Quinn Redeker has been a screenwriter for more than 30 years. He co-wrote the 1978 film "The Deer Hunter," the tale of small-town boys who go to Vietnam with the romance of war in their eyes, but encounter something very different.

Although four writers eventually shared credit on the script, the film began with a story from Quinn called "The Man Who Came To Play." And according to www.hollywood.com, "It was Redeker, often working late in a coffee shop booth, who carved the original blueprint for the film." His version opened with the notorious Russian roulette sequence.

Redeker has also appeared in more than 70 TV series and shows, including roles on "Sea Hunt" (1960), "Bonanza" (1963), "Ironside" (1968), "Adam-12" (1972), "The Bob Newhart Show" (1975), "Kojak" (1974/1976), "The Rockford Files" (1977), "The Six Million Dollar Man" (1974–1977), "Starsky and Hutch" (1975/1979), "Fantasy Island" (1983), "The Michael Richards Show" (2000), and "CSI: Miami" (2003). Redeker is also well-known for his roles on "Days of Our Lives" (1979–1987) and "The Young and the Restless" (1979–1980 and 1987–1994). In addition to his small-screen roles, Redeker landed roles in big-screen productions The "Three Stooges" "Meet Hercules" (1962), "The Candidate" (1972), "The Electric Horseman" (1979), and "Ordinary People" (1980).

As a writer, Redeker was nominated for an Academy Award for Best Original Screenplay and a WGA Award for Best Drama Written Directly for the Screen for "The Deer Hunter," along with Deric Washburn, Louis Garfinkle and Michael Cimino.

Redeker was twice nominated for the Outstanding Supporting Actor in a Drama Series Daytime Emmy Award for his role on "The Young and the Restless" (1989 and 1990).Originally from Woodstock, Illinois, Quinn grew up in Seattle and moved to Los Angeles in 1957. He was an All-American Honorable Mention, All-City football player in Seattle. He has four children — two boys and two girls. His father was a banker, and his mother ran a boarding house for divorced women.

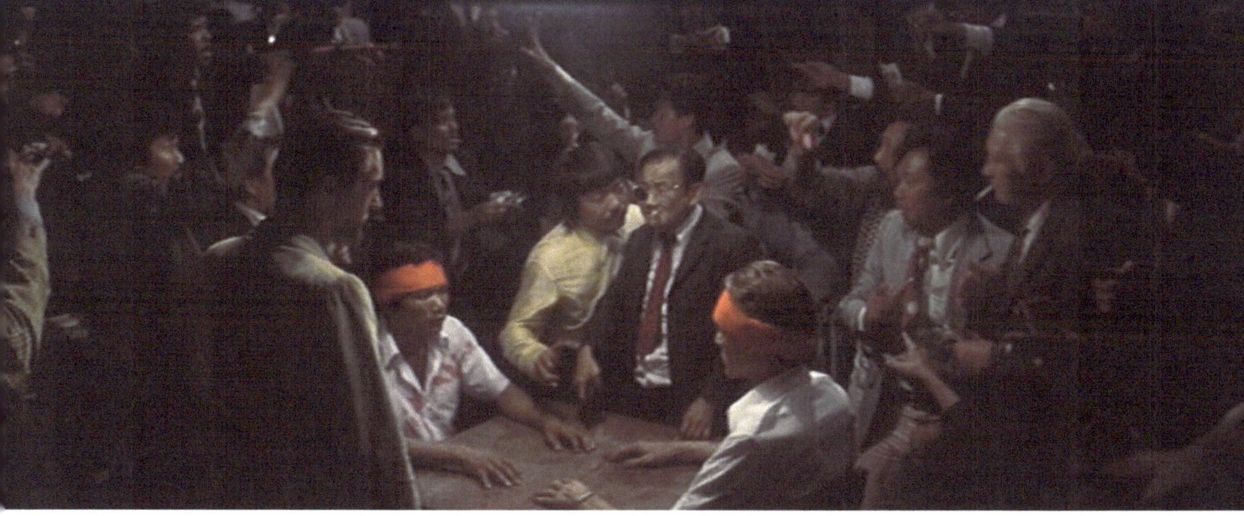

A Conversation with Screenwriter Quin Redeker

As a child, what did you want to become (profession-wise)?

A football player.

In which town did you grow up?

Seattle.

Do you think your background has influenced your current work style? If so, what specific element in your background is most pervasive in influencing your current work style?

Probably metaphysics. In the original script of "The Man Who Came to Play," which became "The Deer Hunter," I hung the Russian roulette in the POW camp in Vietnam on "see the empty chamber." See yourself healthy, and you'll get what you see yourself getting.

What inspires you in the job of being a producer?

To take you someplace you've never been, show you something you've never seen, and make you care. To get your emotional investment on the screen — that's what makes you leave the theater with: "GO SEE THIS MOVIE!" I call it Emotional Architecture.

In which way do you consider yourself an innovative creator?

In every way. Everybody is. Bach, Beethoven, Brahms, Hemingway, Robert Louis Stevenson. All said: "I don't write that stuff, I just hold the pen."

You've never had a hunch? Oh yes you have! There's an old saying: "Your instincts are never wrong; your mind will screw you up every time."

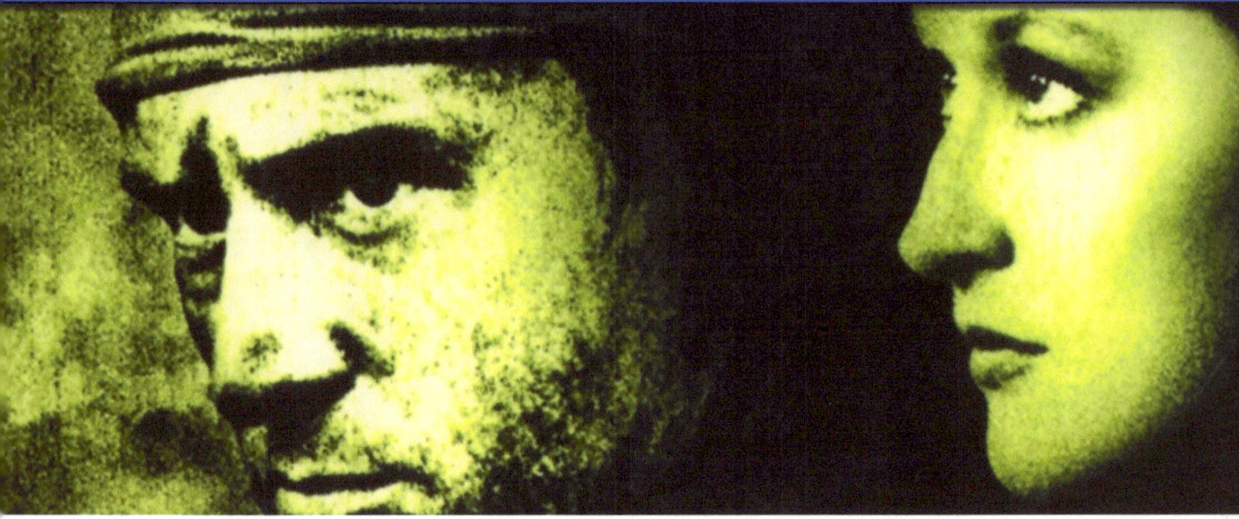

Do you have any other creative ambitions or dreams to which you aspire?

Helping to bring world peace, which I'm becoming more and more convinced lies somewhere in the equation: "Don't shoot at me, sell me something." I recently played President Reagan in Universal's Everybody Loves Whales, with Drew Barrymore and Ted Danson. I think the whole White House staff got cut out of that movie because the script made fun of Reagan, but it inspired me to do a Website as Reagan: "Ronnie at the Ranch." We shot several little two-minute episodes, and they should be edited and on the Web soon.

Which basic elements of creativity did your family teach you?

"When you're 100 years old and going to die tomorrow, the only thing that counts is ... did I enjoy it? What you enjoyed most was love, because love has the biggest power; God is love ... So, whatever it is: "Love it like it is, it gets lovely or you get moved, love does the work. It just sounds ridiculous so don't tell anybody what you're doing."

Do you have a favorite author yourself?

VERY tough question. I probably have to go with F. Scott.; nobody strings 'em better, but there's a Hell of a lot more to writing than writing.

Are you ever afraid you will run out of inspiration and creativity in your job?

All life is creativity; listen!

What is the most difficult thing in your job?

Listening.

What is the most fun part of your job?

Making a propitious difference, especially to women and kids.

Do you expect your way of producing films to change in the future?

Of course. Hopefully they will be a contribution to somebody.

Do you embrace the changes in the film industry regarding social media and technology influences?

Hard to know. They keep changing.

Do you like art? Do you have any preferences for an artist? And/or for creators of artistic work?

If it makes me feel something, you bet. Woody Allen certainly comes to mind. He's innovative, yet he knows who George Cukor was.

In which way do you think creating films, art and design are different and/or similar?

The artist's reflection of their society, their emotional reaction to it, and their attempts to influence everything around it. The means they employ to that end will all be different, but I suspect similar in their intent; I think every artist wants to make a social contribution somewhere in their life.

Do you aspire to collaborate in your creations with an artist from another artistic discipline?

Sure, e.g., "set up" and "punchline" writers are two different guys, but both striving for the same end to the joke.

Do you have a favorite company or exciting other creator with whom you would like to work?

Don't really know for sure; a LOT of people come to mind, but this is a lot trickier than it sounds; rapport is critical here. Collaborating with a brilliant designer/artist that doesn't speak "your" language just won't work. Ever been on a blind date that was magic? Ever been on one that wasn't?

What is your favorite building in the world?

The Eiffel Tower says more just standing there than all the buildings put together in most other countries.

What is your favorite hotel?

This is SO subjective, but the George V in Paris. I took my four kids there when they were growing up, and it was an experience on a cultural level that I'll never forget — and neither will the kids. Years later, I took a girlfriend there, and the Concierge smiled and said, "Oh, hi. How are the kids?"

What would be your ideal home?

A large place that I could house all my friends and a wife and still have a party every night. Because bottom line, it's really about Joie de vivre.

Do you have any dreams for the future?

I don't know. I've written a couple scripts around the relationship therapist, Pat Allen. She says things like: "Men are the stems; women are the flowers," "Men get respect; women get cherished," "Men have to do good to feel good; women have to feel good to do good," "Boys take; men give." I always thought there was an important contribution in a feature around her stuff. But then, my mother ran a boarding house for divorced women, so I guess I would be impressed with her.

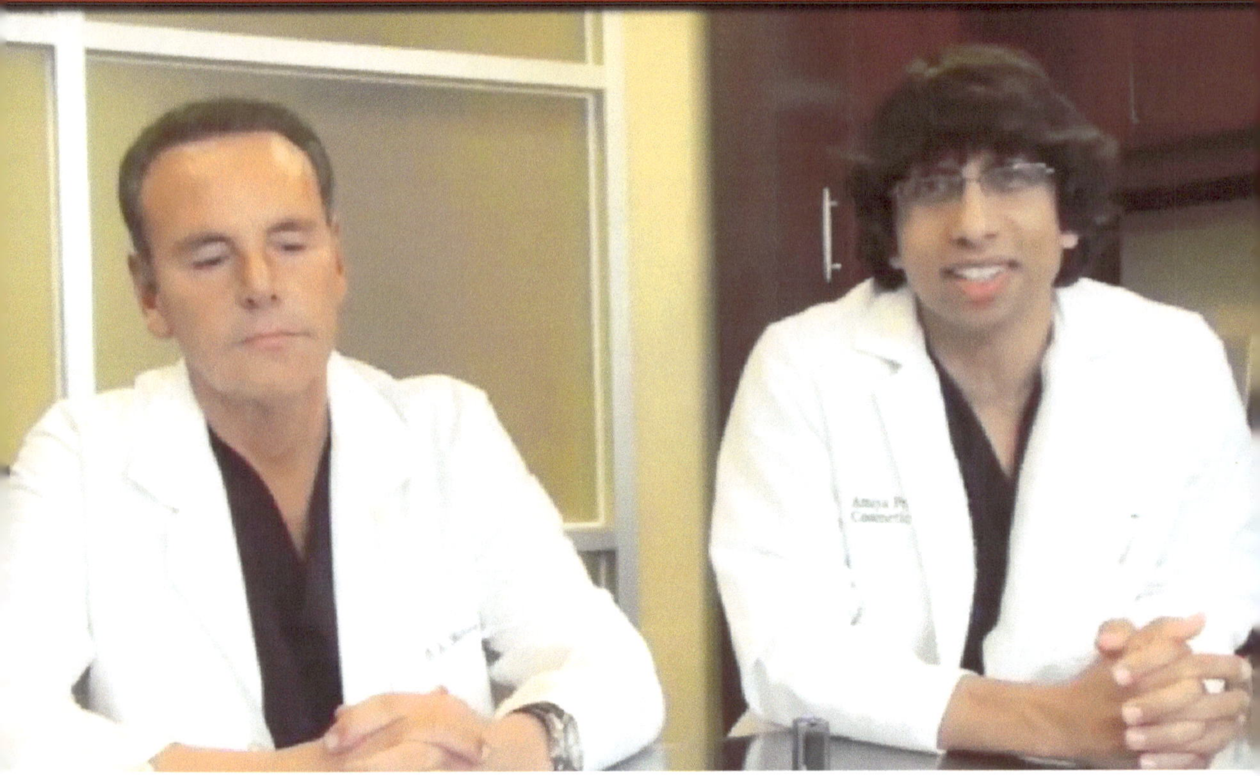

Paired Up for Perfection:
Dr. Gary Hitzig & Dr. Amiya Prasad

Dr. Gary Hitzig was the first medical doctor to successfully clone hair using the FDA-approved ACell wound healing powder ACell MatriStem® MicroMatrix™. He then went on to discover that if you dissolve the MatriStem powder in an arterial blood serum rich in the patient's adult stem cells and inject it into the donor area and top of scalp where hair is being transplanted, the powder and blood serum combination acts like a hair growth accelerator and fertilizer. Patients experience significant hair re-growth in just six months versus 12 months and the area where donor hair has been taken and transplanted is completely healed – with little or no signs of a scar. Gary Hitzig, M.D. is a pioneer in the field of hair restoration surgery. He is the author of Help and Hope for Hair Loss, patented the Hitzig Linear Punch, and has published numerous peer- reviewed articles on hair transplant techniques including Auto Cloning of Beard Hair. Dr. Hitzig has also presented new techniques at medical hair restoration symposiums around the world. ACell's technology is not limited to one market segment (e.g., wound care), but instead can serve as a core technology for treatments across a broad range of human medical conditions.

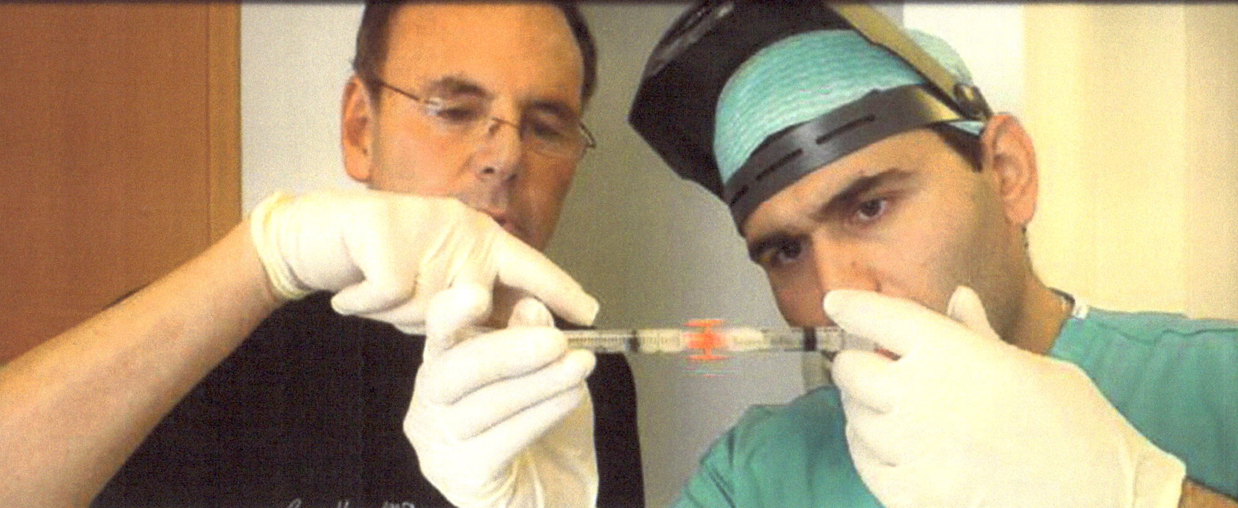

It's a cosmetic team match made in heaven – Gary Hitzig, M.D., a notable hair transplant researcher and surgeon, and Amiya Prasad, M.D., a prominent New York cosmetic surgeon, have merged their specialties into one practice – Prasad Cosmetic Surgery. Prasad Cosmetic Surgery has two Joint Commission certified practices located in Manhattan, Upper East Side and on Long Island in Garden City, NY.

Dr. Amiya Prasad is a renowned cosmetic surgeon with a specialty in facial rejuvenation. He is among only a small group of medical doctors worldwide to earn a certified cosmetic oculofacial (eyes and face) plastic surgeon designation. Dr. Prasad developed the highly specialized ocular cosmetic surgery division at Brookdale University Hospital in Brooklyn, NY and has been in private practice since 1998. His reputation for exceptional and natural cosmetic results has increased his popularity around the world and made him sought after by patients around the world. Dr. Hitzig will be offering this impressive hair transplant procedure at Prasad Cosmetic Surgery along with his ACell application to aid healing in cosmetic surgeries.

"Amazing medical research keeps the medical field advancing with better treatments and better results," said Dr. Hitzig. "My research and work using the ACell wound healing powder in hair transplantation has shown impressive results in promoting hair growth and wound healing. This same technique will benefit Dr. Prasad's cosmetic surgery patients. Teaming up together was a logical step to advance both of our medical specialties." said Dr. Prasad,"Dr. Hitzig and I have built successful private practices for each of our medical specialties. The timing was right to combine our expertise into one practice and use Dr. Hitzig's proven results with ACell to further advance the field of cosmetic surgery and speed up our patients healing following surgery."

About Prasad Cosmetic Surgery

Founded by renowned cosmetic surgeon, Dr. Amiya Prasad, Prasad Cosmetic Surgery is a boutique practice providing hair loss and facial rejuvenation solutions with natural results. Dr. Gary Hitzig, a nationally known hair restoration surgeon and researcher, recently joined the practice. Prasad is the author of The Fine Art of Looking Younger. Hitzig is the author of Help and Hope for Hair Loss. Prasad Cosmetic Surgery has two Joint Commission certified practices located in Manhattan, Upper East Side and on Long Island in Garden City, NY.

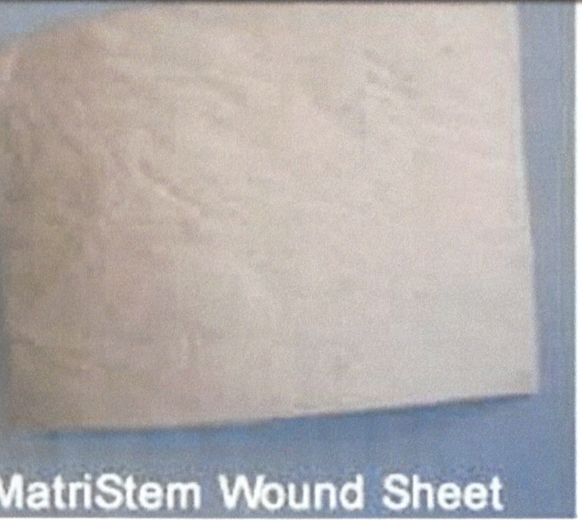

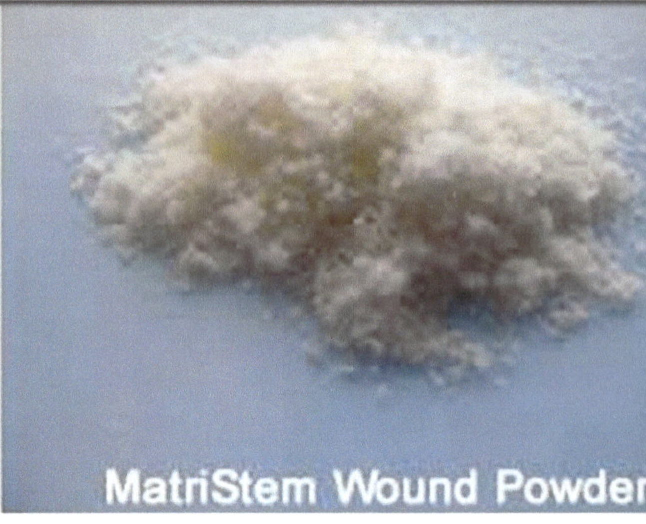

About ACell

ACell's patented Extra cellular Matrix (ECM) products are covered by multiple 510(k) clearances and address important unmet clinical needs, providing safe, effective and therapeutic outcomes. Derived from porcine urinary bladders and referred to as UBM (urinary bladder matrix), trademarked as MatriStem™, ACell's core technology is a naturally occurring, non-crosslinked, completely restorable acellular biomaterial. A similar "first generation" ECM technology has been used to treat over 500,000 patients with remarkable effect. ACell's MatriStem products are the next generation of ECM technology due to its unique characteristics featuring a basement membrane surface which is ideal for epithelial cell growth in many applications.

"We are growing new hair in prior donor scar sites as well as duplicating (growing multiple hairs from a single transplanted beard or donor hair) in the bald recipient area," states Dr. Ted Chaglassian, a Board Certified Plastic Surgeon and former Chief of Plastic Surgery at Memorial Sloan-Kettering Hospital and Attending Physician at Columbia Presbyterian Medical Center in NYC. He further states: "Where we go from here is anyone's guess but the future of cloning growing hair has just been made a reality in the present!"

We will now be expanding the study by accepting a select few additional patients to work on using the Regenerative FDA cleared MatriStem MicroMatrix. The MatriStem MicroMatrix products are unique in that they fundamentally change healing by triggering abundant new blood vessel formation at the wound site and also recruit to that site numerous cell types, including progenitor cells, which have the potential to differentiate into numerous types of site specific tissues. During the healing process, the injured tissue is remodeled as the MatriStem product is completely reabsorbed, leaving new tissue where scar tissue would normally be expected, which may also include new hair! For more information, please look at www.acell.com

Philosophy: Combination Method Most Effective

At the most recent International Society of Hair Restoration Surgery meetings, many surgeons from around the world acknowledged that the most effective treatment for most patients was a combination method of surgery. Utilizing single follicular units for hairline work and using various larger size grafts for supporting density created the best balance of patient satisfaction and cost savings. Many of these surgeons who initially treated patients with follicular units expressed patient dissatisfaction with both density and cost. Faced with the dilemma that most prospective patients do not have unlimited time, financial resources or donor hair; the hair transplant surgeon should be able to offer methods that can achieve a natural cosmetic appearance while remaining affordable to the average patient.

Procedures involving 1500 to 4000 grafts with teams of 4 to 8 assistants working on a single patient for over 8 hours can be unnecessarily dangerous both to the patient and the ultimate cosmetic result. Such complexity, repetition, varying skill levels of staff and handling and manipulation of tissue cannot be performed consistently in most environments with a high level of quality. These type of procedures in most cases cannot be performed "cost effectively" for the doctor or patient. Patient dissatisfaction with density versus cost are not always soothed with "how natural it looks". The issue of these lengthy procedures may become moot in the U.S. as some states are planning legislation to limit in-office cosmetic procedures to 4 hours and that procedures taking longer will only be allowed to be performed in a hospital or licensed ambulatory facility.

Creating a "Perfect Fit"

Linear slot grafting was developed so that a slightly larger 4 to 10 hair graft could be transplanted without the cosmetic limitations of round grafts or the compression of slits. The multi-blade scalpel can excise donor strips with a width equal to the length of the slot incision. This makes it easy to dissect narrow (0.5mm) linear hair bearing grafts. These narrow linear grafts contain "Coupled Follicular Units" (CFU's). These CFU's are groups of follicular units in natural distribution. The spacing between follicular units is the same as it is in the donor area. With the use of the Redfield Slot Punch* (Redfield Corp., Montvale, NJ) a similar size sliver of bald recipient tissue is removed creating a "perfect fit" for the linear graft. The receptor scalp integrity is not altered or compromised because corresponding tissue replaces the bald tissue removed and the ultimate growth appearance is natural because the hairs are not compressed or distorted. It also exponentially increases the speed of the procedure and significantly lessens the X factor (manipulation, drying, crushing and striping of grafts) thereby insuring minimal hair loss in the transfer.

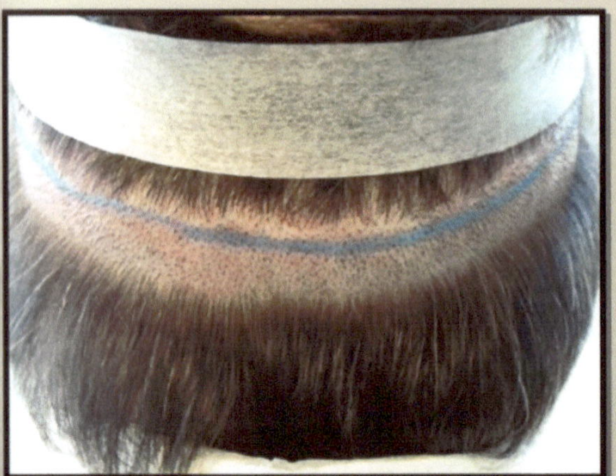

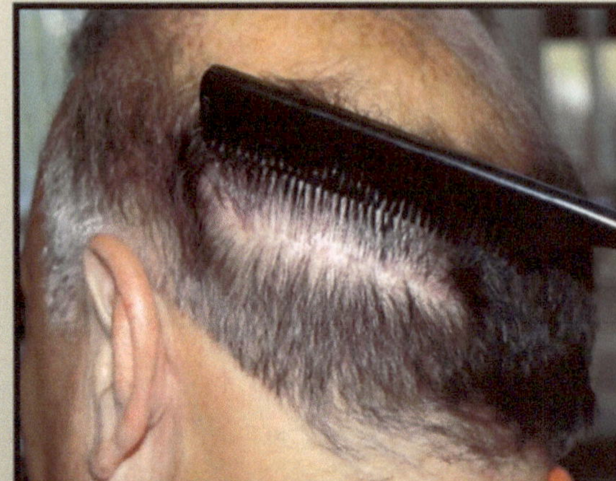

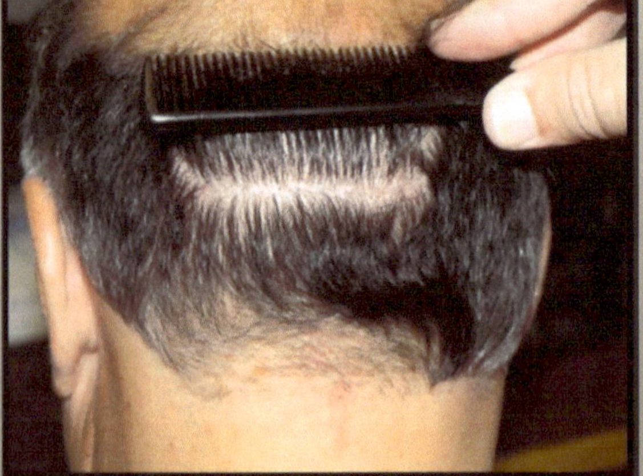

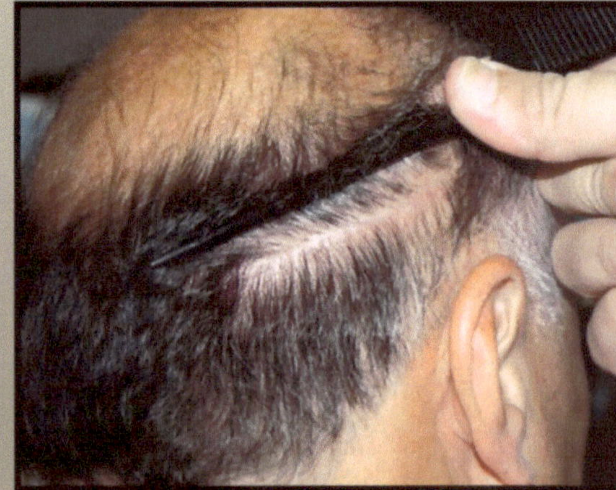

A Conversation with Dr. Amiya Prasad

As a child, what profession did you want to pursue?

As a child I was always drawn toward science and art. I spent much time creating models of rockets and other machines to understand how they worked. I considered being an engineer. But as I continued in school, I found that I loved to draw and my art teacher told me to consider a career in art. But I was more interested in finding a combination of both fields. This is how I ended up in cosmetic surgery.

In which town did you grow up?

I grew up in Bull's Head on Staten Island, NY. I went to college and medical school in New York City so I am a real native New Yorker.

What inspires you in the job of being a cosmetic and reconstructive surgeon and a hair restoration specialist?

I am inspired by helping people regain their confidence. So many branches of medicine deal with the breakdown of physical health, but in my profession, I get to restore happiness and see people take pleasure in their appearance. For most people, this positive outlook has a remarkable effect on their every day lives. They feel empowered to take on new challenges whether it's in their careers or in their personal lives.

In which ways do you consider yourself an innovative creator?

One of the drawbacks to the training of an aesthetic surgeon is that the process does not necessarily select for individuals with a creative or artistic perspective. Many of the stereotypes of surgeons on TV do come from a kernel of truth.

There are many arduous steps that include a battery of tests on meaningless minutiae and an initiation process that is sometimes more like a fraternity hazing than a true passing on of skill from a master to a student. Many have written about the dysfunctional nature of the crusty surgeons and again, there is some truth in this imagery. If you don't have a passionate or creative spirit, you will walk away from this experience to be a very good technician who understands how to perform an eye lift or a brow lift and can reproduce a procedure when requested to do so. However, I decided during my training that I was fortunate to be able to call upon my artistic skills and see the character of a face. It is my number one priority when I examine a patient to understand the integrity of the face and the relationship of the features to one another. After I have gained an understanding of the person's true appearance, I can focus on bringing about the most natural appearance possible. My goal is to perform a procedure that makes the patient look like themselves, not a plastic surgery patient, but ten years younger.

I like to ask a different set of questions from the surgeons who trained me. I appreciated their expertise and wisdom but I found myself re- thinking how to care for my patients. In the modern world, regardless of your responsibilities, you do not have a lot of free time to wait around and heal from a cosmetic procedure. People lead busy lives with crammed calendars stored on their smart phones. In the older models of aesthetic procedures, the surgeon would make sometimes overly optimistic estimates about when you could return to your normal life. However, the after effects of general anesthesia made the healing time variable and could negatively impact on the recovery experience of the patient. I decided to explore methods to perform cosmetic procedures that would reduce downtime and fit in better with a modern lifestyle. I am pleased to state that we have achieved this goal in my office and we offer all of our procedures with an eye towards quick recovery as one of our most important goals.

Do you have any other creative ambitions or dreams to which you aspire?

Although we have come quite a long way in terms of performing youth restoration procedures, there are limitations that exist. For example, skin cells that have aged cannot be reversed. A face lift can improve the underlying architecture of the face but cannot change the skin. I believe that the next frontier to restoring youth so that you can truly look as young as you feel is to restore youth at a cellular level so that the aging process is actually slowed down considerably. My colleague —Dr. Gary Hitzig — and I have collaborated on a project using ACELL (which is short for Acellular Matrix) and has helped to show regeneration of selected tissues in specific situations. My dream is to expand the use of products such as these to slow down the aging process that we currently face.

I like Bobby Flay, too. I have to admit that I am a Food Network junkie. I love to watch the process of cooking and how it transcends mere food on a plate to a sensory experience. I watch Iron Chef all the time and I am struck by his creativity and genius of execution. Certainly his numerous restaurants are also a testament to that genius. He has created an empire that any business person or chef would envy. You know that when you go into a Bobby Flay restaurant that you will have a consummate dining experience with fresh ingredients and an innovative combination of ingredients that you have never seen before.

Finally, I admire Giovanni Coello, the lead architect of Diversified Design Associates. I met this architect by chance while I was looking for someone to help me set up my offices. He actually listened to the experience that I wanted to create for my patients so that I could convey a sense of calm, confidence, and optimism to my patients when they come to see me. Many of the other architects that I met with were ready to fit my office into a medical "template" that resembled all the other offices that they'd built — with a few superficial differences. Giovanni understood the details such as lighting, color, materials, and other matters of décor that would create an efficient but professional and soothing atmosphere. He has designed both of our offices and I have received numerous compliments on them. One of the things that he taught me was that I am able to communicate much about my philosophy and approach to patients before they even meet me just by the look and feel of my office. He spent a lot of time asking me about what types of patients I have and what their needs would be so that his design could meet all functional and esthetic requirements thoroughly. We have similar goals in that we both live by the principle of making form and function work together so that each benefits the other in our work.

Could we feature your favorite photographer, author, artist, designer, architect, filmmaker, etc. in our publication and/or online?

Yes, Bobby Flay or the architect that I mentioned, Giovanni Coello.

Do you follow any philosophical or psychological approach in your practice as a surgeon?

I have always admired the principles embodied by companies such as Mac or Zappo's where the priority in designing their products and services stresses the need to keep the "end-user" in mind. In other words, a consumer-oriented focus is of paramount importance. I have always preached to my staff and to all who ask me about this that you can't provide a beneficial service unless you have "walked a mile in their shoes." I strive to live by this principle with every procedure I perform and with any modifications that I develop in the course of my work.

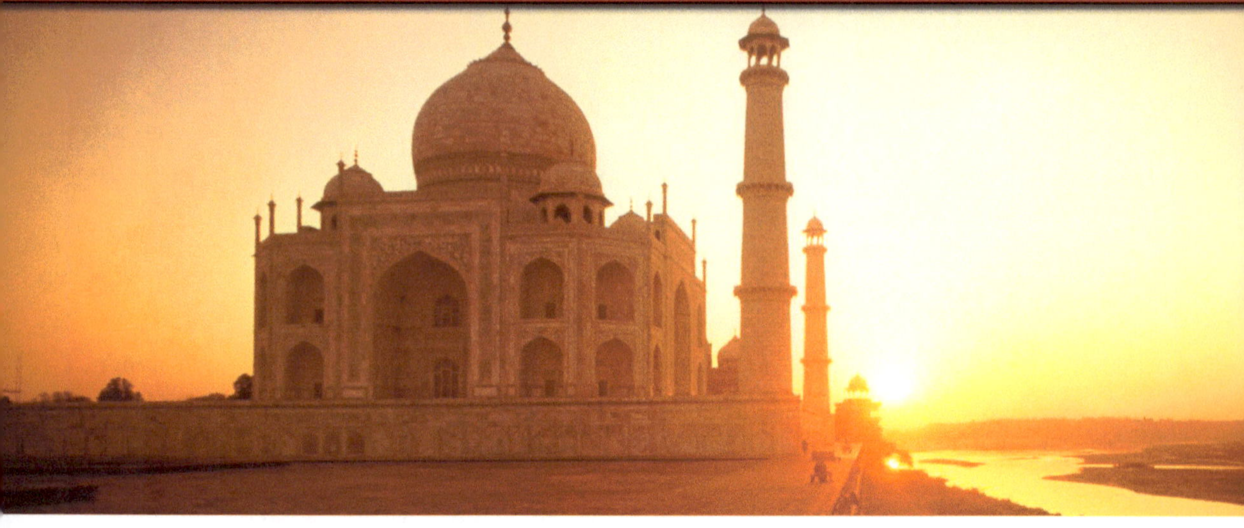

What is your favorite building in the world? List as many as you like and provide a reason for each.

I have a few: the Guggenheim - the layout and circular flow suggests infinite possibilities. The Taj Mahal - I admire the advanced engineering and mathematical skills that utilize many tricks to enhance the perspective of this monument. The inlaid semi-precious stones have been placed with special glue that remains a well-guarded secret to this day. The stones have remained untouched for centuries. All of these efforts were brought about because of the love of a king for his wife, which is a beautiful story.

Washington Monument - a modern building that reminds one of Ancient Egyptian Obelisks.

What is your favorite hotel? List as many as you like and provide a motivation for each.

Soho Grand - a really funky atmosphere that feels very urban when you are there. It's the quintessential New York City hotel.

The Venetian Hotel in Las Vegas - it's so fun to admire the over-the-top efforts where there is virtually no restraint in the architecture. The upstairs mall with the replica of the outside sky as the ceiling is a masterpiece.

Oberoi Hotel at Taj Mahal - this building is a wonderful place to feel what it must've been like to live in a palace in the 17th century when the Taj Mahal was built. Every room has a view of the monument. There are beautiful sculpted gardens and outdoor mosaic pathways with a magnificent pool and spa to promote the atmosphere of stepping back in Mughal times in India.

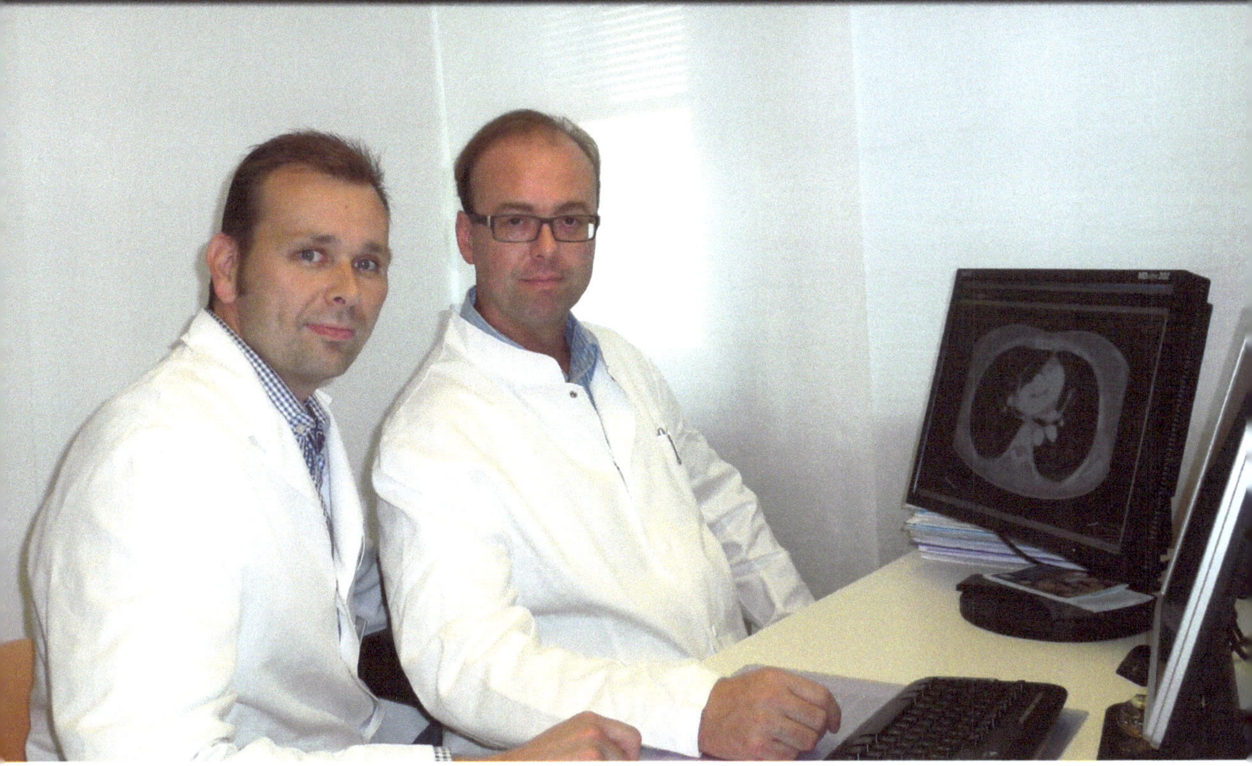

Dr. Rainer Ehmann & Dr. Thorston Walles

Innovative Cancer Detection Methods

For centuries dogs have been used to help humans in several different fields. They've worked as service dogs for those with disabilities and visual or hearing impairments. They've worked with fire departments as rescue dogs. They've worked with the police to find missing persons or concealed drugs. And now, they're helping doctors to detect lung cancer.

When Dr. Rainer Ehmann, a physician in a private outpatient clinic in Stuggart, Germany first approached Dr. Thorston Walles, a surgeon at the Schillerhoehe Hospital about conducting research on the use of sniffer dogs to detect lung cancer, Dr. Walles was hesitant. He called the theory that dogs could sniff out lung cancer in its early stages "esoteric nonsense." With Dr. Ehmann's persistence, Dr. Walles finally agreed and the two worked together to determine if dogs could really be used for cancer research.

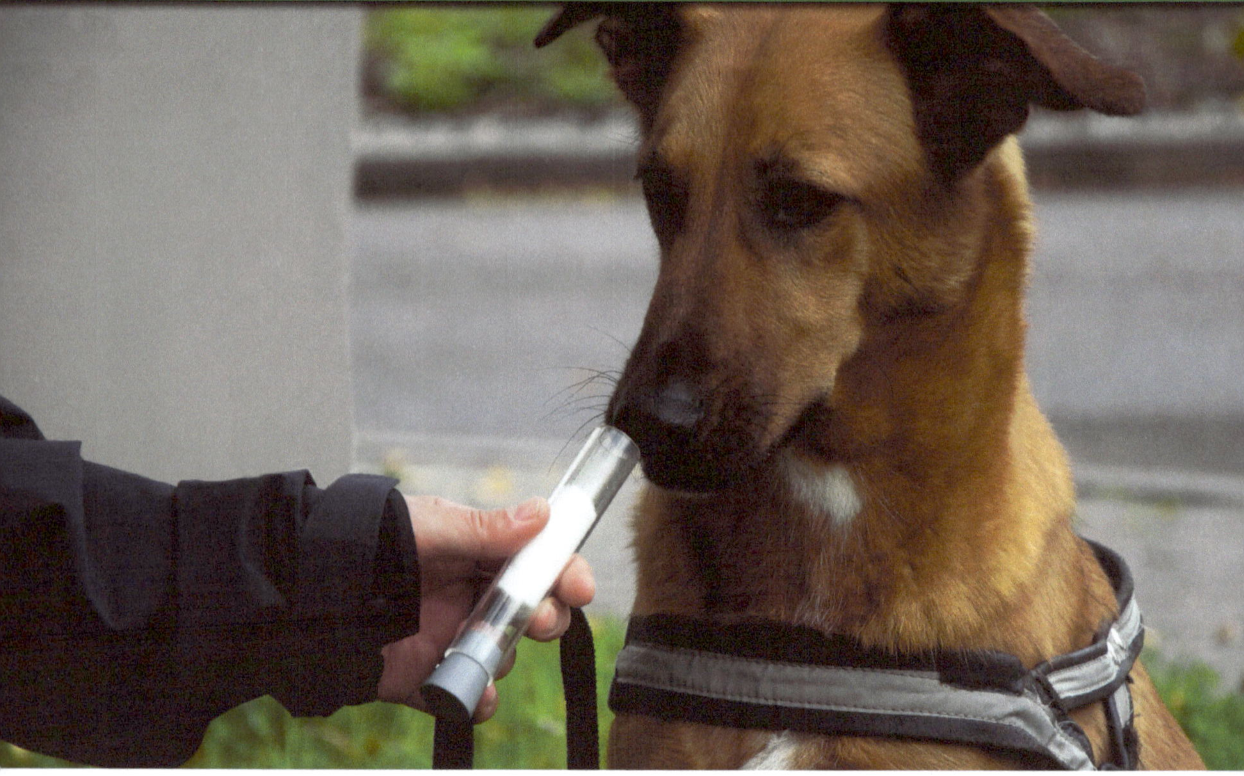

Sniffer dogs can be used to detect lung cancer.

Sniffer dogs could be used for the early detection of lung cancer, according to new research published in the European Respiratory Journal. The study, carried out by researchers from Schillerhoehe Hospital in Germany, is the first to find that sniffer dogs can reliably detect lung cancer.

Lung cancer is the second most frequent form of cancer in men and women across Europe with over 340,000 deaths per year. It is also the most common cause of death from cancer worldwide. The disease is not strongly associated with any symptoms and early detection is often by chance. Current methods of detection are unreliable and scientists have been working on using exhaled breath specimens from patients for future screening tests.

This method relies on identifying volatile organic compounds (VOCs) that are linked to the presence of cancer. Although many different technological applications have been developed, this method is still difficult to apply in a clinical setting as patients aren't allowed to smoke or eat before the test, sample analysis can take a long time and there is also a high risk of interference. Because of these reasons, no lung cancer-specific VOCs have yet been identified.

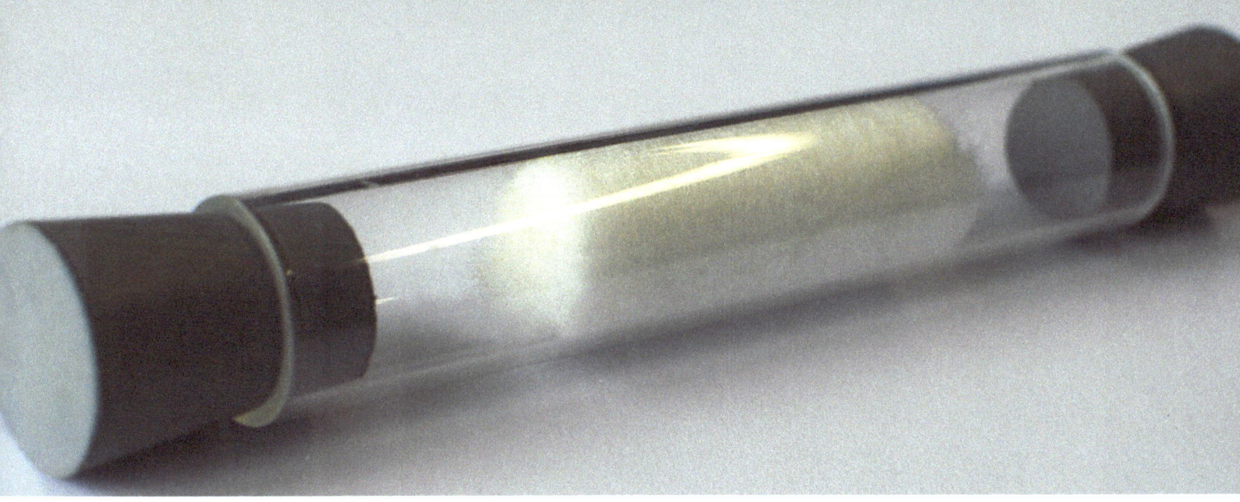

This new study aimed to assess whether sniffer dogs could be used to identify a VOC in the breath of patients. The researchers worked with 220 volunteers, including lung cancer patients, chronic obstructive pulmonary disease (COPD) patients and healthy volunteers. They used dogs that had been specifically trained. The researchers carried out a number of tests to see if the dogs were able to reliably identify lung cancer compared with healthy volunteers, volunteers with COPD and whether the results were still found with the presence of tobacco.

The dogs successfully identified 71 samples with lung cancer out of a possible 100. They also correctly detected 372 samples that did not have lung cancer out of a possible 400. The dogs could also detect lung cancer independently from COPD and tobacco smoke. These results confirm the presence of a stable marker for lung cancer that is independent of COPD and also detectable in the presence of tobacco smoke, food odors and drugs.

Author of the study, Thorsten Walles from Schillerhoehe Hospital, said: "In the breath of patients with lung cancer, there are likely to be different chemicals to normal breath samples and the dogs' keen sense of smell can detect this difference at an early stage of the disease. Our results confirm the presence of a stable marker for lung cancer. This is a big step forward in the diagnosis of lung cancer, but we still need to precisely identify the compounds observed in the exhaled breath of patients. It is unfortunate that dogs cannot communicate the biochemistry of the scent of cancer!"

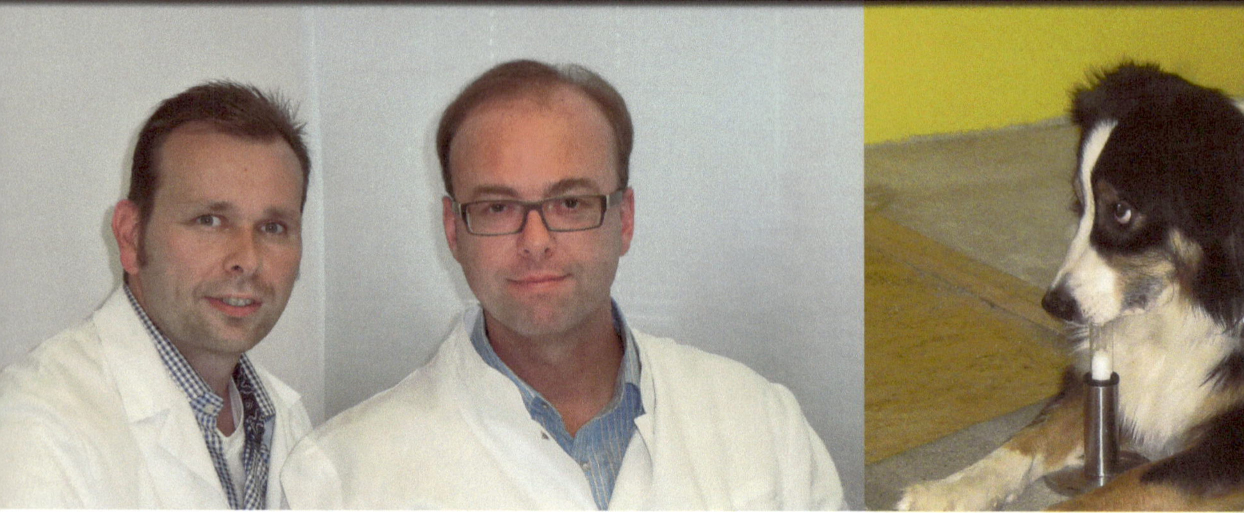

A Conversation with Dr. Ehmann and Dr. Walles

As a child, what did you want to become (profession-wise)?

Dr. Ehmann: I wanted to become a farmer, as I admired living in close relationship to animals and plants. Later that wish was replaced by the dream of being a musician; feeling music is one of the most reliable means for transmitting emotions – and keeping them in mind.

Dr. Walles: This and that – ideas changed a lot that time .....

In which town did you grow up?

Dr. Ehmann: In Stuttgart, during my childhood labeled as the "big city between forests and vineyards," nowadays a place charmingly combining industry, culture and beautiful natural surroundings. Dr. Walles: Nordhorn, a rural country in the north of Germany

Do you think your background has influenced your chosen profession in health care? If so, what specific element in your background is most pervasive in influencing your current approach in your health care profession?

Dr. Ehmann: An open minded education with social emphasis, providing a big deal of freedom in choosing my own way.

Dr. Walles: I cannot tell whether and how my background influenced my current profession.

What inspires you in the job of being a doctor/researcher?

Dr. Ehmann: I am inspired by helping patients find their way to heal, improve or live with a disease, as well as having nice colleagues and co-workers.

Dr. Walles: I am inspired by identifying the fundamentals behind ostensible complexity.

In which way do you consider yourself an innovative creator?

Dr. Ehmann: Making efforts to find or develop integrative and interdisciplinary diagnostic and therapeutic approaches.

Dr. Walles: In no way.

What do you consider as a masterpiece you have created or worked on in your health care field?

Dr. Ehmann: Perhaps you should ask my patients to find out ...

Dr. Walles: I'm still working on it.

How did you get the idea for using dogs to sniff out lung cancer?

Dr. Ehmann: In the late nineties I read a 100-year-old article from a Swiss TB sanatorium reporting that a senior consultant's dog seemed to have learnt selecting patients with an active TB disease before they had been detected by clinical and X ray investigation. Later, in 2006, Californian researchers published a study showing amazing results with dogs trained to detect cancer using breath samples of patients.

What were your thoughts when Dr. Ehmann approached you about researching a dog's ability to sniff out cancer?

Dr. Walles: Esoteric nonsense.

What do you consider to be the next steps in that research?

Dr. Ehmann: Finding a reliable combination of methods for early detection of lung cancer, including the valuable sensory capabilities of sniffer dogs.

Dr. Walles: Reproduce our findings, investigate the detected specificity further and draw the line back to "real science."

Did or do you have any other creative ambitions or dreams to which you aspire?

Dr. Ehmann: Learning from other medicines and cultures, and integrating key parts of them into our quite "technical-prone" medicine.

Dr. Walles: I'm still looking for them.

Do you have a favorite health care professional or institution you look up to yourself?

Dr. Ehmann: I have many, depending on their clinical specialty or scientific focus.

Dr. Walles: No one specific.

Are you ever afraid you will run out of inspiration in your job?

Dr. Ehmann: No – my patients provide me with new inspiration every day!

Dr. Walles: A little less every day.

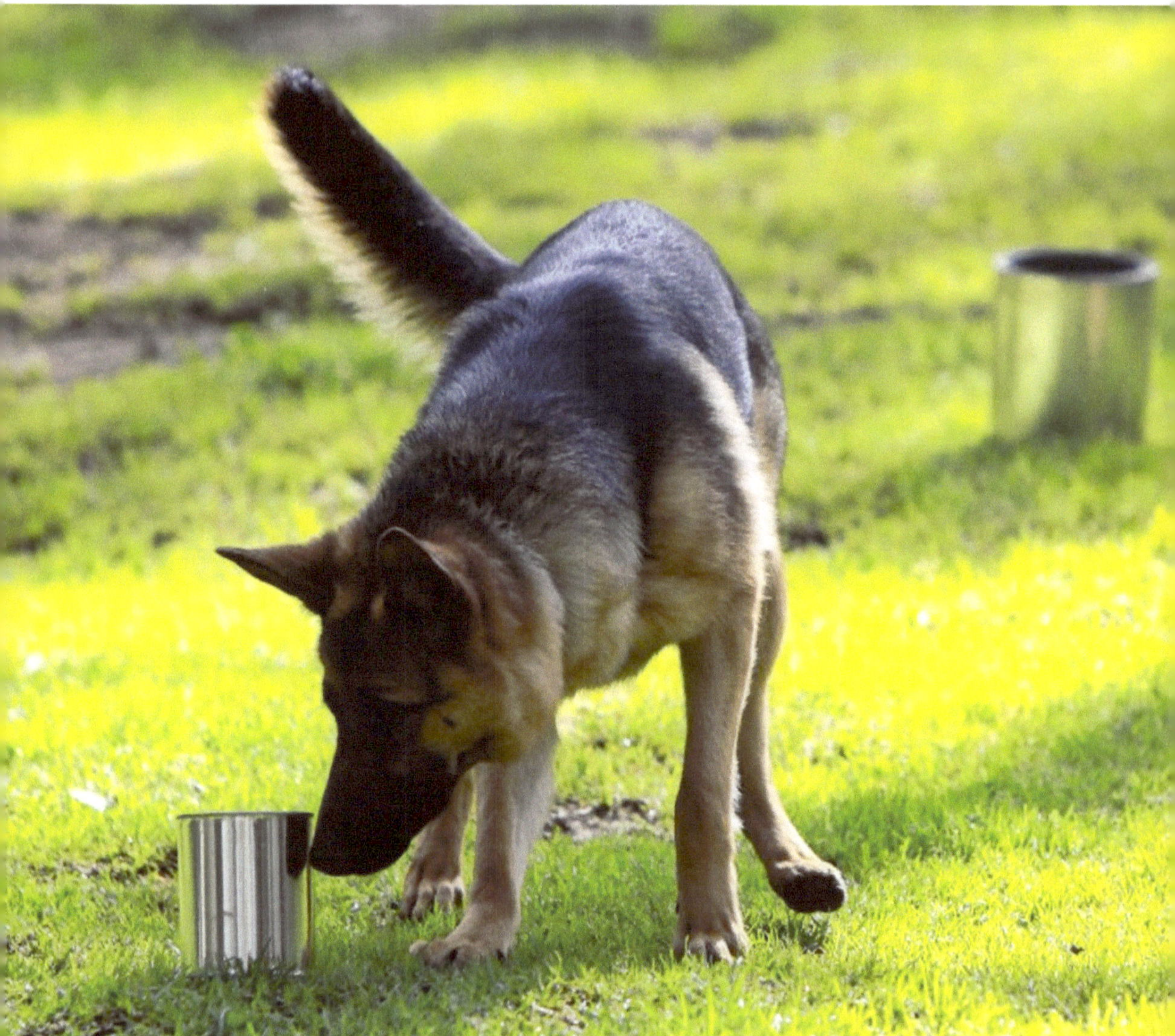

What is the most difficult part of your job?

Dr. Ehmann: Daily bureaucracy and the administrative limitations of our present health care system.

Dr. Walles: Waiting for results.

What is the most fun part of your job?

Dr. Ehmann: Dealing with a large variety of different people, finding an individual way of communicating with each of them.

Dr. Walles: Getting good results.

Do you expect your health care profession to change in the future?

Dr. Ehmann: Sure, and I hope the change will lead to a more individual, more integrative and more preventive approach to medicine.

Dr. Walles: Yes, I anticipate an increase in diversification and specification.

Do you embrace the changes in the health care industry regarding social media and technology influences?

Dr. Ehmann: I am rather skeptical. It depends on whether they will really ease our work or lead to more safety - without developing themselves as a new focus.

Dr. Walles: I will have to, won't I?

Do you like art? Do you have any preferences for an artist? And/or for creators of artistic work? (Creators can also be chefs, designers, photographers, fashion designers or inventors.) If so, why is that? What special quality do you like in their work or personalities?

Dr. Ehmann: Two of my favorites:

1.The Iranian artist Laleh Khorramian (living in New York as far as I know), especially for her creative and ingenious ideas captured in her video productions.

2. The Canadian dancer and choreographer Eric Gauthier (living in Germany) for the thrilling dance performances of his troupe, and that he had enough strength and creativity to built up his team of dancers despite the existing traditional state ballet in Stuttgart.

Dr. Walles: As an academic surgeon you again and again have the opportunity to work with innovative characters – if you want to.

Did or do you follow any philosophical or psychological approach in your profession?

Dr. Ehmann: My most important ones: Albert Schweitzer's "respect for life" towards every individual, and Mahatma Gandhi with his ideas how societies could find ways to develop in justice and harmony.

Dr. Walles: "New paths originate by walking them." (Franz Kafka)

Do you have any dreams for the future?

Dr. Ehmann: First, more time to cultivate my friendships. Second, always finding "good angels" giving me a helping hand to realize at least some of the ideas mentioned above.

Dr. Walles: Not walking alone.

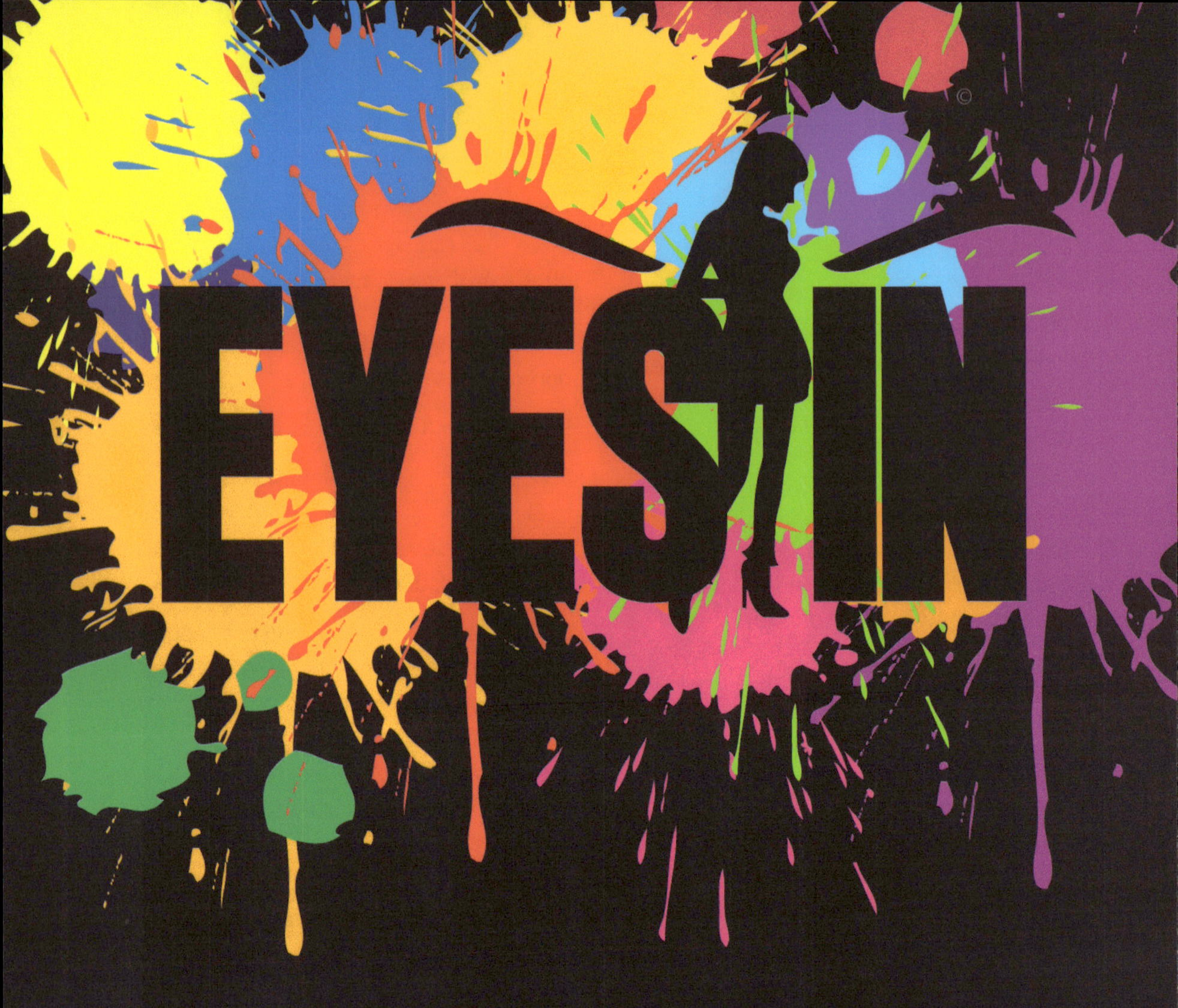

Promoting the World's Innovative Creators & their Masterpieces

With EYES IN™ author & art director Vivian Van Dijk has chosen a collection of self-publishing materials from the World's Innovative Creators & their Masterpieces. This EYES IN™ book spotlights innovations in the fields of architecture, art, beauty, books, culinary arts, culture, design, fashion, film, health, music, photography, real estate and travel. It is a must read for anyone who wants to stay informed on global trends, artistic intellect, innovative thinking and sustainable solutions shown by upcoming and celebrity creators in these areas. EYES IN™ delivers a state-of-the-art visual experience into the minds and works of the most stunning creators. The book is a road map that can teach through the transparent creators' interviews how to get inspiration and aspiration on how to fulfill a person's innovative and aesthetic dreams in different professions. This path from dreams to reality can contribute to significant positive developments worldwide.

www.ingramcontent.com/pod-product-compliance
Lightning Source LLC
LaVergne TN
LVHW070128110826
845147LV00002B/207